Research Methods for Creating and Curating Data in the Digital Humanities

RESEARCH METHODS FOR THE ARTS AND HUMANITIES

Forthcoming Titles
Research Methods for Law, 2nd edition
Edited by Mike McConville and Wing Hong Chui

Research Methods for History, 2nd edition
Edited by Lucy Faire and Simon Gunn

Published Titles

Research Methods for Creating and Curating Data in the Digital Humanities
Edited by Matt Hayler and Gabriele Griffin

Research Methods for Reading Digital Data in the Digital Humanities
Edited by Gabriele Griffin and Matt Hayler

Research Methods for Memory Studies
Edited by Emily Keightley and Michael Pickering

Research Methods for English Studies, 2nd edition
Edited by Gabriele Griffin

Research Methods in Theatre and Performance
Edited by Baz Kershaw and Helen Nicholson

Research Methods for History
Edited by Lucy Faire and Simon Gunn

Practice-led Research, Research-led Practice in the Creative Arts
Edited by Hazel Smith and Roger T. Dean

Research Methods for Cultural Studies
Edited by Michael Pickering

Research Methods for Law
Edited by Mike McConville and Wing Hong Chui

WITHDRAWN

Research Methods for Creating and Curating Data in the Digital Humanities

Edited by Matt Hayler and Gabriele Griffin

EDINBURGH
University Press

Edinburgh University Press is one of the leading university presses in the UK. We publish academic books and journals in our selected subject areas across the humanities and social sciences, combining cutting-edge scholarship with high editorial and production values to produce academic works of lasting importance. For more information visit our website: www.edinburghuniversitypress.com

Edinburgh University Press Ltd
The Tun – Holyrood Road
12(2f) Jackson's Entry
Edinburgh EH8 8PJ

Typeset in 11/13 Ehrhardt by
Servis Filmsetting Ltd, Stockport, Cheshire,
and printed and bound in Great Britain by
CPI Group (UK) Ltd, Croydon CR0 4YY

A CIP record for this book is available from the British Library

ISBN 978 1 4744 0964 3 (hardback)
ISBN 978 1 4744 0966 7 (webready PDF)
ISBN 978 1 4744 0965 0 (paperback)
ISBN 978 1 4744 0967 4 (epub)

Contents

Acknowledgements

The editors would like to thank the University of Birmingham's College of Arts and Law for generously providing a grant to make the colour-printing of the images in this volume possible.

Matt Hayler would like to thank Brian and Jackie Hayler, Richard Lee, Lorna Lee and Tatiana Cutts for being family and helping me work on this project across three cities and two universities in not many months. He would also like to thank the Department of English Literature at Birmingham University for all of their support.

Gabriele Griffin would like to thank the University of Umeå's Media and Communications Department, and in particular Professor Britta Lundgren and the Dean, Per-Olof Erixon, for the visiting professorship period in 2014 during which this project was begun. She would also like to thank the University of Uppsala for a brief visiting professorship in 2014–15 during which the project was further developed.

Finally, the editors would like to thank the commissioning and production team at Edinburgh University Press, in particular Jackie Jones and Adela Rauchova. Their great support for this project has always been appreciated.

CHAPTER I

Introduction

Matt Hayler and Gabriele Griffin

The Digital Humanities (DH) is in many respects nothing new. Its histories have been traced a number of times (e.g. Schreibman et al. 2004; Kirschenbaum 2012; Deegan and Hayler 2016), and its definitions and emphases unpacked and challenged (see, for example, Gold 2012). Something that might be recognised, if not named, as Digital Humanities or 'Humanities Computing' (see, for example, McCarty 2014) dates back to at least the 1980s and arguably the 1970s or 1960s. With code-crackers recruited via cryptic crossword to Bletchley Park during the Second World War, Alan Turing's speculations about machine intelligence following his work on the German Enigma code or the gender politics that can be traced from Ada Lovelace assisting Charles Babbage with theorising the earliest mechanical computers through to the word 'computer' well into the twentieth century, commonly referring to a woman sat at a desk calculating, cracking or connecting data, we might accurately say that modern computer science and humanistic concerns have never been neatly separated. The Digital Humanities, however, are still in the process of making themselves distinct from this broad backdrop, and in this collection and our companion volume on reading digital data (Griffin and Hayler 2016), we make the case that distinctive (if iterating) research methods, and reflection on the rationale behind those methods, are one means through which Digital Humanities marks itself out as a particular field.

In the volume on reading data (Griffin and Hayler 2016) our contributors explore both new ways of reading and new things to read: new techniques such as large-corpus data-mining and new texts like born-digital pages and social media feeds. The work presented here, instead, focuses on *production*, the making and collecting together of digital data. Creating, coding and 'building' have become increasingly important terms for marking out the distinctiveness of what DH does. Within the field, the desire for scholarship to result in, or emerge out of, the production of new digital artefacts (e.g. tools, apps, visualisations, games, archives) has been more or less problematically captured in the phrase 'more hack, less yack' – stop simply talking or theorising and start *making*.[1] This collection is at once committed to the hack of DH, to emphasising what digital building does for scholarship in the twenty-first century, but also to the importance of discussing acts of making and the ways in which they are always theory- or value-laden, as research is never neutral; there is, we contend, always importance to the yack.

As will be seen from each of the chapters here, the bringing together of materials always re-conditions how each element is received; the making of any new digital artefact (which includes collections and archives) is always shot through with both theory and unrecognised assumptions that later need to be teased out and analysed so that the item might give up at least some of its secrets. By exploring and furthering our understanding of the effects that lead to, and emerge from, the acts of creation and curation, the writers in this volume demonstrate how such acts constitute research methods in their own right – something is brought out in the doing that would otherwise have remained hidden. This view of practice as theory has gained increasing prominence in the past two decades, following on from the incorporation of many 'making-training' institutions such as art colleges and conservatoires into the academy and specifically universities where the question of the meaning of making in the context of research gained traction, not least through the establishment of the so-called research assessment exercises.[2] The concomitant rise of the 'employability' agenda and of 'transferable skills' has also promoted practice-orientation which, in the context of English studies, for example, has led to the establishment of creative writing courses where the act of making, i.e. writing texts of various kinds, has itself been figured as a form of research. Hence we now have volumes such as Hazel Smith and Roger Dean's (2009) *Practice-Led Research and Research-Led Practice in the Creative Arts* which explicitly engage with questions of how making is and articulates research. The act of writing enables revelations that are distinct from writing about writing. Such issues are also evident across a range of other disciplines, such as philosophy, science and technology studies, and cognitive science where the relationship between the human and the material in action has been increasingly scrutinised.

In this vein, the post-phenomenological philosopher Don Ihde (1990)[3] outlines four modes of technological relationship: embodied, hermeneutic, background and alterity.[4] In embodied relationships the tool, such as a hammer or tennis racquet, disappears; we do not pay attention to the thing that we are using, just the task that we are undertaking. In a hermeneutic relationship we look through the technology, such as with a telescope or microscope – we bring new ways of looking into being. Background relationships are an invisible relationship where we set a technology going and then it looks after itself even as it conditions our experience of the environment, like an air-conditioning unit. Alterity relationships are slightly different, bringing our focus onto the technology itself, such as using an ATM machine where our attention is brought explicitly to the device. In this surprisingly comprehensive taxonomy, Ihde reveals that the majority of our interactions are not focused on the tools that are used to facilitate them; rather, technologies most often (and most profoundly) shape our experience as they slip outside of our awareness, melting away while we think about other things. We raise this idea because DH's interest in making can get into these same investigations by another door – through building, the builder either comes to know the effects of various tools and platforms in the use of them, or is better able to reflect on their effects after the fact. The accumulation of expertise through getting one's hands dirty is quite different from theorising from the sidelines (as the philosophy of technology from the mid–late twentieth century onwards has attested[5]). One obvious indicator of this is many academics' comments – including within in the contributions in this volume – about how time-consuming, challenging and distinctive Digital Humanities can be, something which most only discover in the actual doing.

Taking our line about the effects of building above, of course, raises an immediate question: who is 'the builder' here? As all the contributions to this volume indicate, digitising and curating digital data is a collaborative effort involving multiple disciplines, skills and tools. It may start with a researcher or an academic (or a mixed group) having an idea and then looking for the technical expertise, hardware and software to develop the project. This is a crucial and, for the most part, still wholly unexplicated aspect of Digital Humanities work where the engagement with technicians, technology experts and technologies is often left unaddressed, even by those who engage in such collaborations. Indeed, it can be surprisingly difficult to get experienced researchers to discuss this dimension of their work. There are a number of possible reasons for this. The development of digital tools has proceeded at such a pace that, for starters, most academics have little knowledge of what tools and technologies there are, how they might be used and what they might do, even within these academics' own areas of expertise. At the same time, many academics who engage in Digital Humanities 'making' (for example, digitising and curating texts) tend to work with a very limited range of hardware and software, not least because, as the various chapters in this volume indicate, much of this practical research is extremely time-consuming and utilising even one tool to a proficient level – a skill which may become obsolete in the course of a three- or five-year research project and/or be superseded by newer tools – requires a long process of training. Secondly, because there is still little to no systematic tuition in the use of many digital tools, they remain something of a black box for many academics. Thirdly, unused to research collaborations in many Humanities disciplines, academics can find it difficult to conceptualise how to engage in such collaboration, never mind finding technicians and technology-savvy colleagues with whom to engage. Fourthly, there continues to be, at an institutional level in higher education, very little sense that knowledge of and proficiency with technology needs to be acquired through training and practice which in turn takes an investment of time. The prevailing view seems to be that technological know-how is somehow acquired osmotically, or simply just *is* – some have it, some do not – but with no sense of how those who have it got it. It has been rendered an invisible process, something acquired in secret when it needs to be, at least in part, formalised and made visible.

This invisibility, at least to some extent, has some counterparts in the chapters that follow. The contributors are mostly academics rather than, for instance, technicians, even though – as the chapter on 'Curating Mary Digitally' makes clear – technicians (and the technologies that they marshal) have a crucial influence on the digital production of knowledge and are, indeed, co-producers of knowledge rather than the servants of knowledge-makers. Not every chapter here, however, acknowledges this as fully (or, in a couple of instances, at all). We raise this from the outset to note a general trend within the field – this absence is resonant with the current landscape. One reason for this, here and elsewhere, may well be that the technical process of digitisation is often either demanding to explain (thereby taking up too much space in chapters and articles investigating other aspects of the work) or, in its very technicality, beyond the academics who are principally involved in different areas of the digital project being undertaken. Nonetheless, we have been struck by how much this issue of collaboration in the process of digitisation still requires explication and engagement, and that the academic–technician relation in particular needs to be addressed.

In discussions of the relation of the human and the material this issue is also often circumvented, for instance by homogenising 'the human' without attention to the differential relations diverse knowledge producers with differing levels of expertise may be able to have to the non-human world. Such entanglements between embodied humans, their material technologies and their cultural milieu are beginning to be discussed more frequently in various threads in contemporary cognitive science regarding the effects on thought of embodiment and external supports such as tools. In *How Things Shape the Mind: A Theory of Material Engagement* (2013), Lambros Malafouris, for example, discusses how clay to be thrown on a wheel pushes back against the potter. A pot is not simply the product of the potter's mind, of a neatly planned intent, but born of an entanglement between the potter's brain, body, the clay and the conditions of the day – humid air allows for certain techniques and prevents others; a more dense clay allows for greater height, but less dramatic shapes.[6]

> We should assume . . . that every mental recourse needed to grow
> a vessel out of clay may well be extended and distributed across the
> neurons of the potter's brain, the muscles of the potter's sense organs,
> the affordances of the wheel, the material properties of the clay, the
> morphological and typological prototypes of existing vessels, and the
> general social context in which the activity occurs . . . I do not mean
> to deny that an intricate computational problem may well arise for the
> brain the moment the potter touches or is touched by the clay; I simply
> mean to emphasize that part of the problem's solution is offered by the
> clay itself. (Malafouris 2013: 213 and 219)

The expert potter thinks alongside, with and through the clay, the wheel and her arms and hands, and it is only their actions together that determine the final shape of the pot. Such 'intra-action', in Karen Barad's (2007) terms, means that tools co-determine their products and the thinking of their users, and this is as true for the digital productions discussed here as it is for the analogue realm of clay, humidity and the actions of the potter's hands. It extends out even further when we consider the entailed system required to make a digital product. The web of builders (including academics and technicians working from different, even opposing traditions), consumers, software and hardware, communities and their concomitant expectations of use and discourse, and the recalcitrant nature of data itself – all combine to create a network of production well worth investigating in its own right, not just as a source of objects, but as a site of new developments in thought, practice and stance toward the world; the actants and networks that Bruno Latour describes (e.g. 2007) can be analysed in action as well as described in theory.

However, as already indicated above, the discussion of such action qua action is less evident in this volume which pursues the matter of digitising and curating predominantly from the researcher's or academic's perspective, not least because they are our intended audience. As with our volume on reading digital data (2016), the chapters here instead often either explicitly or implicitly address what it is like to act as part of a team and the ways in which DH research leads to co-produced knowledge. This volume is therefore also aimed at researchers working in the field who would like to see how others are doing it, as well as at those new to the Digital Humanities at any level who are interested in what its methods might include and be useful for. But we do also see it as part of a call for further discussion to take place around the issues raised above. It certainly offers at least some preliminary examples of how to go about this task and why it might be worth doing so, even as it often focuses on the advantages of the outcomes of building after it has occurred. These include, for instance, the benefits of the digitisation of collections for audiences, both scholarly and lay, who might otherwise not be able to access their contents or, on another level, the ways in which seeing artefacts and texts in digitised form may enable experiences or (re)constructions that are not possible in the material world away from the liberties offered by the virtual. This volume, then, is about what the research methods required of academics in acts of making have to offer the Digital Humanities and Humanities research more broadly.

In the next chapter, 'Choices in Digitisation for the Digital Humanities', Simon Tanner, Laura Gibson, Rebecca Kahn and Geoff Laycock explore the ways in which Digital Humanities research and scholarship has been significantly enhanced by the process of digitisation in the last twenty years. They pay particular attention to the mass conversion of analogue materials to digital, including the growth of the mass digitisation of books, newspapers and primary source materials such as manuscripts, arguing that this has enhanced scholarly practice and enabled fresh research insights while the digitisation of rare and special collections has also brought together online otherwise hidden collections for study. The chapter analyses the process of digitisation, the tools and mechanisms, and offers a critical appraisal of the selection criteria for materials to be digitised and the ways in which these choices can affect Digital Humanities research opportunities. This discussion covers a range of technical areas including scanning, digital photography, multi-spectral imaging, rekeying, metadata, crowdsourcing and optical character recognition (OCR). Crucially, this is about more than just capturing novels; the chapter explores the digitisation of a wide range of resources including images, audio–visual material and handwritten and small-run texts alongside the more familiar capture of mass print works. Tanner et al. also consider some of the ethical and moral issues thrown up by the selection process, such as copyright and publication rights that have left the Digital Humanities with a digitisation agenda which focuses primarily on pre-1920s content that is already out of copyright and may therefore escape legal wrangling. Issues of equality, democratisation, digital colonialism and gender balance in digitisation are explored in the context of how digitisation choices can be freeing or more oppressive through the repetition of westernised collection practices in digital form. In line with our discussion above, the chapter highlights the choices available for digitisation as a means to enhance the Digital Humanities while also considering the consequences of the tools and the practices surrounding hardware and software as co-producers of knowledge entangled with their makers and users – Tanner et al. demonstrate that choices, and the reasons that they must be made, are never neutral or consequence free.

The third chapter, 'Curating the Language of Letters: Historical Linguistic

Methods in the Museum', similarly focuses on acts of curation, but does so within the specific context of the heritage industry. Mel Evans details how the wealth of digitised and visualised artefacts and objects, and the interactive experiences that accompany them, have a significant impact on the industry, expanding the opportunities to engage non-traditional user groups among heritage visitors. As with Tanner et al.'s discussion, Evans at once acknowledges the huge benefits which digitisation has provided for the sector while paying particular attention to the challenges that remain in knowing how best to utilise these new technologies for the purposes of curation. For Evans, these concerns come from knowing (particularly when confronted by more obscure, esoteric or difficult items such as historical correspondence) how Digital Humanities methods can offer a way of creating new exhibits and displays that serve the needs of the heritage organisation and its expanding visitor base. The chapter unpacks a curatorial method through a case study of the Living Letters prototype, an AHRC-funded start-up project which sought to use digital technology as a platform to open up historical manuscripts that comprised part of a heritage organisation's history. Working with Norton Priory, Cheshire, the project explored how traditional methods of curation for written documents could be augmented with media expertise and academic research practices, based on the potential for digitised, narrative-based and interactive displays of the letters. After outlining the key stages and main questions raised by the project, the chapter concludes with a discussion of two important issues: first, the benefits arising from the curatorial project from the perspective of an academic researcher and, second, the opportunities and challenges for digital curation in the future that must balance curatorial needs with cost and expertise.

In 'Connecting with the Past: Opportunities and Challenges in Digital History', Thomas Nygren, Zephyr Frank, Nicholas Bauch and Erik Steiner outline the aspects of digitisation that most significantly impact upon the field of academic History. They argue that the digitisation of historical sources has increasingly compelled historians to navigate in digital environments and that this increased availability of digital material and the capacity for digitally processing historical artefacts has both great potential for empowering research and is already having a significant impact on the discipline. At the same time, since considerable digital data growth can be expected in the coming years as the technologies that can be deployed become more accessible, user-friendly and domain-science orientated, the expansion of digital archives and the development of novel digital tools will also pose further challenges for historians. Nygren et al. demonstrate that critical knowledge and understanding of digital media needs to be augmented considerably in order to take full advantage of contemporary research opportunities and navigate the potential downsides – by better knowing the tools, their capabilities and their limitations, researchers will be able not only to employ existing tools better, but also to know what to call for in future iterations. This chapter therefore discusses how the creation of data and the use of new digital tools supports a variety of types of historical research, but also problematises developments of ongoing historical research in digital environments.

Stephen Hilyard moves us away from the curation of existing texts in 'The Object and the Event: Time-based Digital Simulation and Illusion in the Fine Arts', instead exploring a particular kind of building in fine-art practice: simulations. To date, the integration of digital tools into fine art practice has been arrayed around three principal motivations which, Hilyard argues, may be conveniently identified via typical subject matters: technological capabilities as a 'wonder show' in which the demonstration of new capabilities is an end in itself; digital technology as a subject matter in its own right; and finally art which critiques the deployment of digital technology in mass media, commerce and/or systems of power. This chapter argues that one particular subset of capabilities provided by digital media tools has yet to be widely exploited in the field of fine art, namely the ability of digital tools to create convincing simulations or, as Hilyard puts it, the computer's ability to lie convincingly. Recent advances in the digital production of verisimilitude provide artists with a wealth of opportunity to create visual metaphors which allow or provoke the viewer to consider questions of subjectivity, contingency, cultural mediation and relativism in the context of lived experience in the actual world. Hilyard is clear that, for him, such new visual language appeals not so much to the concept of the dissolution of 'reality' in Jean Baudrillard's familiar terms of 'simulacra and simulation', but rather this is a new way of dealing with the notion that we live in a web of illusion (*maya*), or experience the world at the mercy of our own minds, a concept at least as old as western philosophy. Hilyard contextualises his discussion by describing the ways in which fine art photographers realised the implications of digital simulation early on, recognising its relevance to the debates in their own field concerning the idea of the 'decisive moment' and the problematic nature of the photograph as index. He argues, however, that outside of the comparatively narrow field of fine art photography, for many years few artists made use of digital tools in this way. By exploring contemporary work by new media and moving image artists, Hilyard goes on to show how such work both catches up with fine art photography's lead and extends the potentials it first identified around the power of the digital image. Hilyard's own work exemplifies one artistic strategy of creating near simulations that are designed to hover in the 'uncanny valley' between the apparently real and the obviously synthetic. The power of such work relies on the tension between the viewer not being able to help but 'believe their eyes', based on their prior experience of judging the reality of moving images, and their intellectual understanding that they must be being fooled due to the fantastical nature of the subject matter. Hilyard's main point here is that viewers appear to distinguish between individual objects depicted in a simulation, which they understand as 'real', and the event or narrative depicted, which viewers recognise as impossible. Though Hilyard speaks to a very different kind of building than Evans or Tanner et al., his exploration of audience responses, the possibilities and challenges produced by digital technologies, and his awareness of the interplay between data and user in producing (sometimes troubled or selective) knowledge clearly aligns this chapter with others in the volume and positions art practice along the same continuum of value for research as curation, archiving and the development of new tools.

In the sixth chapter, Lisa Otty and Tara Thomson explore 'Data Visualisation and the Humanities'. The chapter begins with a broad consideration of what visualisations are and how we might understand them, extrapolating from the premise that visualisations occupy an ambiguous and sometimes conflicted position as at once thinking processes, analytical tools and presentation tools. The chapter considers the role of visualisations in research and the factors that make visual experience distinctive, discussing the cultural assumptions that underpin our responses to visual images (ideas of immediacy, transparency, etc.) and exploring how such assumptions might shape a viewer's reception of visualisations. Otty and Thomson conclude their first section with a discussion of some of the mechanics of vision (colour, detail, etc.) that can impact on how viewers experience visualisations and briefly discuss the criteria against which the effectiveness of visualisations might be measured. The second section of the chapter focuses on case studies of creating and working with visualisations in the research process and in teaching. Discussing a variety of examples created using freely available software programs, this section explores the challenges faced and choices made in creating visualisations, outlining some of the insights that they facilitated and, in key instances, discussing their reception. The chapter concludes with a move beyond the authors' own research to consider some further particularly interesting and impressive examples of complex visualisations, offering a sense of the 'blue sky' possibilities inherent in visualisation and offering a real sense of the role of this kind of digital creation as research practice.

In 'Curating Mary Digitally: Digital Methodologies and Representations of Medieval Material Culture', Cecilia Lindhé, Ann-Catrine Eriksson, Jim Robertsson and Mattis Lindmark detail the *Imitatio Mariae: Virgin Mary as a Virtuous Model in Medieval Sweden* project and its new methods and tools for representing medieval artefacts. The project was developed in close collaboration between researchers and computer technicians and is therefore an ideal case study for the issues surrounding creative Digital Humanities projects produced by teams rather than lone or small groups of academics. Instead of thinking in terms of collecting, preserving and exhibiting collections of medieval artefacts, the *Imitatio Mariae* team created various digital interactive installations as well as alternative ways of presenting and archiving research material in virtual environments. Their chapter outlines the conceptual and theoretical framework of the installations and archive, explaining their ties to aesthetic theory (for example H. U. Gumbrecht's writings about the production of presence) and ancient and medieval rhetoric, especially the concepts of *memoria, ductus* and *ekphrasis/enargeia*. In this way, Lindhé et al. demonstrate the ways in which theoretical sophistication and historical awareness can be built into the practices of collection and creation. The installations and the archive not only orchestrate the Swedish medieval church as a multi-modal and performative space, but they further investigate digital technology as a critical perspective on medieval materiality (and more generally on knowledge production within the Humanities). Instead of conforming to an interface that merely presents a collection in a more traditional way, this chapter describes how the team tried to design scholarly tools that revise, question and describe the formative stages of the research process while also demonstrating the potential for new digital methods to represent medieval materiality.

Chapter 8, 'Raising Language Awareness Using Digital Media: Methods for Revealing Linguistic Stereotyping', sees Mats Deutschmann, Anders Steinvall and Anna Lagerström detailing another kind of creativity: the creation of a research methodology that could not have existed, even in abbreviated form, before contemporary computing. Deutschmann et al. explore language's close connection with identity, its links to nationality, but also the conscious and unconscious associations of language output and group identity (e.g. class, gender, generation, ethnicity) that we deploy whenever we interact with someone linguistically. They cite a long history of research into the ways in which individuals are judged in terms of intellect and other character traits on the basis of their voice quality, intonation and accent, a process which affects 'identification', the ongoing process of identity construction that takes place during all human interaction. The chapter, then, gives an account of several methods for raising awareness of language issues and identity (such as stereotyping) using digital media. Working in a virtual world environment with digital representations of speakers (avatars), Deutschmann et al. used avatar manipulations and so-called voice morphing tools with the aim of exposing students to different disguised 'versions' of the same real speaker (by, for example, manipulating impressions of gender). The chapter demonstrates how the students' judgement of the same person differed greatly depending on how the latter had been digitally manipulated, and an approach to using this revelation as a starting point for a discussion about language and identity. The authors argue that such an approach has great implications for language-awareness-raising activities, particularly in the vocational training of a diversity of people on a daily basis (teachers, police, nurses and doctors for example).

From a research methods perspective, the chapter is also particularly useful in demonstrating the limits of current technologies and how approaches often need to be iterated in sympathy with these limitations in order to produce the most effective results.

The final chapter, Marilyn Deegan's 'A World of Possibilities: Digitisation and the Humanities' offers an appropriate bookend to Tanner et al.'s opening piece. Where Tanner et al. broadly discuss the nature and possibilities of the digitisation of materials and introduces the reader to some of the ethical and academic issues that have arisen from its implementation, Deegan, instead, focuses on a series of wide-ranging projects that have drawn on and developed such methods in a variety of forms. In doing this she again explores the potentials and problems of digitisation methods, but approaches the discussion from a different angle, rooting it in practices undertaken (or, in some instances, that are planned to occur). The chapter traces projects across their development and into their use, emphasising how the early choices made before and during digitisation efforts (that Tanner et al. also discuss) pay off in the final user experience. In her discussion of the Rwandan Gacaca archive, Deegan also contributes to demonstrating the dramatic range and significance of political concerns that can be, must be bound up in digitisation projects.

This volume, then, calls for a recognition of two things: firstly, and already established at the heart of the Digital Humanities, that digital building is a research method which will produce its own distinct insights. And, secondly, that such acts are never neutral, whether through intentionally embedding theoretical concerns and political choices into the fabric of what is being constructed or through the unconscious laying-in of values that must later be recognised or teased out by subsequent scholars. In this way building and reading, hack and yack, are intrinsically combined, and sometimes the very same thing, just as the potter must always discover something about the clay and about her hands in the act of working with the world in calling her artwork into being. We hope, therefore, that this volume stands alone and is of use to anyone interested in the practice of academic digital creation, but also that it sits alongside our collection on new reading methods. Together we think that these volumes show some of the potentials for digital work in the humanities: the potential to make new things, the potential to learn new things and the potential to ask new questions through (and despite) the affordances of digital technologies.

NOTES

1. For more on the emergence of this phrase in the field see Nowviskie (2014) and Deegan and Hayler (2016).

2. These transmogrified into the 'Research Excellence Framework' in 2014.
3. Ihde's postphenomenology extends phenomenological concerns, particularly with regard to the role of technology in human action and perception. He is concerned with how humans actually deploy their tools and unites elements of pragmatism and classical phenomenology to explore the effects of embodiment, social forces and material interactions.
4. Matt has written elsewhere about Ihde's work, post-phenomenology, and the effects of the use of technologies and their structuring of our experience of the world (see Hayler 2015, 2016). For more on these particular relationships see Ihde (1990: 72–112).
5. See, for example, Heidegger (1977), Ellul (1964), Clark (2008), Pickering (2011).
6. Matt discusses this entanglement elsewhere (Hayler 2015: 1945).

REFERENCES

Barad, K. (2007) *Meeting the Universe Halfway: Quantum Physics and the Entanglement of Matter and Meaning*. Durham, NC: Duke University Press.

Clark, A. (2008) *Supersizing the Mind*. Oxford: Oxford University Press.

Deegan, M. and Hayler, M. (2016) 'Digital humanities and the future of the book', *Futures for English Studies*. Basingstoke: Palgrave.

Ellul, J. (1964) *The Technological Society*. Toronto: Random House.

Gold, M. K. (ed.) (2012) *Debates in the Digital Humanities*. Minneapolis: University of Minnesota Press.

Griffin, G. and Hayler, M. (eds) (2016) *Research Methods for Reading Digital Data in the Digital Humanities*. Edinburgh: Edinburgh University Press.

Hayler, M. (2015) *Challenging the Phenomena of Technology*. Basingstoke: Palgrave.

Hayler, M. (2016) 'Another way of looking: reflexive technologies and how they change the world', in Rhonda Blair and Amy Cook (eds), *Theatre, Performance and Cognition Languages, Bodies and Ecologies*. London: Methuen.

Heidegger, M. (1977) *The Question Concerning Technology and Other Essays*, trans. W. Lovitt. New York: Garland.

Ihde, D. (1990) *Technology and the Lifeworld*. Bloomington: University of Indiana Press.

Kirschenbaum, M. (2012) 'What is Digital Humanities and what's it doing in English departments?', in M. K. Gold (ed.), *Debates in the Digital Humanities*. Minneapolis: University of Minnesota Press.

Latour, B. (2007) *Reassembling the Social*. Oxford: Oxford University Press.

McCarty, W. (2014) *Humanities Computing*. Basingstoke: Macmillan.

Malafouris, L. (2013) *How Things Shape the Mind: A Theory of Material Engagement*. Cambridge, MA: MIT Press.

Nowviskie, B. (2014) 'On the origin of "hack" and "yack", online at: <http://nowviskie.org/2014/on-the-origin-of-hack-and-yack/> (last accessed 30 August 2015).

Pickering, A. (2011) *The Cybernetic Brain*. Chicago: University of Chicago Press.

Schreibman S., Siemens, R. and Unsworth, J. (2004) *A Companion to Digital Humanities*. Oxford: Blackwell, online at: <http://www.digitalhumanities.org/companion/> (last accessed 30 August 2015).

Smith, H. and Dean, R. (2009) *Practice-Led Research and Research-Led Practice*. Edinburgh: Edinburgh University Press.

CHAPTER 2

Choices in Digitisation for the Digital Humanities

Simon Tanner, Laura Gibson, Rebecca Kahn and
Geoff Laycock

INTRODUCTION

Digital Humanities research and scholarship has been significantly enhanced by the process of digitisation over the last twenty years. The mass conversion of analogue materials to digital, including the growth of the mass digitisation of books, newspapers and primary source material such as manuscripts, has enhanced scholarly practice and enabled fresh research insights. The digitisation of rare and special collections has brought together online collections otherwise hidden from study. This chapter will concern itself with the process of digitisation, the tools and mechanisms, with a critical appraisal of the selection criteria for materials to digitise and the way that choices in terms of digitisation processes affect Digital Humanities research opportunities. The intent is to highlight the choices available for digitisation as a means to enhance the Digital Humanities while also considering the consequences of such choices.

WHAT IS DIGITISATION?

In the *Oxford English Dictionary* (*OED*), digitisation refers to the 'action or process of digitizing; the conversion of analogue data (esp. in later use images, video, and text) into digital form' (*OED* 2015). This definition provides the focus for this chapter which views digitisation as the intricate and multifaceted material process of converting analogue forms of information storage into digital bits. The *OED* traces the term digitisation back to its use in the 1950s in relation to computing science. Depending on a person's linguistic origins and preferences, it can be spelt with an 's' or a 'z'. Digitisation is some-times used interchangeably with 'digital imaging' or 'scanning' but these are merely mechanisms within the process for capturing a digital picture that is sampled and mapped as a grid of squares known as picture elements (pixels). Many other processes exist within digitisation. Other decisions within the process might include:

- assessment and selection of originals for digitisation;
- feasibility testing, costing and piloting;
- copyright clearance and intellectual property rights management;
- preparation of original materials, including conservation;
- benchmarking of processes and technologies;
- digital capture, including scanning, digital imaging, optical character recognition (OCR), digital recording for audio/video;
- quality assessment and assurance;
- metadata for discovery, data management, preservation and administration;
- storage solutions for long-term preservation and sustainability of the digitised content;
- delivery mechanisms to get the end digitised content to the user;
- workflow processes to effectively manage the flow of activity;
- project management (of crucial importance) to ensure time, money, risk and deliverables are well managed.

This non-exhaustive list includes just some of the processes. No digitisation activity should proceed without knowing the plan and technologies for each one. Underlying these are a range of other issues specific to each form of original material, to each information goal desired from digitisation and the intended functional outcomes.

Since digitisation relates to processes, it is often treated as a neutral tech-nology or naturally beneficent activity. Consideration of the varied facets and components of these processes demonstrate that digitisation has so many aspects that its impact is intrinsically linked to the wider context of its application. Digitisation, especially of cultural heritage, brings 'a curious and unprecedented fusion of technology, imagination, necessity, philosophy and production which is continuously creating new images, many of which are changing the culture within which we live' (Colson and Hall 1992: 75). Michelle Pickover, curator of manuscripts at the University of the Witwatersrand in South Africa, argues that 'Cyberspace is not an uncontested domain. The digital medium contains an ideological base – it is a site of strug-gle' (Pickover 2005: 8). We will explore these specific issues in more detail later in this chapter. Maintaining a critical appraisal of the selection criteria for materials to digitise remains important as choices made during the digitisation processes significantly affect Digital Humanities research opportunities.

THE BENEFITS OF DIGITISATION TO DIGITAL
HUMANITIES RESEARCH, LEARNING AND TEACHING

Memory institutions (including libraries, archives and museums) have historically focused upon archiving, managing and preserving what can be termed *containers* of information: boxed letters, reports, documents, paintings, film or photographs. These collections frequently form the backbone of primary sources used by humanities scholars in their research and so are also an important corpus for Digital Humanists. These physical, primary carriers of recorded information and knowledge content are a form of semantic memory and were the main focus of efforts to enable description and discovery by archivists and librarians in the past (Reisberg 2013: 206). In short, the route to acquiring the content of these documents was inherently wrapped up in a search for the container (Tanner 2006: 19). With the increased adoption of digitisation came the opportunity for content to be not only inferred but directly managed, preserved and utilised. However, combined with an accompanying deluge of information, this opportunity renders new challenges for scholars as sorting useful source material from the chaff becomes more difficult. The materiality and nature of the analogue thus has an abiding impact upon the digitised content.

> To some extent, the 'shapes' of the containers of information have
> been retained in a virtual world . . . But in a world where information
> and content increasingly are unbound from containers, the containers
> cannot act as guides . . . (De Rosa et al. 2003: 98)

One of the core benefits of digitisation for the Digital Humanities has been the growth in digital content that may be investigated, parsed, re-used and mined for humanistic research purposes. A digitised resource should thus enable, from a Digital Humanities perspective as described by John Unsworth, a 'list of functions (recursive functions) that could be the basis for a manageable but also useful tool-building enterprise' (Unsworth 2000: 1), namely (but not exclusively):

- discovering
- annotating
- comparing
- referring
- sampling
- illustrating
- representing.

The general public desires these functions as much as scholars do. As such, addressing these functional requirements when digitising for the digital humanities not only fulfils scholarly requirements but is also likely to attract a wider base of appreciative users.

LEARNING AND TEACHING

Educational benefits are gained from a wide variety of activities introducing people to newly digitised information and experiences. Education benefits should aim to include all members of society, not just university students or schoolchildren: there is a hunger for learning and for resource discovery at all levels and Digital Humanities resources are frequently used beyond academia. For instance, the Fine Rolls of Henry III regularly gain over 5 million hits per year (DDH 2014).

> Now I enter the classroom and I think, most of the content that I have to deliver and a whole lot more, is floating around them right now. What I need to do is inspire them and give them the tools to harness that information and harness the skills of other people to do the things they want to get done.[1] (Bradwell 2009: 25)

Digital Humanities digitised resources can encourage a more exploratory, research-based approach to teaching and learning. Once available digitally, materials produced for one context can be used in many others: advanced research projects can be used by students in a wide range of contexts and backgrounds, including schools, colleges and life-long learners.

RESEARCH

Research benefits accrue when we invest in deepening our understanding of the world and build upon the intellectual legacy of previous generations. Digitised resources continue to transform the research process. The researcher can now ask questions that were previously not feasible. They can engage in new processes of discovery and focus their intellect more on analysis than data collation. Digitised resources transform the research process:

- New areas of research are enabled.
- Rich research content is now widely accessible through innovative interfaces and friendly research tools. Examples include:
  - Connected Histories;[2]
  - DigiPal: the Digital Resource and Database for Palaeography, Manuscript Studies and Diplomatic;[3]
  - HathiTrust Digital Library;[4]

- NINES (Networked Infrastructure for Nineteenth-Century Electronic Scholarship);[5] and
- EHRI (European Holocaust Research Infrastructure),[6] among many others.[7]
- The researcher can now ask questions that were previously not feasible.
- Researchers can engage in a new process of discovery and focus their intellect on analysis rather than data collation.

A bedrock of scholarship is the ability to share, discuss and reference thoughts, ideas and discoveries. Scholars require access to the accumulated knowledge of human endeavour to move research and discovery forward. However, the sheer volume, value, fragility, complexity and dispersion of physical assets mean that they can never be fully displayed, accessed or made widely available in that form. Scholars travel to libraries around the world if they want to compare sources which is both costly and time-consuming. Now they can access materials in digitised form which may well have been reunified through a Digital Humanities scholarly edition or resource. In addition to reunifying primary sources, digitised resources enable new tools to facilitate research once they have be brought together again. For instance:

> Jane Austen's Fiction Manuscripts Digital Edition offers unprecedented opportunities for new scholarship, particularly in exploring the creative laboratory of her novels . . . It also makes the manuscript sources freely available to the wider public.[8] (Tanner 2011: 16)

CRITICAL STRATEGIC CHOICES IN DIGITISATION

Stakeholders and selection

The digitisation of cultural heritage collections by memory institutions is never a neutral process and involves a number of different stakeholders (individuals, groups or organisations that are affected by the digitisation project), possibly with conflicting interests. Past decisions made about which items should be included in our collections still influence decisions we make today. None of these past decisions were inevitable and often reflect biases at that time. Identifying and engaging with the stakeholders is an important first step in the digitisation process if we are to avoid producing projects that simply embody and reinforce historical power imbalances that exclude and offend certain stakeholders. Stakeholders may include:

- institutional staff
- governments
- users

- funders
- creators
- source communities: 'the communities from which . . . collections originate' (Peers and Brown 2003: 1).

In young or developing technical environments, it may be the case that projects are initiated because they align with institutional interests or the route to funding is straightforward. National-level strategy often sets a precedent, particularly in cultural heritage digitisation, and while this makes it likely that high-profile cultural heritage materials will be the focus, it is important that all stakeholders are addressed in these decisions, as they have an impact not only on the types of materials selected, but on the way the digitised materials may be presented.

Historically, in new technical environments – that is, during the period of experimentation, before something becomes 'business as usual' – it is often the passionate, the visionary, the expert and the collection owners who define and decide what materials or data are digitised. This can leave the beneficial stakeholders being 'told' what constitutes good digitised content or what they should be digitising. While this may change as technology and access to the means of digitisation becomes more ubiquitous, the precedent established by past digitisation sets a trajectory that can be difficult to change in the future. Consequently, selection and appraisal are important processes in digitisation planning since they make transparent how and why value judgements were made, making it easier to navigate a balance between elite and beneficial stakeholders. Even if we were to digitise every artefact or document held by our memory institutions without 'discrimination' – what Mats Dahlström, Joachim Hansson and Ulrika Kjellman understand as 'mass digitisation' – we are not engaging in a neutral process, but are replicating a worldview inherent in our collections and at the expense of other narratives. 'Critical digitisation' where 'at every step one can make choices, select, leave out and interpret' (Dahlstrom et al. 2012: 262) means the digitisation process 'merely adds an additional layer of complexity' since decisions made today about what to digitise are also neither made independently of prevailing worldviews nor of historical circumstances (Pickover 2014: 3).

Given that many marginalised communities have been denied ownership over cultural heritage collections that reside in both public and private institutions, making these digital items available online can further exacerbate this loss of ownership since, in the online sphere, they are open to even wider 'misappropriation and misunderstandings by outsiders' (Srinivasan et al. 2009: 175). Indeed, a western predilection for open access is not universal and sits uncomfortably with structures of access in other communities that are based around kinship and other ties whereby it is deemed undesirable, or even dangerous, for the unintended or uninitiated person to access certain items and knowledge (Brown and Nicholas 2012; Christie and Verran 2013; Ngata et al. 2012). Similarly, a western idea that the digital object is a surrogate of the original is not universally accepted. For example, certain Maori groups do not understand the digitised version of an object as distinct from the original since it is imbued with the same power and so deserving of great respect (Ngata et al. 2012).

Navigating the balance between elite and beneficial stakeholders depends on:

• thorough stakeholder mapping;
• serious engagement with all stakeholders;
• framing and interrogating past and present decisions from different stakeholder perspectives;
• critical engagement with the criteria used in decision-making workflows;
• recognising that success indicators might vary between stakeholders and so be more difficult to define. (This question of measuring success is discussed further below.)

The Digital Humanities open up possibilities for extracting new meanings from digitised assets, but this is only possible if the motivations for creating the assets in the first place are able to balance transparency with flexibility.

ETHICAL AND MORAL FRAMEWORKS

While recognising that digitisation projects are fraught with obstacles, there are persuasive arguments that digital resources can, potentially, bring 'a range of opportunities' to some of the world's most marginalised groups, particularly through supporting and preserving local identities (Boast et al. 2007). The Australian Ara Irititja project is one example. Ara Irititja is a database of over 50,000 digital images and sound recordings of indigenous Australian *Anangu* culture collected from public and private collections since 1994. Ara Irititja is housed on computer stations at the museum in Adelaide and eleven mobile *niri niri* computer workstations located throughout the remote *Pitjantjatjara* lands. These *niri niri* are unique workstations that are capable of withstanding a plethora of pests, from mice to spilled drinks (Christen 2006).

The methodology for developing Ara Irititja was community oriented, meaning that the Pitjantjatjara Council was involved in decisions about collecting and software design before these activities commenced. Significantly, the database was built 'using Pitjantjatjara access parameters – gender, kin relations, and country knowledge – to sort and present data' (Christen 2006: 57). Many of the project's complexities are to do with the database structure itself since some men's objects cannot occupy the same space as women's objects and this rule applies in digital as well as physical spaces (Hughes and Dallwitz 2007). Accepting these parameters required a shift in thinking for many non-Anangu people involved in the project. The solution has been splitting data between three structurally identical databases:

- open items
- men's items
- women's items.

The restricted databases are never stored on the same computer. Data is further sorted into six fields that are labelled using Pitjantjatjara language, but reflect standard museum catalogue categories:

- photos
- documents
- sound
- movies
- objects
- maps.

A further set of data fields provide space for including such information as object number, collection, date and copyright, as well as a free information field that 'allows multiple storylines to coexist' (Christen 2006: 58). Access, however, is defined in four categories of privilege:

- open access;
- operator;
- sorrow (view and edit items concerning deceased people);
- offensive (view and edit items considered offensive).

The community controls who has access to which materials and they password protect this.

What Ara Irititja highlights is that conducting ethical digitisation projects requires serious engagement with all stakeholders so that their needs and concerns are clearly understood, as discussed in the preceding section. In some cases this may mean reassessing widely practised approaches to organising and accessing data and subsequently developing innovative alternatives. Of course, these ethical decisions are impacted by the intended outcomes of the project.

ECONOMIC AND LEGAL FRAMEWORKS

When businesses like Google look at libraries, they do not merely see temples of learning. They see potential assets or what they call 'content' ready to be mined. Built up over centuries at an enormous expenditure of money and labor, library collections can be digitised en masse at relatively little cost – millions of dollars, certainly, but little compared to the investment that went into them. (Darnton 2009: 1)

The purpose of the digitisation project has an impact on the way the resulting data is managed. If digitisation was part of an institution's ongoing internal processes (such as the photographing of museum objects) there may be a different legal infrastructure for the management of the materials as opposed to a funded project to digitise materials for increasing access, developing research infrastructure or preservation concerns. While the reasons for digitisation may change, what remains unchanged is the need to produce a framework that avoids locking digital content away. Darnton's concerns expressed above point to an overall anxiety, often cited in the cultural heritage sphere, that large multinational corporations digitise materials for future exploitation and 'ownership'. The HathiTrust lawsuit in which the Authors Guild of America alleged that the HathiTrust's digitisation of works to use in a full-text search database (as well as the Orphan Works Project developed by the University of Michigan) constituted copyright infringement is one example of how litigation can have a chilling effect on digitisation (HathiTrust Digital Library 2015). While the ruling in the HathiTrust case was eventually made in favour of the libraries, the Orphan Works Project (orphan works are defined as those which are subject to copyright but whose copyright holders cannot be identified or contacted) was abandoned, meaning that a great deal of content which might otherwise be available in the public domain has been rendered inaccessible as a result of copyright anxiety.

In fact, if humanities scholars and cultural heritage practitioners wish to avoid their creative content being mined by web businesses such as Google, there is an urgent onus on them to exploit both the content in their collections and the networked, peer-driven nature of the Web to showcase their collections and data themselves. In this context, institutions can make use of legal frameworks already in existence, such as:

- open licensing
- open access classifications
- public domain.

Making use of these tools to facilitate the sharing of content is based on the premise that researchers and professional staff are familiar with both the rights status of the materials or data they are working with and the range of options available to them. However, anxiety around licensing and ownership, fears about the risk of 'watering down' the value of content via free sharing and a lack of clarity about the copyright status of materials are often cited as reasons not to make materials available.

The reality in many cultural heritage organisations is that digital content, while possibly expensive to create, is not a profitable revenue stream in museums, galleries and archives. In research undertaken in US art museums, founded on a previous study in UK and European institutions, Tanner has shown that 'the level of revenue raised by museums through imaging and rights is small relative to the overall revenue earning capacity of the museum' (Tanner 2004: 40). If the revenue from these services is relatively small, museums need to find other sources. However, this does not mean that the reproduction and distribution of digital data cannot be used to bolster other sources of income within a structured legal and rights management framework.

CASE STUDY — THE RIJKSMUSEUM

> With the internet, it's so difficult to control your copyright or use of images that we decided we'd rather people use a very good high-resolution image of the 'Milkmaid' from the Rijksmuseum rather than using a very bad reproduction. (Taco Dibbits, Director of Collections, Rijksmuseum, in Siegal 2013)

The argument is sometimes made that restricting access to content acts as a quality control mechanism, preventing the proliferation of poor-quality content or data and preserving an institution's intellectual property. However, the reality is often the opposite: replication and re-use of content are two of the main activities on the Internet and are difficult and expensive to control. Ensuring quality reproduction of your data is actually easier if it is made readily and freely available.

The Rijksmuseum in the Netherlands argued that the digital reproduction of an object would raise public interest and might lead directly to people buying tickets to the museum. As a result, the museum made all out-of-copyright digitised objects available as public domain objects, including masterpieces by van Gogh, Vermeer and Rembrandt. The combination of high-quality, freely re-usable digital images in the public domain has resulted in a data set which is well used and web-users have creatively remixed images to produce:

- make-up palettes based on the colour palettes of the Dutch Masters;
- a range of jams inspired by foods in the paintings;
- spectacle frames based on great artwork frames.

Creative re-use has also translated into viable business models for the Museum – the total revenue from the Museum's image bank grew from just under €125,000 in 2010 when no material was freely available to €181,000 in 2012 after the data sets were released. Visitor numbers to the museum have also increased, from 896,000 in 2010 to over 2 million in 2013 (Reijksmuseum 2012). However, it is also important to note that this amount is only 0.2 per cent of total revenue for the Museum overall (Pekel 2015). When revenue amounts are so small and the potential pay-off for open sharing is evident, the case for open licensing with due diligence is compelling.

TYPES OF OPEN LICENCES

Scholarly publishing and open access

The infrastructure with which most academics are familiar are those governing the use of academic and scholarly content and communications. These are usually referred to as either Green or Gold open access, or free and *libre* open access. In principle, open access refers to the way data and scholarly communications are published. Traditionally, peer-reviewed journals were bought by individuals or licensed from publishers but these arrangements were typically expensive and made much of the published research inaccessible to the developing world and unaffiliated researchers. It also created a false economy around access to publication, ensuring that many researchers in the developing world were unable to find publication outlets for their research (Gray 2010). With the advent of digital communication and online publishing, the sharing of scholarly communications became much easier and increasing numbers of academics began sharing their work online. As the system evolved, many funders mandated that the results of any funded research be openly licensed. At the time of writing, in 2015, these include private funders such as the Bill and Melinda Gates and MacArthur Foundations in the USA, national research councils like the UK Arts and Humanities Research Council (AHRC) and the Wellcome Trust, and the European Commission (ROARMAP 2015). US funders such as the US National Endowment for the Humanities likewise show strong support (St Louis 2014).

Orphan works and the public domain

While these models govern the publication of digitisation outputs, research data and scholarly communications, there are other open-licence scaffolds which can be used for the free sharing of other types of content. Orphaned works, mentioned above, are a significant stumbling block in mass digitisation projects, particularly in the cultural heritage sphere. Many copyright reform campaigners argue that orphan works should be licensed specifically for the public domain, thus entering the body of works whose intellectual property rights have expired, been forfeited or are inapplicable. The public domain makes works available to anyone, and includes items such as the works of Shakespeare and Beethoven and Newtonian physics. Most countries have balked at mandating the public domain status of orphan works and have offered hybrid solutions in their copyright law. In the European Union, a statutory exception-based model requires member states to establish a statutory exception to the rights and permits uses of orphan works if a 'diligent search' is performed and no rights holders are located. Once a work is deemed orphan in one member state, it is considered orphaned in the entire Union (European Commission 2014). In the UK, an independent review of the UK intellectual property system in 2011 stated that the orphan works problem represented the 'starkest failure of the copyright framework to adapt' and warned that 'as long as this state of affairs continues, archives in old formats will continue to decay and further delay to digitisation means some will be lost for good' (Hargreaves 2011: 38). At the time of writing, the UK solution is similar to Europe's whereby the management of rights is the UK Intellectual Property Office's responsibility. For anyone working with cultural heritage or humanities data, it is essential to know the copyright status of materials before digitising and attaching a licence.

DIGITISATION TOOLS

Having decided that digitisation would aid a Digital Humanities process and after considering these vital strategic issues, there are further choices to be made in terms of tools and technologies. A narrow delineation of these has been selected for this chapter so as not to repeat content appearing elsewhere in this book. We focus on digital imaging, capturing sound and vision, text capturing and metadata.

Large-scale digitisation

The body of materials that need to be digitised may be very large scale if the drivers for digitisation activity relate to capturing analogue materials for long-term preservation and access. This creates a set of choices incumbent with challenges that require both careful management and well considered process design. A process that works for a few thousand items will be unlikely to scale to tens of thousands of items, and certainly not to the millions of items seen in the Google Books or the HathiTrust's digital library (Conway 2010).

To avoid inconsistencies in the resulting digital content due to human error or the misuse of technology, the most effective way to consider large-scale digitisation is to view the challenge in terms of an industrial production line with tools, technology, checks and balances in place to ensure consistent and measurable output. Planning then becomes the most important step because there is an opportunity not only to assess the quantity, condition and range of the materials, but also a chance to trial production processes and factor in the elapsed time for certain tasks to be completed. Looking at a large-scale digitisation project in this way allows the scale of the task to be understood in context and makes setting up a digitisation facility or outsourcing the activity to another organisation more realistic and achievable (National Archives 2015).

With large-scale projects, the materials are often in many different formats and conditions; some of the materials may need conservation treatment before they can be digitised. Each different material type will require its own capture approach, for example digital photography, flatbed or dedicated book scanners. Protecting the integrity of the original materials while capturing images on an industrial scale is challenging in terms of workflow, cost efficiency and the management of people, time and space resources. Given these variables, it is vital to carry out a detailed survey during planning to understand the range of materials that are to be captured.

The survey should ideally involve the following investigations:

• quantity assessment of the materials to be captured;
• condition assessment of the materials to assess if conservation work is required;
• condition assessment to ascertain the safest digitisation processes for the materials and the proportion of materials to which each capture method will apply;
• assessment of the required pre-scanning preparation steps;
• assessment of the unique identifiers available for the digital master files created by the project and any links to metadata sources such as existing library or archive catalogues;
• assessment of which aspects of the information contained within the digitised materials may need to be captured in the form of text or other metadata.

The different assessments listed above help to build a picture of the eventual digitisation workflow that will be employed and are all vital to a successful project.

The quantity assessment is the core of the survey and it is worth taking sufficient time to complete to a reasonable level of accuracy (+/− 5 per cent is advisable) as the quantities of materials will determine the effort required to complete the project in the agreed time frame. Digital Humanities projects are often externally funded and must be completed within specified time frames, therefore the core feasibility of the project is dependent on ensuring sufficient resources are assigned.

As a large collection may have varying quantities of different material types it is also key to understand the proportion of different material types across the entire corpus. This has an impact on resource planning as well as on the areas which may require greater conservation focus. This is particularly important within archives where the holdings are often unique and are always irreplaceable. For this reason the protection of the original material is the prime aim of the project. At the survey stage it is also a good idea to look at the pre-preparation steps that may be required before digitisation can take place. Rolled maps or drawings may need to be flattened, historic steel staples, paperclips or pins may need to be removed and so on. Some projects also use the digitisation process as an appropriate time to re-house materials into chemically inert polyester enclosures or acid free boxes. If the goal is to digitise 90–100,000 images per day from historic newspapers then it is a good investment to spend resources at the preparation phase unbinding newspapers where possible and ironing sheets flat for fast, accurate imaging (Tanner 2013).

Armed with survey information, a better picture of the project activity will emerge. It is sound practice at this stage to carry out timed trials of all stages in the proposed production process in relation to the different material types. The quantity of materials that are processed in a fixed time frame can be combined with the quantity information gathered as part of the survey to unlock the amount of resources that will be required for the project. With the variables of quantity, project duration (often a fixed quantity) and throughput it is possible to calculate the amount of digitisation machinery, staffing, space and management resources required to deliver the project successfully. A healthy contingency must be introduced (15 to 20 per cent) to allow for the relatively small sample set of data assessed at the pilot stage.

As consistency of output is a key driver it may be advisable to manage the production process using commercial project and workflow management software tools such as Goobi or DigiFlo (Goobi 2015; DigiFlo 2015). When designing the workflow, formal feedback loops should be built in to identify material which fails quality assurance checking so that it can flow back through the production process for correction. Reporting is also vital because with large projects it is difficult to identify bottlenecks in the processes. If different streams of capture (for different materials) are taking place simultaneously there needs to be a method of assessing whether they are on track or whether more resources may be needed to deliver the project on time. The larger the project is, the more important using industrial tools becomes. Monitoring and understanding the live state of a production process makes it possible to manage resources and identify problems before they have catastrophic impact.

Figure 2.1 Superb preparation facilities at the Swedish National Archives department for digitisation: Media Conversion Center (MKC). (Source: Simon Tanner.)

DIGITAL IMAGING

Digital imaging is the process of capturing a representation of a physical object, whether paper, photographic, artistic or any other material format. A digital image is 'stored in numerical form, for potential display, manipulation or dissemination via computer technologies . . . a digital image is like any other computer data file, just a long code of ones and zeroes, using information as its raw material' (Terras 2008: 6). The decisions faced by digitisation are driven by the digital format to be created, but most importantly by the format and nature of the original analogue object itself.

Imaging of fragile originals

Most image materials to be captured will need a high level of fidelity to the original. The process of capturing colour images from fragile originals is effectively a series of informed decisions. There is no standard approach that will fit every material type but safety for the original is the most important consideration. Originals can be damaged through handling or through exposure to the heat and light of the digitisation process itself. The basic principle should be to capture all the information needed from an original in one digitisation activity to reduce the risk to the original from multiple handlings. When we think of fragile originals we should consider that these may be on many different kinds of substrates:

- parchment
- papyrus
- canvas
- paper
- glass
- film
- fabric, etc.

and are likely to include:

- manuscript images
- paintings
- drawings
- different types of photographs (film negatives, glass plate negatives, slides, prints)
- stained glass
- fabrics
- maps
- architectural drawings, etc.

There are two types of technology available for digitising these objects: scanning and photographic capture. The methods of operation of scanning equipment vary and it is not the intention of this chapter to give details of such methodologies – JISC Digital Media, however, provide an excellent set of online guides (JISC 2015).

There are a few rules of thumb to keep in mind when making choices:

- Choose a mechanism and resolution to capture the smallest significant detail. What is 'significant' will differ across material types and the nature of the content – for text it might be punctuation, for medieval manuscripts it might be the pores of parchment skin side.
- Choose a standard colour space and manage this rigorously to ensure consistency of colour.
- Choose either TIFF or JPEG2000 as the master image file format for long-term preservation. See Buckley's report for the Wellcome Trust Library on JPEG2000 for guidance (Buckley 2009).
- Consider using the IIPImage server system for web-based streamed viewing and zooming of ultra-high-resolution images (IIPI 2015).

Allowing time for expert conservators to assess the materials at this early stage will enable estimates to be made about the length of time and resources required to carry out any conservation work. It may be the case that a substantial proportion of the materials need to undergo some form of treatment before digitisation can be carried out safely. Ascertaining the conservation load on the project at this stage is wise. When using digital cameras to capture materials, the key considerations are the way in which the original is supported and lit. For bound materials, particularly those with fragile bindings, it is good practice to use a conservation cradle to support the volume and protect the bindings. Pages can be kept open with conservation weights and 'snakes' for effective capture of individual pages. For more modern or robust bound volumes there are a variety of 'v-cradle' book scanners available which hold the volume open at a 100° angle while two digital cameras capture both pages simultaneously. These come in various levels of automation from completely manual to robotic book scanners which are capable of turning the pages using robotic arms and slight vacuums to turn the page.

Some materials may have hidden content that will only become visible through imaging beyond the human visual spectrum. This includes hidden or lost text in palimpsest, the effect of tarnishing of substrates, obscuring artefacts such as foxing or chemical erosion, overpainting, blackened in fires or simply being too fragile to unroll. Such imaging encompasses infra-red (IR), ultra-violet (UV) and multi-spectral imaging. UV imaging is generally considered too damaging for organic substrates to be a normal digitisation mechanism and it is good practice to remove UV light from the digitisation studio (DFG 2013: 12). IR is often used to recover text lost in historical manuscripts, such as the Dead Sea Scrolls (Tanner and Bearman 2009). New techniques in multi-spectral imaging are being successfully used to observe features in documents and art not possible by other techniques. Notable examples include the Archimedes Palimpsest (Netz and Noel 2011), carbonised scrolls from Herculaneum (Chabries et al. 2003) and the diaries of David Livingstone (Knox et al. 2011). The Archimedes Palimpsest is the most striking, not least as the original images are made freely available to scholars. The project has revealed to the world the lost ideas of the ancient Greek mathematician and physicist Archimedes (287–212 BC) whose discoveries underpin much of modern physics. This work was quite literally brought out of the dark by digitisation. As Will Noel stated, 'from beneath the pages of the prayer book a second book emerged – a virtual Archimedes' (Tanner 2011: 15).

CAPTURING SOUND AND VISION

Humanities scholars are increasingly using time-based media in research and relying on digital means to represent and discover content. Primary sources in sound and vision are very desirable and most useful if available in digital form, be it film, news, music, video or oral histories. In principle, the conversion of audio or video from an analogue medium to a digital data file is simple – just replay to record it digitally. However, complexity occurs in the detail. Apart from finding playback equipment for the dozens of types/formats of physical carriers, the ongoing problem of digitally capturing video and audio is the resultant file sizes. Time-based media are resource hungry in terms of the file storage required, time to digitise, cost of equipment and bandwidth to deliver. Highly skilled vendors are capable of converting audio and video and many scholars will want to outsource such work.

To illustrate these issues, the British Library Sound Archive is at the pinnacle of sound preservation and digitisation. Their 'Save our Sounds' project looks to raise £40m to digitise the country's sound archive of more than six million recordings (BBC 2015) and already has £9.5m 'to digitise and publish online up to 500,000 rare and unique sounds' (Ranft 2015). While costly, not doing it will be more culturally costly: 'Archival consensus is that we have approximately 15 years to digitise our sound collections, before they become unreadable and are effectively lost' (British Library 2015: 10). The risks for sound and film archives are the twin fires of technology obsolescence and format degradation. The substrates upon which analogue film, video and sound is recorded are degrading fast and even with good conservation effort may become unplayable in the very short timeframe identified by the British Library. Further to the problem of damage and decay are the difficulties in finding playback mechanisms that still work for the many and varied formats – technological obsolescence in the playback of all analogue media is beset with a lack of equipment, spares and experienced operators.

When viewing video or listening to audio, the digital content has to go through a process of compression and decompression (codec). There is initial compression at the production end using a suitable codec (for example Sorenson, Qdesign) to gain the desired file size, frames per second, transmission rate and quality for video. This content may then be saved in a file format suitable for the architecture of the delivery network and expected user environment (for example, MP3 or MP4). For digitisation, the amount and form of compression will be the most difficult choice to be made as retaining suitable quality and searching for possible savings in file size must be balanced. The issues are too extensive to deal with effectively here but there is excellent guidance available from the US Federal Agencies Digitisation Guidelines and the European PrestoCentre (US Federal Agencies Digitization Guidelines 2015; PrestoCentre 2015).

CAPTURING TEXT

'Humanists have been capturing, analyzing, and presenting textual data in digital form for as long as there have been computers capable of processing alphanumeric symbols' (Deegan and Tanner 2004: n.p.). Text capture is a process rather than a single technology. It is the means by which textual content residing within physical artefacts (such as books, manuscripts, journals, reports, correspondence and so on) may be transferred from that medium into a machine-readable format (Schantz 1982). In some cases digital images of text content are sufficient to satisfy the end users' information needs and provide access to the resource in an electronic format that can be shared online. This sort of digital presentation of text resources is particularly useful for documents where transcribing the content would be difficult, such as for handwritten letters or personal notes.

Machine readable text may be gained through the various text capture processes listed below. Rather than presenting the end user with an electronic 'photocopy' of the page, machine readable text makes additional computing functions possible, the most important of which is the ability to index and search text. As a digital text repository grows the only efficient way to navigate through it is via search tools supported by good indexing which is made possible by machine readable text. Thus text capture is a process that should be designed to add value to the text resource. Inherent in the concept of adding value is an assessment whether the cost of delivering the benefit was commensurate with the value added. The more automated the capture process the easier it seems to justify the cost for the benefit across a large corpus.

The main methods for text capture are (in order of popularity):

- optical character recognition (OCR) – sometimes also known as intelligent character recognition (ICR);
- rekeying;
- handwriting recognition (HR);
- voice or speech recognition.

We will focus upon OCR and rekeying as the most efficient and effective mechanisms of text capture.

Optical character recognition

OCR is a type of document image analysis where a scanned digital image containing either machine printed or handwritten script is input into an OCR software engine and translated into a machine readable digital text format (like ASCII text). OCR works by first pre-processing the digital page image into its smallest component parts with layout analysis to find text blocks, sentence/ line blocks, word blocks and character blocks. Other features such as lines, graphics and photographs are recognised and discarded. The character blocks are then further broken down into component parts, pattern recognised and compared to the OCR engine's dictionary of characters from various fonts and languages. Once a likely match is made, this is recorded and a set of characters in the word block are recognised until all likely characters have been found for the word block. The word is then compared to the OCR engine's dictionary of complete words that exist for that language. These factors of characters and words recognised are the key to OCR accuracy.

Gaining character accuracies of greater than 1 in 5,000 characters (99.98 per cent) with fully automated OCR is usually only possible with post-1950s printed text. Accuracies averaging 95 per cent (5 in 100 characters wrong) is more usual for post-1900 and pre-1950s text; anything pre-1900 will be fortunate to exceed 85 per cent accuracy (15 in 100 characters wrong). Thus OCR for historical materials is usually hampered by the expensive and time-consuming need for manual or semi-automated proofreading and correction of the text (Holley 2009).

OCR as a technology is significantly affected by the following factors:

- scanning methods;
- nature of original material;

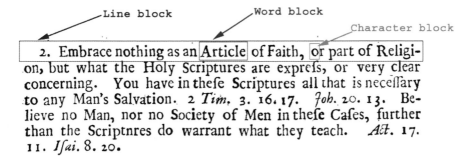

Figure 2.2 By combining character, word and line blocks, the OCR engine can deliver high levels of accuracy. (Source: Simon Tanner.)

- nature of printing:
  - uniformity
  - language
  - text alignment
  - complexity of alignment
  - lines, graphics and pictures
  - handwriting;
- nature of document;
- nature of output requirements.

If our processes should orientate towards the intellectual aims desired from a resource, then the means of measuring success should also be defined by whether those aims are actually achieved. This means exploring the potential benefits of measuring success in terms of words – and particularly those that have more significance for the user searching the resource. When we look at the number of words that are incorrect rather than the number of characters, the suppliers' accuracy statistics seem a lot less impressive. For example, given a newspaper page of 1,000 words with 5,000 characters, if the OCR engine yields a result of 90 per cent character accuracy, this equals 500 incorrect characters. However, considered in word terms, this might convert to a maximum of 900 correct words (90 per cent word accuracy) or a minimum of 500 correct words (50 per cent word accuracy), if an average word consists of 5 characters. The key consideration when utilizing OCR is the usefulness of the text output for indexing and retrieval purposes. If it were possible to achieve 90 per cent character accuracy and still get 90 per cent word accuracy, then most search engines utilizing fuzzy logic would get in excess of 98 per cent retrieval rate for straightforward prose text (Tanner 2009).

When we assess the accuracy of OCR output, it is vital we do not focus purely on statistical measures but also consider the functionality enabled through the OCR's output, such as:

- search accuracy;
- volume of hits returned;
- ability to structure searches and results;
- accuracy of result ranking;
- amount of correction required to achieve the required performance.

Rekeying

Rekeying is a process by which text content in digital images is manually keyed via a keyboard. It is differentiated from copy typing by the automation and industrialisation of the process.

Rekeying is usually offered in three forms:

- double rekeying;
- triple rekeying;
- OCR with rekeyed correction.

In rekeying, the digital image of the text is viewed at high magnification in one window and keyed into a separate window (usually in specially designed software). Double and triple rekeying are variations on a quality assurance method. In double rekeying the same digital image of text is keyed by two different keying operators with no conferring over their interpretation of the text. This output is then automatically compared by a computer and a third person (usually in a supervisory role) is shown the two texts overlaid with the differences highlighted. The third operator makes the casting vote in deciding which version is correct. In this way high levels of accuracy can be reached by reducing keying errors introduced by human error. Triple rekeying uses three keying operators and would expect to achieve 99.99 per cent character accuracy while double rekeying typically achieves 99.96–99.98 per cent character accuracy.

METADATA

Given that humanists and librarians will almost certainly be capturing primary source data at a high quality and with long-term preservation as a key goal, it is important that this data be documented properly so that future curators and users understand what it is they are dealing with. Metadata is one of the critical components of digital resource conversion and use, and is needed at all stages in the creation and management of the resource. Metadata is defined in the OED as a 'set of data that describes and gives information about other data' (OED 2015). Metadata is structured information about a digital object that allows systems, and therefore users, to find the object and define it. Metadata describes, explains, locates or otherwise makes it easier to retrieve use or manage an information resource (NISO 2004: 1).

> Any creator of digital objects should take as much care in the creation of the metadata as they do in the creation of the data itself – time and effort expended at the creation stage recording good-quality metadata is likely to save users much grief, and to result in a well-formed digital object which will survive for the long term. (Deegan and Tanner 2004: n.p.)

Metadata is vitally important to digitisation and the Digital Humanities because it is the gateway to interrogating large bodies of digital materials for research needs. If metadata about a digital collection is well organised then the possibilities for collating and interrogating digital resources become functionally endless.

Metadata is split into different logical types, all of which relate to the digital object:

- *Descriptive metadata* – describe the resource to aid finding and identifying it. Common attributes for this type of metadata could include its title, creator/author and keywords together with a brief description of the contents.
- *Structural metadata* – describe and chart how complex objects are ordered in the digital object, for instance showing how a map with its annotations fits into the wider Geographical Information System (GIS).
- *Administrative metadata* – place where information that helps to manage the digital resource is stored. This may be information about file types, creation dates, copyright and intellectual property information, access rights and information about digital preservation or the long-term archiving and preservation of the digital object.

Metadata is often held in the open-source XML language. This brings many advantages to Digital Humanists, such as providing a means to ensure platform independence, multi-lingual character support, easier interoperability and extensible open standards (McDonough 2009). XML operates in a cascading structure which relates the smallest piece of information all the way up the tree to the highest level of collection information thus keeping information organised and in a direct structural relationship at all times. For users, this means that the databases can operate very quickly and deliver the results instantly. XML-based content standards, such as the Text Encoding Initiative (TEI), have been widely adopted by Digital Humanists and, with librarians, they have further developed other XML-based metadata standards (McDonough 2009).

Metadata is organised into schemas. There are many internationally accepted and freely available metadata schemas (a selection is listed below) that can be used. To a large extent they are interoperable, meaning that a system using one type of schema will often be able to understand and interrogate a group of materials organised using a different metadata schema thanks to established links or mappings between them. Here are a few examples of different metadata schemas:

- CCO: Cataloguing Cultural Objects
- CDWA: Categories for the Description of Works of Art
- DC: Dublin Core
- EAD: Encoded Archival Description
- IEEE LOM: Learning Object Metadata

- ISAD(G): General International Standard Archival Description
- ISAN: International Standard Audiovisual Number
- MARC: Machine-Readable Cataloguing
- METS: Metadata Encoding and Transmission Standard
- MIX: Metadata for Images in XML
- MODS: Metadata Object Description Schema
- OAI-ORE: Open Archives Initiative Object Reuse and Exchange
- PREMIS: Preservation Metadata Implementation Strategies
- RDA: Resource Description and Access
- TEI: Text Encoding Initiative.

(JISC Digital Media, 2015; Library of Congress 2015)

While the above is by no means an exhaustive list, it serves to illustrate the wide variety of standards available. Using metadata effectively opens opportunities for data-mining projects that interrogate multiple data sets to allow broader research outcomes. These often allow further analysis of the same data set in fresh ways by relating it to different sources, such as mapping data or eye witness testimonies (Hagood 2012).

CONCLUSIONS

Digitisation potentially offers enormous possibilities for innovative research in the humanities. However, ensuring that this potential is met effectively, efficiently and ethically requires recognising the need to make careful, critical choices at each stage of the project. Far from being a straightforward, single process, digitisation involves multiple steps and mechanisms at every stage. This chapter has highlighted some important issues and choices faced by individuals and institutions embarking on digitisation projects during the planning and implementation stages, ranging from stakeholder analysis, selection criteria, dealing with intellectual property rights and orphan works to selecting the most appropriate tools to digitally capture items and then make them usefully available to researchers. Knowing these choices and what they involve should allow practitioners to make better, well-informed choices about digitisation projects that lead to exciting results and new research possibilities in the Digital Humanities. As our technology capabilities increase, it is critical that Digital Humanists continue to keep the perspectives of scholars, archivists, librarians and communities in mind in order to preserve information which may have already survived for hundreds of years and keep it available, relevant and valuable to future generations of researchers.

NOTES

1. Quote by Dr Michael Wesch, Kansas State University who is the 2008 CASE/Carnegie US Professor of the Year for Doctoral and Research Universities.
2. Connected Histories <http://www.connectedhistories.org/>
3. DigiPal <http://www.digipal.eu/>
4. HathiTrust <https://www.hathitrust.org/>
5. NINES <http://www.nines.org/>
6. HRI Portal <https://portal.ehri-project.eu/>
7. Further examples can be found at the DH Commons <http://dhcommons.org/projects>.
8. Professor Kathryn Sutherland, University of Oxford, is the Principal Investigator of the Jane Austen's Fiction Manuscripts Digital Edition available at <http://www.janeausten.ac.uk/index.html>.

REFERENCES

BBC (2015) 'British Library seeks £40m to "save" sound archive', *BBC News*, 12 January. Online at <http://www.bbc.co.uk/news/entertainment-arts-30781320> (last accessed 3 August 2015).

Boast, R., Bravo, M. and Srinivasan, R. (2007) 'Return to Babel: emergent diversity, digital resources, and local knowledge', *Information Society*, 23 (5): 395–403.

Bradwell, P. (2009) *The Edgeless University: Why Higher Education Must Embrace Technology*. London: Demos. Online at <http://www.demos.co.uk/publications/the-edgeless-university> (last accessed 3 August 2015).

British Library (2015) *British Library Annual Report and Accounts 2014/15*. London: British Library. Online at <http://www.bl.uk/aboutus/annrep/2014to2015/annual-report2014-15.pdf> (last accessed 3 August 2015).

Brown, D. and Nicholas, G. (2012) 'Protecting indigenous cultural property in the age of digital democracy: institutional and communal responses to Canadian First Nations and Māori Heritage Concerns', *Journal of Material Culture*, 17 (3): 307–24.

Buckley, R. (2009) 'JPEG 2000 as a preservation and access format for the Wellcome Trust Digital Library', in S. Tanner (ed.), *Report for the Wellcome Trust*. London: King's College London. Online at <http://wellcomelibrary.org/content/documents/22082/JPEG2000-preservation-format.pdf> (last accessed 3 August 2015).

Chabries, D. M., Booras, S. W. and Bearman, G. H. (2003) 'Imaging the past:

recent applications of multispectral imaging technology to deciphering manuscripts', *Antiquity*, 77: 296, 359–72.

Christen, K. (2006) 'Ara Irititja: protecting the past, accessing the future – indigenous memories in a digital age', *Museum Anthropology*, 29 (1): 56–60.

Christie, M. and Verran, H. (2013) 'Digital lives in postcolonial Aboriginal Australia', *Journal of Material Culture*, 18 (3): 299–317.

Colson, F. and Hall, W. (1992) 'Educational systems: pictorial information systems and the teaching imperative,' in M. Thaller (ed.), *Unspecified Images and Manuscripts in Historical Computing*. Gottingen: Scripta Mercaturae Verlag, pp. 73–86.

Conway, P. (2010) 'Preservation in the age of Google: digitization, digital preservation, and dilemmas', *Library Quarterly: Information, Community, Policy*, 80 (1): 61–79.

Dahlström, M., Hansson, J. and Kjellman, U. (2012) '"As we may digitize" – institutions and documents reconfigured', *LIBER Quarterly*, 21 (3/4): 455–74.

Darnton, R. (2009) 'Google & the future of books', *New York Review of Books*, 56 (2). Online at <http://www.nybooks.com/articles/archives/2009/feb/12/google-the-future-of-books/> (last accessed 3 August 2015).

DDH (2014) 'Department of Digital Humanities at King's College London internal web analytics for the Fine Rolls of Henry III project prepared in response to the Research Excellence Framework'.

De Rosa, C., Dempsey, L., Limes, R., Shepard, L. and Wilson, A. (2003) *The 2003 OCLC Environmental Scan: Pattern Recognition: A Report to the OCLC Membership*. Dublin, OH: OCLC Online Computer Library Center. Online at <https://www.oclc.org/reports/escan.en.html> (last accessed 3 August 2003).

Deegan, M. and Tanner, S. (2004) 'Conversion of primary sources', in S. Schreibman, R. Siemens and J. Unsworth (eds), *A Companion to Digital Humanities*. Oxford: Blackwell. Online at <http://www.digitalhumanities.org/companion/> (last accessed 31 July 2015).

Deutsche Forschungsgemeinschaft (DFG) Subcommittee on Cultural Heritage (2013) *DFG Practical Guidelines on Digitisation*, DFG form 12.151 – 02/13. Online at <http://www.dfg.de/formulare/12_151/12_151_en.pdf (last accessed 3 August 2015).

Digiflo (2015) Online at: <http://digiflo.in/> (last accessed 3 August 2015).

European Commission (2014) 'Orphan Works' Online at http://ec.europa.eu/internal_market/copyright/orphan_works/index_en.htm> (last accessed 3 August 2015).

Goobi (2015) Online at <https://www.goobi.org/en/> (last accessed 3 August 2015).

Gray, E. (2010) 'Access to Africa's knowledge: publishing development research and measuring value', *African Journal of Information and Communication*, 10 (1): 4–19.

Hagood, J. (2012) 'A brief introduction to data mining projects in the humanities', *Bulletin of the American Society for Information Science and Technology*, 38 (4): 20–3.

Hargreaves, I. (2011) 'Digital opportunity: a review of intellectual property and growth', UK Intellectual Property Office 38, May. Online at <http://www.ipo.gov.uk/ipreview-finalreport.pdf>.

HathiTrust Digital Library (2015) 'Information about the Authors Guild Lawsuit'. Online at <http://www.hathitrust.org/authors_guild_lawsuit_information> (last accessed 3 August 2015).

Hedstrom, M. (2003) 'Research agendas set course for digital archiving and long-term preservation', *RLG DigiNews*, 7: 6. Online at <http://worldcat.org/arcviewer/1/OCC/2007/08/08/0000070519/viewer/file3170.html> (last accessed 7 July 2015).

Holley, R. (2009) 'How good can it get? Analysing and improving OCR accuracy in large scale historic newspaper digitisation programs', *D-Lib Magazine*, 15 (3/4). Online at <http://www.dlib.org/dlib/march09/holley/03holley.html> (last accessed 3 August 2015).

Hughes, M. and Dallwitz, J. (2007) 'Ara Irititja: towards culturally appropriate IT best practice in remote indigenous Australia', in L. E. Dyson, M. Hendriks and S. Grant (eds), *Information Technology and Indigenous People*. Hershey: IGI Global, pp. 146–58.

IIPI (2015) http://iipimage.sourceforge.net/ (last accessed 3 August 2015).

JISC Digital Media (2015) 'Putting things in order: a directory of metadata schemas and related standards'. Online at <http://www.jiscdigitalmedia.ac.uk/guide/putting-things-in-order-links-to-metadata-schemas-and-related-standards> (last accessed 3 August 2015).

Knox, K. T., Easton, R. L., Christens-Barry, W. A. and Boydston, K. (2011) 'Recovery of handwritten text from the diaries and papers of David Livingstone', *Proceedings of International Society for Optics and Photonics, Conference, San Francisco, California*. Conference Vol. 7869.

Library of Congress (2015) 'Metadata for Digital Content (MDC). Developing institution-wide policies and standards at the Library of Congress'. Online at <http://www.loc.gov/standards/mdc/index.html> (last accessed 3 August 2015).

McDonough, J. (2009) 'XML, interoperability and the social construction of markup languages: the library example', *Digital Humanities Quarterly*, 3: 3. Online at <http://digitalhumanities.org/dhq/vol/3/3/000064/000064.html> (last accessed 3 August 2015).

National Archives (2015) 'Digitisation at the National Archives'. Online at

<http://nationalarchives.gov.uk/documents/information-management/ digitisation-at-the-national-archives.pdf> (last accessed 3 August 2015).

National Information Standards Organization (NISO) (2004) *Understanding Metadata*. Bethesda, MD: NISO Press. Online at <http://www.niso.org/ publications/press/UnderstandingMetadata.pdf> (last accessed 3 August 2015).

Netz, R. and Noel, W. (2011) *The Archimedes Codex: Revealing the Secrets of the World's Greatest Palimpsest*. London: Weidenfeld & Nicolson.

Ngata, W., Ngata-Gibson, H. and Salmond, H. (2012) 'Te Ataakura: digital Taonga and cultural innovation', *Journal of Material Culture*, 17 (3): 229–44.

OED (2015) *Oxford English Dictionary Online (OED)*. Online at <http:// www.oxforddictionaries.com/definition/english/metadata> (last accessed 20 July 2015).

Peers, L. and Brown, A. (2003) *Museums and Source Communities: A Routledge Reader*. London: Routledge.

Pekel, J. (2015) *Democratising the Rijksmuseum*. Amsterdam: Europeana Foundation. Online at <http://pro.europeana.eu/publication/democratising-the-rijksmuseum> (last accessed 20 July 2015).

Pickover, M. (2005) 'Negotiations, contestations and fabrications: the politics of archives in South Africa ten years after democracy,' *Innovation*, 30: 1–11.

Pickover, M. (2014) *Patrimony, Power and Politics: Selecting, Constructing and Preserving Digital Heritage Content in South Africa and Africa*. Paper presented at IFLA WLIC 2014, Lyon, France, 16–22 August. Online at <http://library.ifla.org/1023/1/138-pickover-en.pdf> (last accessed 3 August 2015).

PrestoCentre (2015) Online at <http://www.prestocentre.org> (last accessed 4 August 2015).

Ranft, R. (2015) '£9.5m boost from Heritage Lottery Fund for our Save our Sounds campaign', *British Library Sound and Vision Blog*, 20 May. Online at <http://britishlibrary.typepad.co.uk/sound-and-vision/2015/05/95m-boost-from-heritage-lottery-fund-for-our-save-our-sounds-campaign. html#sthash.o1JT1zAa.dpuf> (last accessed 3 August 2015).

Registry of Open Access Repository Mandates and Policy (ROARMAP) (2015) Online at <http://roarmap.eprints.org/view/policymaker_type/ funder.html> (last accessed 3 August 2015).

Reijksmuseum. (2012) *Annual Report: 2012*. Online at <https://www.rijks-museum.nl/en/organisation/annual-reports> (last accessed 3 August 2015).

Reisberg, D. (2013) *The Oxford of Cognitive Psychology*. Oxford: Oxford University Press.

Schantz, H. (1982) *The History of OCR, Optical Character Recognition*. Manchester Center, VT: Recognition Technologies Users Association.

St Louis, S. R. (2014) 'Digital humanities and open access: an interview with Brett Bobley of the National Endowment for the Humanities', *Right to Research Blog*, 24 October. Online at <http://www.righttoresearch.org/blog/digital-humanities-and-open-access-an-interview-wi.shtml> (last accessed 2 August 2015).

Siegal, N. (2013) 'Masterworks for one and all', *New York Times*, 28 May. Online at <http://www.nytimes.com/2013/05/29/arts/design/museums-mull-public-use-of-online-art-images.html?_r=o> (last accessed 3 August 2015).

Srinivasan, R., Enote, J., Becvar, K. and Boast, R. (2009) 'Critical and reflective uses of new media technologies in tribal museums', *Museum Management and Curatorship*, 24 (2): 161–81.

Tanner, S. (2004) 'Reproduction charging models and rights policy for digital images in American art museums: a Mellon Foundation study', King's Digital Consultancy Services, King's College London, London. Online at <http://www.kdcs.kcl.ac.uk/innovation/us-art.html> (last accessed 5 August 2015).

Tanner, S. (2006) 'Managing containers, content and context in digital preservation: towards a 2020 vision', in *Proceedings of Archiving 2006*. Arlington, VA: Society for Imaging Science and Technology, pp. 19–23.

Tanner, S. (2011) 'Inspiring research, inspiring scholarship. The value and benefits of digitised resources for learning, teaching, research and enjoyment', *Proceedings of Archiving 2011*. Arlington, VA: Society for Imaging Science and Technology, pp. 77–82.

Tanner, S. (2013) 'World class digitisation in Sweden', *When the Data Hits the Fan Blog*, 12 March. Online at <http://simon-tanner.blogspot.co.uk/2013/03/world-class-digitisation-in-sweden.html> (last accessed 3 August 2015).

Tanner, S. and Bearman G. (2009) 'Digitising the Dead Sea Scrolls', in *Proceedings of Archiving 2009*. Arlington, VA: Society for Imaging Science and Technology, pp. 119–23.

Tanner, S., Muñoz, T. and Ros, P. H. (2009) 'Measuring mass text digitization quality and usefulness: lessons learned from assessing the OCR accuracy of the British Library's 19th century online newspaper archive', *D-Lib Magazine*, 15 (7/8). Online at <http://www.dlib.org/dlib/july09/munoz/07munoz.html> (last accessed 3 August 2015).

Terras, M. (2008) *Digital Images for the Informational Professional*. Aldershot: Ashgate.

University of Michigan (2012) 'Orphan Works Project'. Online at <http://www.lib.umich.edu/orphan-works> (last accessed 3 August 2015).

Unsworth, J. (2000) *Scholarly Primitives: What Methods do Humanities Researchers Have in Common, and How Might Our Tools Reflect This?* Paper presented at the Humanities Computing: Formal Methods, Experimental Practice Symposium, King's College London, London. Online at <http://people.brandeis.edu/~unsworth/Kings.5-00/primitives.html> (last accessed 3 August 2015).

US Federal Agencies Digitization Guidelines (2015) Online at <http://www.digitizationguidelines.gov/> (last accessed 4 August 2015).

CHAPTER 3

Curating the Language of Letters: Historical Linguistic Methods in the Museum

Mel Evans

INTRODUCTION

An estimated 20 million historical texts were available in digital formats in 2010 (Hu et al. 2013). The impact of this vast, virtual pool of language, words and cultural heritage on academic research cannot be underestimated. It changes the kinds of research questions one can ask, the methodologies that can be applied and the ways in which data is interpreted and presented. The study of historical languages and literatures, in particular, has been revolutionised by the ability to explore documents in digital modes, taking non-linear as well as linear approaches towards their contents. For historical linguistics, the emergence of corpus methods has transformed how scholars engage with historical language. Studies using digitised text resources can undertake larger-scale, macro-level investigations of language than were previously possible, using purpose-built corpora that span geographic regions, social groups (i.e. gender), genres and temporal periods. They also permit more fine-grained, micro-level investigations using investigative software packages and data visualisation techniques to explore the practices of particular individuals and specific communicative acts such as family relationships or royal discourse (see, for example, Nevalainen and Raumolin-Brunberg 2003; Nurmi et al. 2009; Evans 2013) at a level of detail not feasible or readily achievable with traditional resources and methods alone.

Digital technologies have also had a profound impact on the heritage industry. Virtual representations of historic artefacts have transformed how users can interact with objects, while preserving the fragile originals. Audio tours and, more recently, mobile applications, promote autonomous interaction between an audience and a museum's exhibits, all of which help traditional and non-traditional audiences to engage more fully with their cultural heritage. However, the application of digital technologies within the heritage industry has largely been object-oriented. As a consequence, many organisations' textual objects – the archives of official documents, expenses records and correspondence – remain under-utilised. Although historical manuscripts constitute the language or literature scholars' bread and butter and have driven the advances in digital methodologies within these academic fields, the same manuscripts are often perceived as being difficult, problematic material for heritage audiences. This is for reasons of incomprehensibility (handwriting, spelling, language), complexity of function (genre conventions, e.g. royal proclamations), difficulties of display (preservation concerns, 'uninspiring' appearance) and mundanity (utilitarian, e.g. expenses records) (Allyn et al. 1987).

This chapter discusses the ways in which digitally informed methods and findings from historical linguistics can aid the curation of historical manuscripts – specifically correspondence – for heritage organisations. The historical linguist's approach, I argue, can transform data (material that may be linguistic, demographic, physical or similar) into information (the meaning that is created when specific data is selected as appropriate for attention) of relevance for heritage audiences (Jones and Hafner 2012: 19). With the digital tools now available, this information can be presented in flexible, manageable ways that allow a heritage visitor to make links with their existing concepts and structures, enabling knowledge creation (ibid.). More specifically, I consider the collaborative potential arising from the approach of the academic who locates and unlocks the data of historic texts, and the needs of a heritage organisation that wishes to interpret and display their archival documents to visitors with reference to one case study: the AHRC-funded web prototype *Living Letters*, designed in partnership with Norton Priory, Cheshire, and Adair Richards Associates.

HISTORICAL LINGUISTICS IN THE DIGITAL AGE

Corpus linguistics is now a widespread methodology for exploring large quantities of language data. This approach uses large collections of electronic texts (corpora) ranging in size from thousands to billions of words, to identify linguistic patterns not discernible to the human eye, and complements other methodologies, such as qualitative categorisation or experimental elicitation (see Archer, in Griffin and Hayler 2016). Since its emergence in the mid-twentieth century, techniques for corpus data manipulation have become increasingly diverse and sophisticated. The linguistic analytical tools include word frequency lists, which extrapolate words into types (forms) and tokens (frequency of recurrence) – this can be used for authorship attribution analysis among other purposes (see Burrows 2002); keyword analysis, which identifies items that occur more or less frequently than a reference corpus predicts and can be used to reveal ideological standpoints (see, for example, O'Halloran's (2010) study of *The Sun*'s 2004 reporting of EU migration); and N-gram analyses, which extract recurrent strings (phrases) of any length and have, for example, informed our theoretical appreciation of language as operating in 'units of meaning' (Greaves and Warren 2010: 221). These linguistic tools are increasingly accompanied by data visualisation techniques (see Archer 2009).

Historical linguistics has flourished in this new research environment. The typical process for the historical linguist using digital resources comprises three stages: data set creation, data analysis and interpretation. The first stage typically includes the identification of relevant texts, their preparation through transcription, spelling normalisation and other formatting and mark-up decisions. This stage has been transformed from a lengthy, laborious and often arbitrary process due to the availability of electronic resources, either through databases of images or existing corpora that may be adapted or adjusted as appropriate. The latter include the landmark *Helsinki Corpus* (see Rissanen et al. 1993), the socially representative *Corpus of Early English Correspondence* (http://www.helsinki.fi/varieng/domains/CEEC.html), the *Corpus of Historical American English* (Davies 2010) and *Electronic Text Edition of Depositions* (Kytö et al. 2011), among many others. The rapid expansion of corpus resources has been matched by an expanding preparation toolkit, such as the spelling normalisation software VARD (Baron 2013), which automates spelling standardisation using a learning algorithm, and the Text-Encoding Initiative (see <http://www.tei-c.org>), which promotes a universal system for annotation and encoding of electronic texts, ensuring compatibility and coherence across resources.

The second stage is the analysis of the data, which may examine specific linguistic forms, the language of particular individuals or groups, or the relationship between texts and other socio-historical phenomena. Again, digital tools such as concordance software (e.g. AntConc (Anthony 2014)) and data visualisation allow the full potential of these large corpora to be accessed and interrogated. These tools allow the linguistic data to be explored non-linearly, harnessing the computer to identify patterns not visible to the human eye and, vice versa, to counter a human researcher's identification of non-existent trends.

The third and final stage is the interpretation of the data, the means by which the linguistic forms, numbers and patterns are contextualised and framed within existing or new theoretical models. While interpretation remains the preserve of the human investigator, the wealth of tools for data creation and analysis enrich and enhance the scope of those interpretations – for instance, the finding that women led language change in historical periods, a pattern comparable to present-day trends, is less likely to have been appreciable on a smaller, non-digitally assisted scale (Nevalainen and Raumolin-Brunberg 2003: ch. 5).

A useful complement to historical linguistic research is the large-scale digitisation projects of archives and repositories across the world. Although these are not usually developed with linguistics specifically in mind, the documents and images can aid the interpretation of historical language. For example, *State Papers Online* allows a researcher to examine images of the manuscripts transcribed in the text corpora and thus place the linguistic data within its material as well as historical context. In some ways, the non-linguistic digitised resources encourage traditional (linear) methods of reading, often acting as a virtual substitute for the original manuscript; some early initiatives were criticised for presenting manuscript images within a reading frame that replicated the materiality (e.g. page turning) of the physical object (Twycross 2008: 24). However, increasingly, the embedding of XML mark-up means that digitised resources can be explored both linearly (traditionally) and non-linearly.

HISTORICAL LINGUISTICS AND LITERATURE: NON-ACADEMIC COLLABORATION

As Digital Humanities' technologies develop, academic projects are increasingly embracing non-academic perspectives and expertise. One productive area has been the creation and design of scholarly online editions. These can make use of the flexibility of XML to offer their readers multiple versions of the same historic texts. Thus the Bess of Hardwick Project (Wiggins et al. 2013) allows a user to select from modernised, diplomatic (original), XML-visible and PDF versions of Bess's letters. This can better meet the needs and expertise of different users (or the same user on different occasions). The potential for XML mark-up to help 'frame' historical manuscript materials according to very different perspectives is a clear strength of digitised textual resources (see also the *Diplomatic Correspondence of Thomas Bodley* (Adams 2011).

Digital resources can also offer opportunities for interaction between the academy and general public. Within historical linguistics, for example, the open-access concordance interface of the *Corpus of Historical American English* (Davies 2010) allows users to investigate properties of early American English across time and genres, although there is perhaps a steep learning curve for those not familiar with corpus linguistic methods. The potential of interactivity for data creation is also shown in the successful ongoing project 'Transcribing Bentham' (see Moyle et al. 2011), in which users provide transcriptions and metadata for Bentham's manuscripts. Incorporating features such as a transcriber leader-board and a transcription progress chart, the project exemplifies the potential of the read-write web (Jones and Hafner 2012: 42) to engage new audiences with Humanities work and bridge the traditional gap between the 'ivory tower' and non-academics.

However, despite these worthy and ambitious linguistic and literary projects, it is not clear how, or to what extent, the specialised tools, resources or edited materials developed by historical linguists and Digital Humanities scholarship can be used by heritage curators who wish to work with their historical texts as part of a larger repertoire of objects, spaces and social narratives.

CURATION IN THE DIGITAL AGE

The Museum Association defines a curator as someone whose 'core task . . . [is] working with objects – acquiring, researching, storing and interpreting them for the public' (Museum Association, n.d.). It is the latter task – interpretation – to which historical linguistics and Digital Humanities scholarship can potentially contribute. Curatorial approaches to interpretation have undergone a significant theoretical and applied shift, moving away from conceiving of audiences as passive observers of artefacts towards a more interactive relationship between visitors and a heritage site and its contents. Interaction is key, not only for the enrichment of the visitor experience, but in the sustainability of the museum. Sites with limited opportunities for interaction tend to have poorer attendance figures (Walter 1996: 244).

A property that unites traditional and digital approaches to curatorial interpretation is narrative. Narratives are a ubiquitous part of human society and museum- and object-oriented stories can be a productive means for engaging diverse audiences, facilitating an appreciation of the function and sociohistorical heritage of an exhibit. Lwin (2012) studied a human storyteller at the Singapore History Museum and found that the speaker's more successful strategies for engagement were those that responded to and were shaped by the museum collection and the physical space. Of course, having a human storyteller is not possible, nor desirable, for all exhibitions. Traditionally, such narratives might instead be relayed through information boards and accompanying documentation: a strategy that relies on the conduit metaphor of communication, encouraging an audience to adopt a position as a 'receptacle' rather than a 'creator' of information. Digital tools, on the other hand, offer up narratives in more diverse ways – through what Ryan (2003) describes as 'the complete synthesis' of communicative media – thus potentially transforming the traditional monologue to a more dialogic, or even ludic, story.

Audio guides were one of the earliest digital curatorial aids, providing the user with greater autonomy over the kind and timings of information they can access when exploring a museum site, shaping a personal narrative experience. An observational study (Walter 1996) conducted in the mid-1990s found that visitors with audio guides took in more information about the heritage site than those using traditional media. However, Walter found this positive effect was at the cost of the user's greater isolation from their fellow visitors, indicated by lower noise levels and fewer photographs. He also considered the non-linearity of the electronic audio guides to be potentially detrimental, as it removed the 'cumulative narrative' that visitors would normally experience when following the pre-determined 'path' of the space and exhibits. Thus the user lost the curator's interpretative frame that would 'make sense of the site' (Walter 1996: 224). On the other hand, they might make a different (and equally valid) sense of that site through their own meandering.

Walter's study illustrates how curatorial media impact on a museum visitor's behaviour. Interaction with a heritage site is shaped by how we access (i.e. on a page or via audio recording) its information, a process summarised in McLuhan's infamous maxim: 'The medium is the message' (McLuhan 1964). Since the mid-1990s, however, the applications of digital resources have embraced the kinds of narrativity they afford, and it seems less likely that curators today would identify the non-linearity of the audio guides as a purely pejorative outcome. Indeed, digital tools deliberately promote interpretations that challenge or complicate an institutional macro-narrative. One key area is in the interpretation of museum objects. Scholarship on the 'cultural biography of things' has flourished, not least because it provides 'an appealing narrative hook' (Alberti 2005: 561). An object provides a distinct perspective on a community or time period, witnessing the intertwining of that object and its human users (Gosden and Marshall 1999: 169). Objects thus provide a gateway through which a visitor can engage with a museum and the culture(s) that it represents, contributing 'towards public cultural enlightenment' (Sylaiou et al. 2010: 243).

How a curator presents their objects is thus significant for the kinds of narrative interpretation and engagement that results, and even the psychological well-being of the interactor (see Thomson et al. 2012; see also Chatterjee et al. 2009). Sylaiou et al. (2010: 244) use the concept of *presence* to explain how a user's engagement with the object encompasses physical, social and narrative connectedness with the artefact: the greater the level of presence, the greater potential for engagement and enjoyment. However, there are many impediments to a curator's desire for physical and tactile interaction with an object. Few historical objects can be (frequently) handled without risk of damage or decay. And small heritage organisations have a limited collection of objects they can actually display on site, with many pertinent artefacts owned by larger repositories.

The virtual display of objects offers a solution. Indeed, such is the wealth of digitisation projects that terminology has shifted, as Hopes (2014: 500) observes, from discussions of access towards 'a more active language of "participation" and "engagement"' towards digitised objects. There are parallels here with the literary and linguistic digitisation projects noted above. One particularly successful object-focused project was the BBC and British Museum's *History of the World in 100 Objects*. As Neil MacGregor, the curator and author put it to *The Economist* in 2010: 'Objects take you into the thought world of the past [. . .] When you think about the skills required to make something you begin to think about the brain that made it.' The project has a website through which interested parties can explore the curated objects 'by theme' or 'by gallery', offering a simple replica of the physical exhibition at the British Museum which closed in July 2014. As with audio guides, the user is given autonomy in exploring the objects, with some macro-level context provided in relation to the object's thematic category (such as the Victorian tea set, situated in 'Mass Production, Mass Persuasion 1780–1914'). The website uses the multimedia affordances of the web, featuring photographic images of the object, hyperlinks to internal and external content including the radio audio files, live information about the location of the object and textual descriptions of the object. It appears that the website is envisaged for 'at home' browsing that may serve as a catalyst for further investigation.

Other projects seek to recreate a museum object more dramatically. The Augmented Representation of Cultural Objects (ARCO) software aims to provide curators with the tools 'for creating interactive virtual museum exhibitions on-line over the World Wide Web and on-site via information kiosks' (Sylaiou et al. 2010: 244). Virtual representations offer new ways of revealing the narratives embedded within museum objects, and increasing sophistication in interface design suggests that users' engagement and enjoyment continues to rise (ibid.). Given the relatively youthful state of digitisation and digital curatorial aids within the museum and heritage context, it is perhaps unsurprising that work is only now beginning to assess and critique how users actually engage with digital artefacts and thus account for 'the difference in experience of visiting museums and visiting their websites' (Hopes 2014: 499).

The on-site and off-site dimension is significant, as it reflects curators' hopes of engaging non-traditional audiences by breaking down the traditional bounded space of the museum as a solely geographic space: one might describe this as helping to 'demuseologise' museum objects. Visitors' own narrative contributions based on these objects allow for interactivity and greater engagement; for instance, the *Art of Storytelling* project developed a website to run concurrently with the museum-based kiosks and information stands, with users providing narrative interpretations of a pre-selected range of objects (Fisher et al. 2008). Although the proportion of participants is generally only a small percentage of overall visitors, providing an opportunity for multiple means of engagement is an important facility for attracting and maintaining diverse audiences for heritage organisations.

The digitally informed approaches to object curation show the potential for greater interactivity, transforming how narratives around heritage spaces and objects are constructed and interpreted. Yet the role of textual objects and ways in which digital media can aid the interpretation of their complex properties is notable by its absence. The texts that represent perhaps the most prototypical narrative form (linguistic) have surprisingly been overlooked.

INTERPRETING HISTORICAL CORRESPONDENCE

Historical manuscripts, such as correspondence, have a similar range of properties, and thus potential for interactivity, as other museum objects. They have a macro-narrative, the overarching sequence of events in which they played a part, as well as their own micro-narratives comprising the intersection of their writer(s)'s skill, communicative purpose and awareness of genre conventions. Letters are an especially rich example. They offer a snapshot from a larger conversation and are constructed from specific linguistic and material forms that themselves have social resonance and interactive significance. As objects, they are relatively plentiful. They represent individuals across the social spectrum including individuals from lower social ranks and women. They often survive in their original form, bearing traces of their transmission and receipt. And they are recognisable to present-day audiences. Even with the growth of electronic communication, letters carry salience as a genre that provides a useful starting point for a modern audience's interpretation.

In recent years, academic scholarship has explored the complexity of linguistic and material meanings bound up in historical correspondence. Letters are relatively short, interactive texts with distinctive genre conventions and social rules for interaction. Corpus analysis has provided insights into the social dimensions of language variation and change using personal letters as data; they are considered more 'speech like' than many other written documents, and thus provide evidence of morphological, syntactic and lexical properties associated with the spoken as well as the written language of a given period, such as the progression of the change from the third-person singular verb-ending *eth* to Present-Day English *-s* (e.g. *runneth* and *runs*) (see Nevalainen and Raumolin-Brunberg 2003).

Letters are thus rich and vibrant documents, and academic research would seem to provide the heritage curator with plenty of material to inform the design of exhibits for non-academic audiences. And yet, it appears that letters (as with manuscripts more generally) are largely under-utilised. Some languish in glass cases or, when the original manuscripts are not available, in high-quality photographs that form part of the written exhibit. Perhaps the appearance of a historic letter suggests that the visitor will be able to recognise and interpret the meaning of the document more independently than when examining more obscure objects such as military artefacts or antique porcelain. Letters are also, or at least appear to be, rather traditional and conventional. They are linear and textual in form, and therefore may perhaps appeal less to the developers and curators who wish to explore the new opportunities for interactivity and engagement that the non-linear affordances of the web and social media provide. However, as the scope of academic studies indicates, historic correspondence is multi-layered and complex. Consequently, the ability for a visitor to interpret these documents is impoverished through a lack of interpretative aids, compounded by the typical use of traditional presentation formats, and unlike the more innovative presentation of non-textual objects and their digital displays.

One representative example observed recently by this author is a letter written by Robert Dudley, Earl of Leicester, to Queen Elizabeth I in 1588, which forms part of an exhibition exploring their relationship at Kenilworth Castle. The original letter is kept at the British Library and so, understandably, the exhibition uses a high-quality photograph to display the letter on an information board with a written gloss. The letter has significant annotations and contextual significance. Elizabeth added the phrase 'His Last Letter' to the document, following Dudley's sudden death days after its composition. However, the letter itself is not transcribed – despite reference to some of its contents in the accompanying gloss – and other linguistic features are not mentioned, despite their potential relevance to the exhibition's themes: for example, Dudley's self-reference as Elizabeth's 'ôô', an iconic representation of Elizabeth's nickname for him, her 'eyes' (see May 2004). While one might argue that the visitors are given the opportunity to make such interpretations for themselves, I suggest that the document's visual and linguistic properties – written in secretary hand, full of epistolary abbreviations, using Early Modern English syntax and lexis – present a substantial barrier for even the most interested general visitor. Elsewhere in Kenilworth's exhibit, visitors are invited to try the weight of a gauntlet of the kind worn by Dudley and to inspect the manufacturing method of a tapestry, but they are not encouraged to investigate the linguistic and material construction of Dudley's last letter.

This may in part be due to the lack of curatorial methods that allow the rich data held within a historical letter to be appropriately unpacked and opened up for visitors on a par with the non-textual objects surveyed above. Digital approaches which have provided rich and multiplex perspectives on the linguistic and material data of a historical manuscript for academic researchers offer an opportunity to remedy this for heritage organisations and enable museums and other organisations to make better 'use' of their archival resources and the data within them. As the websites for *100 Objects* and the *Art of Storytelling* demonstrate, digital media do not have to be particularly innovative at a technological level. Rather, the innovation lies in its application, to allow curators to facilitate their visitors' interpretations of the document. Here, academic methods – corpus analyses, XML mark-up, data visualisation – provide a starting model, where both the approach and findings can be reframed for the non-academic audience within a museum context.

'LIVING LETTERS': A PROTOTYPE PROJECT

The prototype website interface 'Living letters' was part of the Arts and Humanities Research Council's Collaborative Arts Triple Helix (CATH) project, which ran in collaboration with the Universities of Birmingham and Leicester in 2013–14. CATH was interesting in 'exploring the barriers to, and opportunities offered by, cross-sector collaboration' (CATH 2014) between academics, small cultural organisations, and small medium enterprises. 'Living Letters' was one of the successful triplets awarded a small grant of £4,000. In addition to the present author (the academic), the triplet comprised Adair Richard Associates Ltd, who undertook the technological development of the prototype, and Norton Priory, managed by Frank Hargrave, who wished to make better use of their correspondence relating to the site's history.

As a technological project, the premise of 'Living Letters' was simple: to offer a web-based interface that would allow users to investigate the different levels or layers of data within a historical letter. Visitors interested in learning about the heritage site would use this interface either remotely or at an on-site computer kiosk, similar to the ARCO and *Art of Storytelling* projects discussed above. Therefore it was essential that the curation of the letter data made best use of the technological opportunities of web media, if the interface was to improve upon the traditional exhibition methods of glass cases and information boards. The approach therefore focused on the most commonly cited, positive features of web technology: multimedia, hypertext and interactivity (Jones and Hafner 2012: 35).

For the purposes of curation, multimedia allow data to be conveyed in different modes, including text, images, audio and video, increasingly ubiquitous for many web users. Choice of media shapes the kinds of interpretations that can be made (Ryan 2003). The second affordance, hypertext, is the structural 'heart' of the Internet, exemplifying postmodern ideas about non-linearity of reading. In hypertext environments readers have more autonomy (although they are still steered by the creator or curator), a dimension that has clear relevance for museum curation and audience engagement. Within a museum context, these web-based ways of reading would appear to be appropriate for the temporal restrictions of a typical museum visitor (on- or off-site), which impede the more sustained engagement needed for longer, linear texts (for further discussion of the impact of media on reading practices see Carr 2010). Finally, interactivity reflects the attributes of the 'read–write' web (Web 2.0), which promotes participation through textual (linguistic, filmic, etc.) contributions. Although the latter is less relevant for the 'Living Letters' prototype, there are opportunities for expansion in future work which I outline at the end of this chapter.

The workflow for the prototype project comprised five stages:

1. Select the written objects (letters) for the web interface.
2. Research the data held within those written objects.
3. Select the relevant data as appropriate to the organisation's audiences and curator's needs.
4. Decide how best to 'unlock' that data through media affordances.
5. Create the interface and content, test and refine it.

The 'Living Letters' project focused on two letters linked to Norton Priory. One had particular 'star quality', sent in the name of King Henry VIII to command the execution of the abbot of Norton following a riotous protest at the priory's planned dissolution in 1536 (see Cook 1966). The other was addressed to Henry VIII, reporting a local landowner's arrest of the Abbot. The two letters thus fit into a macro-level narrative that has resonance for Norton's present-day physical state (i.e. the fact that the monastery is in ruins), as well as illustrating its role in nationally significant cultural movements (e.g. the Reformation). The texts thus show clear parallels with the kinds of narrative 'hooks' identified as being so profitable for non-textual object curation (Hopes 2014).

The second stage of the project required detailed analysis of the chosen letters. This step largely followed the typical processes of academic research (as outlined above). In addition to the macro-narrative that contextualises the letters, each text (like any object) has its own (related but distinct) biography of its creation and its legacy. It is the specifics of this biography that require the insights of historical linguistic analysis, with elements such as address forms, pronouns and letter subscriptions identified, using a combination of close reading and corpus analysis to corroborate norms and trends in relation to other correspondence of the period. This research was compiled in a dossier that could then serve multiple purposes (for instance, informing the academic's linguistic research as well as contributing to Norton Priory's exhibits).

In the third stage, the academic's research findings were discussed with the other collaborators. At a very basic level, this discussion allowed the value of the data for curatorial purposes to be gauged, based on the collaborators' responses. Information with a tangible connection to present-day forms or practices was deemed most significant – either connected to written communi-

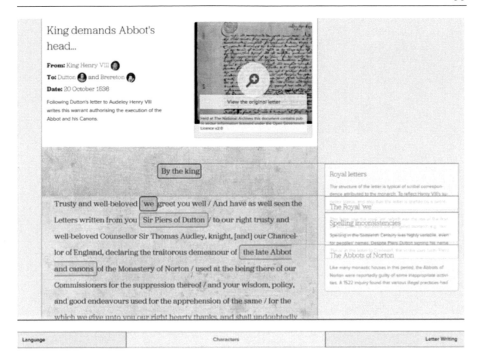

Figure 3.1 Screenshot of 'Living Letters' interface <http://www.livingletters.co.uk>. (Source: The author (2015).)

cation and letters or to linguistic features, for example the lack of any spelling 'standard' for sixteenth-century English writers entailing variable spellings of recipients' names. This strategy follows the pedagogic principle of threshold concepts (see Cousin 2006) in that these recognisable properties offer a route or portal to more complex and unfamiliar ways of thinking and knowing about these objects and their contents. Information that has a link to the historical narrative surrounding Norton was also considered relevant.

The fourth stage focused on how best to curate the selected data through the design of the web-based interface and the media within it. Given the potential for narratives to provide an effective and engaging way of organising complex information, the web interface frames the correspondence as part of a timeline of events. This timeline runs vertically down the screen rather than horizontally (which would parallel conventional (western) conceptualisations of time, reflective of the influence of print) to better suit web affordances such as scrolling tools (see Figure 3.1).

The two letters are foregrounded in the timeline through their presentation as full (modernised) transcripts with a paper-coloured background. Photographic, high-quality images of the letters are situated just above each transcript, with the user given the option to expand the image and investigate more closely. The reason that the photographs are not used for the main image is that their appearance would likely curtail user comprehension and engagement to anything other than a superficial level. Instead, the transcripts contain enough salient visual and linguistic properties to be recognisable as 'a letter' while offering sufficient mediation to allow users to explore the texts in detail. The transcriptions are situated in large boxes which are designed to grab attention through their size, centrality and colour. Other information pertaining to the macro-narrative is placed on the correspondence 'timeline', to show their relation to the main texts. This uses a telegraphic style to convey information succinctly in an attention-grabbing, relatively informal way.

Within the macro-narrative frame, specific linguistic and material aspects of the documents are 'marked-up' for user exploration. From an interpretative perspective, the user starts with a concrete example, such as the phrase 'by the king', and then progresses to consider the feature's significance and meaning for the document and the period more generally. Visually, the information is identified to the user through hyperlinks, which, when selected, link to overlaid box-outs on the side of the screen. The box-outs contain various media. Some are text-based, giving a brief summary of the feature selected (e.g. defining a word that has a different meaning to Present-Day English), while others contain videos, maps or images; more complex topics link to larger overlaid box-outs with a fuller account of the information as well as hyperlinks to external sites. It is up to the user whether they explore any of the media. User autonomy in exploring the 'Living Letters' interface is also supported via the option of toggling the marked-up information on or off on the basis of three categories (characters, letter-writing and language). If we follow Carr's (2010) (not uncontroversial) argument that Internet users can no longer sustain sufficient levels of concentration – or 'deep reading' – to work through textual explanations of these visual, linguistic and socio-historical attributes, this toggle-function adds another degree of choice that better maps onto user's expectations of how web-based information is organised and structured. The media thus shapes the kind of narrative that the user constructs.

The final stage of the project focused on how best to design a usable and aesthetically pleasing interface for the selected information, and was undertaken by the small- and medium-sized enterprises (SME), Adair Richards Associates. In a larger project this would be an iterative process with the input of focus groups representative of both curators and audiences; however, the scope of the prototype meant that the project team were the main contributors to this testing and feedback stage.

As a prototype, the website has many limitations. The main weakness is perhaps the lack of interactivity in a contribution sense, the defining characteristic of Web 2.0. Although the results of interactive museum projects are mixed, with a relatively small percentage of users making the shift from 'read' to 'write', it is nevertheless an important component – particularly as traditional conceptions of what a museum 'is' and what it is 'for' continue to evolve and shift towards a more dialogic, democratic model. There is also scope to pursue more ludic interactions, which would allow a user to consolidate their newly acquired knowledge about historical letters, for instance games housed in the same web interface which encourage the recipient to apply the knowledge acquired through the interface to produce their own epistolary artefacts according to the social and linguistic codes of decorum. A further step might be to extend the interface for use in the school classroom, to work alongside specially tailored teaching materials. This would not only enhance the digital literacy of the students, but enable their engagement with cultural heritage, and specific heritage sites and artefacts.

The prototype also raises practical questions about management and sustainability. From a curatorial perspective, the interface needs to accommodate the needs of any heritage organisation and their textual objects. The curator also needs to know enough about their materials to mark up the data. For 'Living Letters', the academic worked closely with the heritage curator throughout. This would be less practical if the framework were used on a larger scale (i.e. at multiple organisations). In such a scenario, the affordances of social media could be used to construct an institutional, crowd-sourced database of curatorial materials – for example, generic information about epistolary subscription formulae – that could be drawn upon for different curatorial projects as required.

Overall, the technology underpinning 'Living Letters' is relatively simple. But perhaps this simplicity allows for a more effective transformation of the complex data found in historical documents. A common criticism of digital media is the rise of 'information overload' (Jones and Hafner 2012: 19), which denotes the threat that social media and the Internet pose to our ability to process data in any meaningful way (i.e. to render it as information). One might posit that historical letters are themselves guilty of containing too much data to be meaningful to anyone other than the academic researcher. A general reader must first negotiate the visual and linguistic challenges to access the content, situate that content within its socio-historical context, and then reinterpret the visual and linguistic properties in accordance with their contemporary social meanings. Contrary to the critics, therefore, it is precisely the affordances of digital technologies, based on approaches developed within academic research, that allow the complex data to be filtered and framed. A key strength of the web interface in 'Living Letters' is in fact its constraints. The technology forces the curator to be as succinct as possible, being spatially more restrictive than traditional printed information boards or a tour-guide's spoken discourse. Similarly, one is more aware of the mode in which data is presented, with different potential meanings created through video, audio or image.

FROM CREATION TO CURATION:
SOME CONCLUDING THOUGHTS

The starting point for any corpus linguist, regardless of whether her interests are present-day or historical, is data. Data are the foundation from which linguistic patterns can be identified, interpretations made, theories posited and frameworks designed and tested. The development of computational analytic techniques has transformed *how* linguists treat data and *how much* data they can use. Within the Humanities more broadly, historical researchers are increasingly being inundated with data that similarly challenge how they conceptualise and interpret literary and linguistic materials of the past. It is thus a natural step to consider how the traditionally text-centric disciplines of language and literature can frame and share their theories and methods for the benefit of non-academic organisations interested in unlocking their own textual objects. The 'Living Letters' project outlined here demonstrates how relatively simple digital technologies can be repurposed and applied through cross-sector collaboration to allow new audiences to explore and interpret the language and lives of letters of the past within their heritage context.

ACKNOWLEDGEMENTS

With thanks to the CATH Project team: Harrison Brown, Frank Hargrave and Adair Richards.

REFERENCES

Adams, R. (2011) *The Diplomatic Correspondence of Thomas Bodley*. Centre for Editing Lives and Letters. Available at <http://www.livesandletters.ac.uk/bodley/bodley.html> (last accessed 3 May 2015).

Alberti, S. (2005) 'Objects and the museum', *ISIS*, 96: 559–71.

Allyn, N., Aubitz, S. and Stern, S. (1987) 'Using archival materials effectively in museum exhibitions', *American Archivist*, 50 (3): 402–4.

Anon. (2009) 'A history of the world in 100 objects: creative impulses', *The Economist*. Available at (<ttp://www.economist.com/node/15172496 l> (last accessed 3 May 2015).

Anon. (n.d.) 'Careers: Curator', *Museums Association*. Available at: <http://www.museumsassociation.org/careers/9910> (last accessed 28 April 2015).

Anthony, L. (2014) *AntConc*, [computer software] Version 3.4.3. Tokyo: Waseda University. Available from <http://www.laurenceanthony.net/> (last accessed 3 May 2015).

Archer, D. (ed.) (2009) *What's in a Word-List? Investigating Word Frequency and Keyword Extraction*. Farnham: Ashgate.

Baron, A. (2013) *Variation Detection* (*VARD*), [computer software], Version 2.5. Available online at <http://ucrel.lancs.ac.uk/vard/about/> (last accessed 3 May 2015).

Burrows, J. (2002) '"Delta": a measure of stylistic difference and a guide to likely authorship', *Literary and Linguist Computing*, 17 (3): 267–87.

Carr, N. (2010) *The Shallows: How the Internet is Changing the Way We Read, Think and Remember*. London: Atlantic Books.

Chatterjee, H., Vreeland, S. and Nobel, G. (2009) 'Museopathy: exploring the healing potential of handling museum objects', *Museum and Society*, 7 (3): 164–77.

Collaborative Arts Triple Helix (n.d.) 'Mission Statement'. Available at <http://www.cathproject.org.uk/> (last accessed 3 May 2015).

Cook, G. (1965) *Letters to Cromwell and Others on the Suppression of the Monasteries*. London: John Baker.

Cousin, G. (2006) 'An introduction to threshold concepts', *Planet*, 17: 4–5.

Davies, M. (2010) *The Corpus of Historical American English: 400 Million Words, 1810–2009*. Available online at <http://corpus.byu.edu/coha/> (last accessed 3 May 2015).

Evans, M. (2013) *The Language of Queen Elizabeth I: A Sociolinguistic Perspective on Royal Style and Identity*, Transactions of the Philological Society Monograph Series. Chichester: Wiley-Blackwell.

Evans, M., Hargrave, F., Richards, A. and Brown, H. (2014) *Living Letters*. Available at <http://www.livingletters.co.uk> (last accessed 4 May 2015).

Fisher, M., Twiss-Garrity, B. and Sastre, A. (2008) 'The *Art of Storytelling*: enriching art museum exhibits and education through visitor narratives', in J. Trant and D. Bearman (eds), *Museums and the Web 2008: Proceedings*. Toronto: Archives and Museum Informatics. Available at <http://www.archimuse.com/mw2008/papers/fisher/fisher.html> (last accessed 3 May 2015).

Gosden, C. and Y. Marshall (1999) 'The cultural biography of objects', *World Archaeology*, 31 (2): 169–78.

Greaves, C. and Warren, M. (2010) 'What can a corpus tell us about multi-word units?', in M. McCarthy and A. O'Keeffe (eds), *The Routledge Handbook of Corpus Linguistics*, Abingdon: Routledge, pp. 212–26.

Griffin, G. and Hayler, M. (2016) *Research Methods for Reading Digital Data in the Digital Humanities*. Edinburgh: Edinburgh University Press.

Hopes, D. (2014) 'Digital CoPs and Robbers: communities of practice and the use of digital artefacts', *Museum Management and Curatorship*, 29 (5): 498–518.

Hu, B., Rakthanmanon, T., Campana, B., Mueen, A. and Keogh, E. (2015)

'Establishing the provenance of historical manuscripts with a novel distance measure', *Pattern Analysis Applications*, 18: 313–31.

Jones, R. and Hafner, C. (2012) *Understanding Digital Literacies: A Practical Introduction*. London: Routledge.

Kytö, M., Grund, P. and Walker, T. (2011) *Testifying to Life and Language in Early Modern England: Including a CD-ROM Containing an Electronic Text Edition of Depositions 1560–1760 (ETED)*. Philadelphia: John Benjamins.

Lwin, S. M. (2012) 'Whose stuff is it? A museum storyteller's strategies to engage her audience', *Narrative Inquiry*, 22 (2): 226–46.

MacGregor, N. (n.d.) *A History of the World in 100 Objects*. BBC/British Museum Partnership. Available at <http://www.britishmuseum.org/explore/a_history_of_the_world> (last accessed 3 May 2015).

McLuhan, M. (1964) *Understanding Media: Extensions of Man*. New York: McGraw-Hill.

May, S. (ed.) (2004) *Queen Elizabeth I: Selected Works*. New York: Washington Square Press.

Moyle, M., Tonra, J. and Wallace, V. (2011) 'Manuscript transcription by crowdsourcing: transcribe Bentham', *Liber Quarterly*, 20 (3/4): 347–56.

Museum Association (n.d.) See <http://www.museumsassociation.org/careers/9910>.

Nevalainen, T. and Raumolin-Brunberg, H. (2003) *Historical Sociolinguistics: Language Change in Tudor and Stuart England*. London: Pearson Education.

Nevalainen, T., Raumolin-Brunberg, H., Keränen, J. et al. (comp.) (1998) *Corpus of Early English Correspondence*. University of Helsinki, Department of Modern Languages.

Nurmi, A., Nevala, M. and Palander-Collin, M. (eds) (2009) *The Language of Daily Life in England (1400–1800)*. Amsterdam: John Benjamins.

O'Halloran, K. (2010) 'How to use corpus linguistics in the study of media discourse', in M. McCarthy and A. O'Keeffe (eds), *The Routledge Handbook of Corpus Linguistics*. Abingdon: Routledge, pp. 563–77.

Rissanen, M., Kytö, M. and Palander-Collin, M. (eds) (1993) *Early English in the Computer Age: Explorations Through the Helsinki Corpus*. Berlin: Mouton de Gruyter.

Ryan, M.-L. (2003) 'Defining narrative media', *Image and Narrative: Online Magazine of the Visual Narrative*, 6: Medium Theory. Available at <http://www.imageandnarrative.be/inarchive/mediumtheory/marielaureryan.htm> (last accessed 3 May 2015).

State Papers Online (n.d.) Gale Cengage Learning. Available online at <http://gale.cengage.co.uk/state-papers-online-15091714> (last accessed 3 May 2015).

Sylaiou, S., Mania, K., Karoulis, A. and White, M. (2010) 'Exploring the relationship between presence and enjoyment in a virtual museum', *International Journal of Human-Computer Studies*, 68: 243–53.

Thomson, L., Ander, E., Menon, U. et al. (2012) 'Quantitative evidence for wellbeing benefits from a heritage-in-health intervention with hospital patients', *International Journal of Art Therapy: Formerly Inscape*, 17 (2): 63–79.

Twycross, M. (2008) 'Virtual restoration and manuscript archaeology', in M. Greengrass and L. Hughes (eds), *The Virtual Representation of the Past*. Farnham: Ashgate, pp. 23–48.

Walter, T. (1996) 'From museum to morgue? Electronic guides in Roman Bath', *Tourism Management*, 17 (4): 241–5.

Wiggins, A., Bryson, A., Starza Smith, D. et al. (eds) (2013) *Bess of Hardwick's Letters: The Complete Correspondence, c.1550–1608*. University of Glasgow, web development by K. Rogers, University of Sheffield Humanities Research Institute. Available at <http://www.bessofhardwick.org> (last accessed 3 May 2015).

CHAPTER 4

Connecting with the Past: Opportunities and Challenges in Digital History

Thomas Nygren, Zephyr Frank, Nicholas Bauch and Erik Steiner

INTRODUCTION

We are all digital historians now. Scholars access online databases and peruse journals through portals such as JSTOR as a regular part of their practice. Nearly all historians use computers to collect, archive and analyse their sources. Typewriters are dusty relics of a bygone era. The digital is with us everyday, but digital history is something else. It is a broad field characterised by extreme diversity in practice and products. In this chapter, we seek to focus on a specific subset of digital history practices: practices that involve collaborative research through the use of digital tools for analysis and representation. These practices share fundamental and interconnected characteristics. Collaboration is required because the complexity of the tools and methods are such that individual scholars will rarely have the training and capacity to develop these projects on their own. In what follows, we examine three case studies to explain what we mean by collaborative digital history practices. First, however, we shall clarify our terms by addressing some of the critical issues involved in doing digital history. We begin, then, by citing the challenges involved in studying the past by using digital material and tools before moving on to our discussion of accomplishments. In doing so, we also want to make clear that there is no simple template for practising historians to follow. Our discussion of problems with digital history and our description of case studies will emphasise diversity and complexity. This chapter is not a recipe for digital history. Rather, it is an attempt to present a few examples from Stanford's Spatial History Project in order to offer advice for scholars, current or prospective, who are seeking to develop research projects of this nature.

Digital history has been rightly criticised on several fronts. Two major areas of concern have emerged in particular, each of which should be considered before delving into a major collaborative digital history project. The first set of concerns involves problems related to the empirical grounds underpinning digital representations of historical processes. Critics have pointed out the way typical digital representations of the past tend to offer what seem to be complete and definitive accounts of what are, in fact, incomplete and complex records (Prescott 2013). It is a truism that maps, graphs and tables are often taken as objective depictions of historical reality (Drucker 2011; Bodenhamer et al. 2010). There is a danger that the current opportunities for doing exciting work with data and visualisations can seduce the observer. Indeed, seduction per se has been put forward as a challenge: 'GIS [geographic information system] is a seductive technology, a magic box capable of wondrous feats, and the images it constructs so effortlessly appeal to us in ways more subtle and powerful than words can' (Bodenhamer et al. 2010: 17). Therefore, this new practice is estimated, at least in part, to make new demands on critical thinking. On some level, this is, of course, not a problem unique to digital history. Maps and graphs in books have the same characteristics and need to be read and interpreted with the same critical eye. The problem here is greater, however, because with digital tools and web-based publication, the number and apparent sophistication of these seemingly objective representations proliferates. At the same time, all too often, the textual material and the interpretive context tend to fall away or fade into the background.

A second and perhaps even graver set of concerns involves the very practice of exploration and analysis of data through the use of digital tools. As Drucker (2011) points out in a provocative intervention, the term data itself becomes problematic. She suggests the term 'capta', information gained rather than given, as an alternative. If we follow Drucker's lead, assumptions about the unproblematic application of tools to data become problematic, not least because there is a risk that 'data' will be shaped by and for the logic of digital tools. Hence, there will be a tendency to privilege the 'codeable' and the 'clean,' the available and the cheap.

Taken together, these critical perspectives suggest that research should begin with a careful consideration of the pitfalls inherent in digital history. Data should not be taken for granted and tools should not take precedence in the organisation of information and the choice of what is included or excluded from historical representation. This is a tall order and one that ought to give would-be digital historians pause. The point is not to suggest that data exploration is a bad thing. Far from it. Rather, the point and the problem is that without a solid research question framing the enterprise, the 'exploration' is more likely to result in dead ends and spurious results. Researchers should avoid the sequence: tool, data, analysis, result. Rather, begin with the historical question; think about the data as capta; select the right tool; analyse according to the question; and generate results in the plural. Using digital tools in combination with critical interpretations highlighting multiple perspectives can help to achieve nuanced understandings of the past.

If digital history poses problems for research, it also offers rewarding opportunities. Indeed, by responding to the challenges and obstacles, it can produce rich results that go beyond traditional analogue forms. The questions of how digital history differs from traditional history and what the future of studying the past is in terms of research and teaching form an ongoing discussion dating back to the 1980s (Rosenzweig 2011; Sternfeld 2012; Mills Kelly 2013; Dougherty and Nawrotzki 2013). The advantages of digital methods in history are too diverse to summarise here. Instead of a catalogue, we offer three dimensions where these methods have particular purchase and where, we think, they can rightly be thought of as distinct from the affordances of analogue history. The first area of opportunity resides in the dimension of scale and scalability through digital history's capacity to mine, store and process large sets of data. Another distinctive characteristic involves the capacity to explore and represent different perspectives and experiences, sometimes in simultaneous fashion. Finally, digital history can transmute recalcitrant archival information into meaningful relationships with related data (internally or externally) through the process of layering and linking. We offer these ideas in order to move past the platitudes associated with 'interactivity' and 'dynamic visualisation'. The issue is not what digital methods can do, but why, as historians, we ought to contemplate using them. These dimensions of historical practice are just some of the advantages digital history offers the field. Beyond this, there is also the real prospect that digital publication of historical research can enhance modes of scholarly communication. In this regard, the opportunity resides in the integration of sound research practice with mindful design of the digital interface where results are ultimately reported.

CASE STUDIES

To illustrate some of the opportunities and challenges in digital history practices we present three recent projects from a heterogeneous field of research we call spatial history. This practice has a number of names. We use the label spatial history because it is one commonly used by historians. Geographers often call it historical GIS, and it is also known as spatial humanities (Suri 2011). Within this research practice, digital historical data is studied both collaboratively and across disciplinary lines using various types of new technology and visualisations. The extensive use of digital data and tools makes the research practice of spatial history worth reflecting upon when considering the future of historical research.

Spatial history research practices emphasise how history takes place in a historical context (Ethington 2007). Inspired in part by Henri Lefebvre, the historical site is considered a social construction that is perceived, conceived and lived based on geographical preconditions and forces such as power and ideology (Lefebvre 1974; Soja 1989). Spatial historians also refer to Fernand Braudel's *géohistoire* and his description of *la longue durée* in both the creation and analysis of historical maps with multiple layers of data (Braudel 1949; Ethington 2007). It is a truism that people's actions in history have been affected by their context. Yet explicit studies of the spaces and places where people have created their understanding of their own time require concepts and methods of operationalisation that fall outside the frame of many a traditional narrative history. To analyse society, groups and individuals with space as a key category of analysis can contribute to an increased understanding of identity, culture, transactions, structures and actors. A better sense of spatial preconditions enhances the possibility of understanding ways of knowing the world in the past as well as being a key mode in the transfer of knowledge between people and places (Shapin 1998). Sensitivity to the surrounding environment may reduce the risk of tunnel vision among historians (White 2010), in short to account for a broad spectrum of interactions and 'peripheral' as well as 'central' actors and practices. Using illustrations to study the past and connecting historical data to maps is hardly new; what is new, however, is the much greater levels of access to data and the possibility to create dynamic and interactive illustrations in order to analyse information and present research on digital platforms.

CASE 1 – TERRAIN OF HISTORY: YELLOW FEVER EPIDEMIC OF 1850, RIO DE JANEIRO, BRAZIL

Our first case study illustrates several of the challenges confronting digital scholarship in spatial history as well as the potential of the approach hinted at thus far. The questions posed in relation to this visualisation are:

- What is it trying to do?
- How does it address the problems outlined in our introductory remarks?
- What advantages or affordances inhere in the dynamic visualisation of historical materials of this nature?
- What role does collaboration play in building projects of this kind?

The basic intuition behind this visualisation is that the social conditions experienced by individuals and groups can be seen as the result of the complex interplay of factors discernible at different degrees of magnification/ granularity (specific locations, neighbourhood contexts, broader parish-level settings – here translated roughly as 10m, 100m, 1,000m distances or degrees of magnification), which in turn can be represented using digital platforms. The story of death from Yellow Fever in Rio de Janeiro can be told, in part, through the spatiotemporal visualisation of parish records during the period of the epidemic in the early months of 1850.

These records, while often incomplete and sometimes idiosyncratic in content, offer the clearest glimpse we are going to get into the micro-history of death and dying, providing the names, ages, addresses, civil status and relations of decedents. These records constitute the 'capta', the data, for the visualisation we created. As persuasive and rich as data visualisation might be, it remains necessary to narrate the epidemic in prose. Without a story, the images move but the significance of the historical experience remains strangely opaque. Whenever the creators of the visualisation have had occasion to present it in public venues, the storytelling and contextualisation provided to viewers has proven critical in the reception of the visualisation itself – which is one reason why our online version of the project includes a brief introductory text that appears before the interactive material is accessed. The story goes something like this.

> Yellow fever's first days in Rio de Janeiro came on the heels of weeks of rumour and anxiety. The first known cases appeared in January 1850, after the fever reportedly arrived by ship from Bahia in December of the previous year. In spite of the efforts of Rio de Janeiro's medical establishment and associated forces of public order, the disease caused panic and dealt death throughout the city from January through May of 1850, tapering off with the end of the rainy season and the cooler months of winter. The dead numbered at least 4,000.
>
> The effects of the fever were gruesome. Victims evinced symptoms which, although deceptively mild at first, soon progressed to shivers, headache, nausea, vomit of mucous and food, rapid heartbeat, followed by a worsening of the headache and sharp pain in the neck and temples, with further agonising pain in the back. The next stage of the sickness brought a high fever, rapid pulse, further headache and, in some cases, delirium. The victim's tongue turned pallid then swollen and discoloured, and they continued to vomit, now bile and blood. After this agony, according to the doctors who observed the sick and the dying during that awful year, there was a brief period of remission. Some patients emerged from the fever and got well in the following days. For the less fortunate, there was another stage during which the headaches and vomiting reached a terrible climax and the black vomit of congealed blood presaged death.

Patterns of death by fever reveal a strong spatial element to the story. Plotting the addresses of yellow fever victims reveals hotspots of infection in specific neighbourhoods in the parish of Sacramento. The clustering of cases is discerned by visual inspection and confirmed by statistical analysis. There are good reasons to suspect that these clusters were the result of specific environmental conditions prevailing in these locations, coupled with the demographic profile of certain neighbourhoods. Standing water and larger numbers of the disease-carrying mosquitoes likely were found nearby, as well as densely inhabited buildings filled with potential hosts – many deaths, then, and sometimes close together in space and time. Thus the inspiration for this digital history project: visualising intensity in the case of an epidemic.

In approaching this theme, our team created a visualisation that emphasises the different perspectives accorded by the selection of various temporal units. The time of history is variegated. Death comes at one time. The social experience of death is cumulative and varies across space. Intensity, then. How to measure and display such a concept? The visualisation attempts to show how the intensity of deaths from the fever increased dramatically over the months of March and April of 1850. Deaths close in time and space are coded as more 'intense'. The more such deaths cluster, the greater the overall intensity of the social experience. The visualisation attempts to show this through a heat map that can be toggled on or off and viewed at the scale of weeks or months (see Figure 4.1). Deaths from tuberculosis are included as an alternative dataset, helping to put the fever epidemic in context and provide a counterpoint in a form of death that was persistent and distributed rather than clustered and intense.

A dense cluster of yellow fever deaths appears, for instance, at the intersection of Rua da Vala (Uruguaiana) and Rua do Hospício, near the heartland of Rio de Janeiro's artisan community – itself dominated by Portuguese-born men without innate or acquired immunity to the disease. On the right-hand side, the visualisation includes a heat map showing the relative intensity of the deaths from yellow fever in the preceding month (left side). That is, the deaths are remembered visually and summed up according to an algorithm which emphasises proximity in space and time. This is how we try to capture a sense of intensity.

Our first case suggests that variable scales of space and time can be operationalised, up to a point, in the service of revealing patterns in historical experience. These patterns can be visualised and displayed as a sequence, thereby suggesting historical experience as lived through processes taking place in space and time. The limitations, however, are legion. Without the narrative story, the visualisation lacks critical context; it makes its argument on top of a narrative argument that must also be in place and, indeed, precede it. Furthermore, although the project certainly did not depend upon cheap, clean

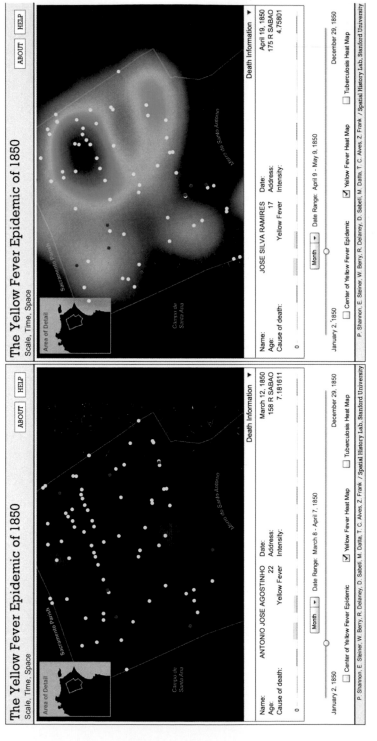

Figure 4.1 Visualization of the yellow fever epidemic in Rio 1850 by Peter Shannon, Erik Steiner, Whitney Berry, Ryan Delaney, David Sabeti, Mithu Datta, T. C. Alves and Zephyr Frank. Available at <web.stanford.edu/group/spatialhistory/cgi-bin/site/viz.php?id=133&project_id=o> (last accessed 20 May 2015). (Source: Arquivo da Curia Metropolitana, Rio de Janeiro: Lista de óbitos da freg. do Sacramento da Sé do ano de 1850, COD.0168.)

and accessible data (the parish records are manuscript books held in church archives), it was limited by what was recorded and how such material could be rendered in graphical terms. The handwriting in the parish ledgers becomes dots on a map or zones of 'heat' as measures of intensity. Our visualisation attempts to avoid the objectification of humans as dots through a feature that allows users to mouse over a given point on the map and call up the name and basic demographic profile of each decedent. Yet this is palliative at best. The view remains somewhat distant and abstract, even as we attempt to explore a concept as visceral as intensity of experience.

The production of the yellow fever intensity visualisation took place in the context of a much larger spatial history project focused on nineteenth-century Rio de Janeiro. Broader lessons from that project should be included here in order to emphasise the challenges as well as opportunities associated with large-scale historical GIS research. The collection of historical GIS data is incredibly time-consuming. While the visualisation itself took perhaps 200 hours to produce, from collecting the data in the archive to geocoding and generating the Flash animation, its production was embedded in a process that required many thousands of hours of labour to create a historical street network and geocoder and to collect the many hundreds of thousands of additional data points for other analytical purposes. The collection and coding of data can become a trap. Time spent in this way is time not spent reading or writing in more conventional scholarship. Projects that look good in isolation can prove to be bad bargains in the larger context. All of which suggests, historical GIS projects should be entered into carefully and the costs and benefits of the approach should be weighted before committing to a major historical reconstruction using digital tools.

CASE 2 – VISUALISING HOLOCAUST GEOGRAPHIES

The goal of understanding and representing the human experience is no more crucial than for traumatic events such as the Holocaust. Historical methods – regardless of whether they are digital – should receive the highest level of scrutiny and their limitations should be clearly acknowledged.

In part for these reasons, engaging in digital, data-driven scholarship of the Holocaust is mostly uncharted territory. This section presents a broad collaborative project examining the geographies of the Holocaust that uses digital methods to reframe this complex history at multiple spatial scales: the personal to the continental. Recent findings and methodological considerations from this project have been presented in Knowles et al. (2014).

Visualising human suffering revives long-standing debates on perspective, objectivity and memorialisation in Holocaust scholarship. Digital methods and a spatial perspective draw strongly from a tradition of abstraction, generalisation and quantification that is difficult to reconcile alongside the deeply personal and emotional experiences of victims and perpetrators. How can you preserve the nuance of individual experiences within large, normalised data sets? How do you characterise and comprehend human trauma in aggregate? How can you avoid privileging abundant but uncomplicated data? And finally, how can you use digital methods in the absence of data altogether?

While Holocaust historians have access to an abundance of data in the form of meticulous Nazi records, these are perilously biased and favour a perpetrator perspective. Equally challenging is a critical lack of consistent data of victim experiences – often overly perfunctory (e.g. coordinates of a victim's timeline), intensely emotional or highly subjective and recounted from traumatic memory. Finally, very little is known from the bystander, those who experienced the Holocaust but participated at a distance are mostly absent in the historical records.

A study of the Budapest ghetto conducted by Cole et al. (2014) examined the evolving distribution of the Jewish population in the spring of 1944. The research was guided by three spatial dualities: visibility/invisibility, centre/periphery and accessibility/inaccessibility. As in the previous case study, the geographic data preparation was substantial, requiring both significant computer digitisation and on-site fieldwork to construct a GIS database with historically accurate street geometries and address ranges in order to geolocate historical addresses. This work alone would constitute a major contribution and useful tool for historians.

Cole et al. (2014) extended this work in two ways. First, they performed traditional spatial analysis on legal Jewish addresses (posted by city officials), examining the dispersion of the population, their visibility to bystanders and access to amenities over time. These quantitative analyses showed mostly unsurprising results but provided texture and evidence to historians' observation that Jews were gradually concentrated over time, and that Jews had different levels of access to foodstuffs and other amenities. While this approach did reveal some nuance in the patterns, it assumed an inappropriately static view of the Jewish population.

Second, the team attempted to examine how Jews may have experienced ghettoisation through different degrees of mobility in the city. The initial maps of mobility quantified distance from each residence to the nearest market hall and colour-coded individual street segments with these values.

In concept these analyses reflected movement, but they collapsed time and were therefore incapable of expressing the dynamic nature of the street experience. The team sought to move beyond these limitations by developing an animated simulation of Jews walking to the market halls. They based this on a shortest-path network analysis, and several essential assumptions on how

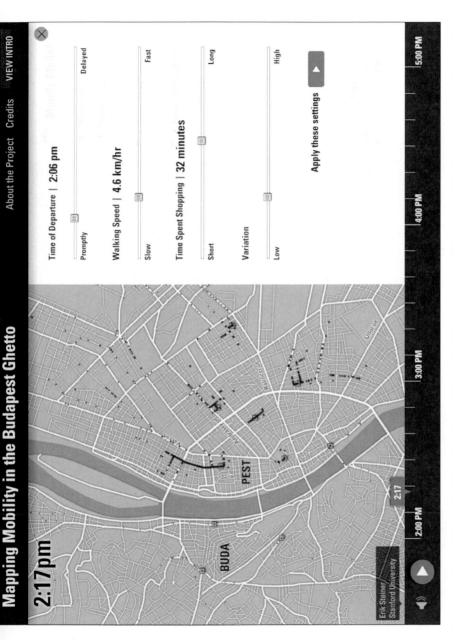

Figure 4.2 An animated simulation of Jewish pedestrian mobility in the Budapest ghetto. Users can modify the assumptions of the model to produce a wide range of possible scenarios. Available at online at <stanford.edu/group/spatialhistory/cgi-bin/site/viz.php?id=411&project_id=0> (last accessed 20 May 2015). (Source: E. Steiner, A. Giordano and T. Cole (2014) 'Mapping Mobility in the Budapest Ghetto', Spatial History Project online visualization.)

fast people could walk and how long they might shop. The model is published online as an exploratory device, allowing users to change the assumptions and re-animate the movement of Jews through the city (see Figure 4.2). By presenting several possible simulated scenarios, the tool represents a kind of new source that allows historians to imagine in what corridors of the city Jews were most active, visible, vulnerable or safe. The tool is allowing the researchers to ask new and more specific questions about survivors' experiences in the city.

The use of simulation models in history might be valuable to digital historians in the absence of complete data, but it also comes with significant technical and philosophical challenges. How do you decide what parameters to include? What assumptions do you make a priori? How do you decide what degree of realism is appropriate? Does simulation constitute invention and thus lack rigour? These questions remain unanswered and were the source of many internal conversations and some conflict within the team. Ultimately, the historians on this project used the visualisation tool to make only cautious observations, thus it arguably failed to realise its potential as a research device.

The Budapest study made spatial arguments at the scale of the city and sought to ground these at the level of the individual street. A second study by Gigliotti et al. (2014) focused on the scale of the individual, seeking to understand how digital methods could help better understand and represent the human experience 'from the bottom up'. This effort tested the limits of how to represent individual experiences and caused the team to question whether these representations fell in the margins between data visualisation and art. The subject of the work was the Germans' last-ditch war effort to evacuate tens of thousands of prisoners from Auschwitz and other concentration camps in the East. This final gruesome stage of prisoner detainment often called the 'death marches' happened on foot over great distances in January 1945 in brutal winter conditions. One clear challenge of analysing this event geographically lay in the fragmentary record (the evacuations were poorly planned and documented by the Germans). The team faced a more substantive challenge, however, in the profound disjuncture between the brutally confined spatial experience of the victims and the wide-angle view of traditional mappings. Attempts at accurately portraying the geography of the evacuations quickly demonstrated the shortcomings of traditional cartography in reflecting on individual experiences or comprehending the places of persecution. These maps seemed to depict exacting and clandestine military movements when they were anything but: this was at once panicked and inefficient labour redeployment, an exhausting and confounding victim experience and a dramatic reveal of the atrocities to local residents.

The team turned its focus to the testimonies of six women who survived the evacuation and described their experiences of a 65km march, the murder of their two close friends and the escape of another. Even with a limited

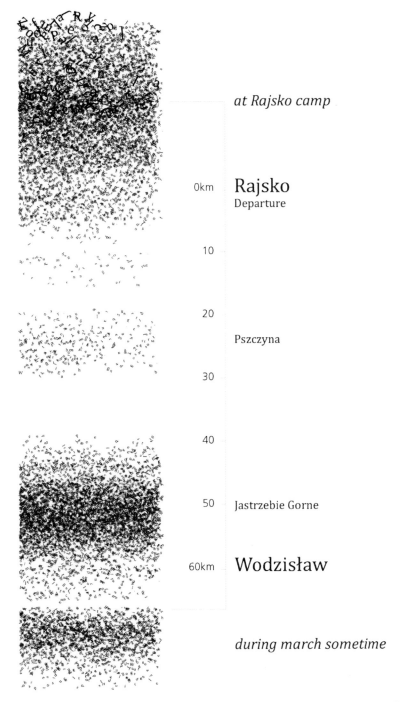

at Rajsko camp

0km   Rajsko
       Departure

10

20   Pszczyna

30

40

50   Jastrzebie Gorne

60km   Wodzisław

during march sometime

Figure 4.3 The textual and textural geography of the testimonies of six female evacuees of the Rajsko subcamp, read top to bottom. (Source: Designed by Erik Steiner. Reprinted with permission from Knowles et al. (2014).)

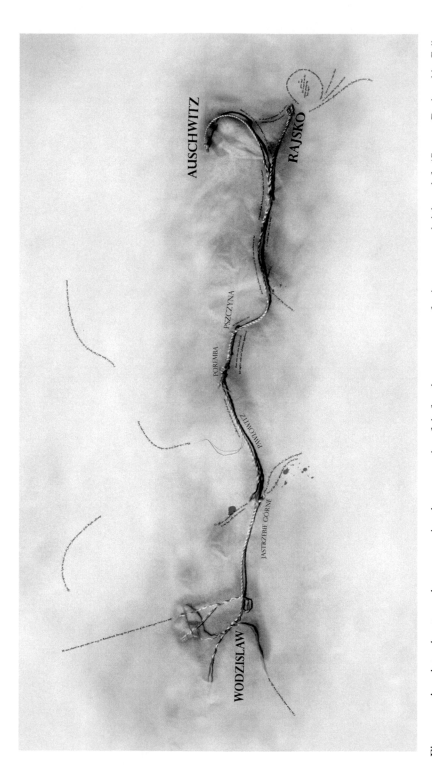

Figure 4.4 A sculptural cartography representing the community of six female evacuees as a fraying rope, read right to left. (Source: Designed by Erik Steiner. Reprinted with permission from Knowles et al. (2014).)

corpus, pseudo text-mining methods were instructive, particularly when the team geolocated the testimony text along a linear path (see Figure 4.3). This mapping was very revealing, unexpectedly showing how memories were unevenly clustered in space while other places were largely forgotten in the thirty years since the experience. What might these silences reflect?

One of the researchers sought to understand these gaps and experience in this geography by visiting the sites and 'rewalking' parts of the journeys in similar conditions. Marc Masurovsky's visit *in situ* revealed a deeper sense of the experience but it was challenging to represent. The team eventually attempted a kind of sculptural inquiry, where Steiner embodied the event through the act of manually fraying a rope that conceptually bound a community across space. This experience and the resulting visual (see Figure 4.4) used non-traditional cartographic techniques, attempting to both generalise the experience of prisoners as well as ground it in individual memories and expressions.

This case study shows how spatial history can draw from but also radically depart from scientific data visualisation methods common in data-driven historical research, edging into the artistic. It seems that one result of a reflexive approach to mapping – that which is aware of the biases of data and the power structures it reinforces – is a more expressive and personal visual aesthetic. Whether this constitutes rigorous objective scholarship is up for debate; the final image extends the abstract visual grammar of the earlier mappings to capture a deeper experience, but it gives up its neutrality along the way. This point highlights a shared challenge across digital history projects that we will discuss in our next case study: given their diversity of form/method and often experimental nature, how do they become scholarly objects and on what grounds should they be evaluated?

CASE 3 − ENCHANTING THE DESERT

The next project in our group of case studies demonstrates an altogether different application of digital tools in understanding the past, and therefore a different type of collaboration, as well. *Enchanting the Desert* is a cultural geography of Arizona's Grand Canyon based on a single historical document: a photographic slideshow consisting of forty-three images made in the early-twentieth century by a commercial photographer named Henry Peabody. The quantity of primary data, in this case, is relatively small. Just 43 landscape photographs of the Grand Canyon, along with Peabody's original typed narrations, provide the focus for this born-digital, interactive web application. Behind the scenes of *Enchanting the Desert*, that is, one will not encounter the massive databases that are sometimes assumed – both inside and outside the

Digital Humanities – to underlay work in digital history. In what is perhaps a return from Franco Moretti's (2013) 'distant reading', *Enchanting the Desert* is in any terms a close digital reading.

The author of the project, Nicholas Bauch, seeks to answer two deceptively simple questions about this historical-geographical document. Where was Peabody standing when he took his pictures, and what human stories are attached to the geological features that appear throughout the slideshow? What, in other words, did viewers actually see when, from thousands of miles away, they watched the slow, monotonous advance of picture after picture, a cascade of foreign-seeming imagery with little to no spatial orientation? To answer these two questions is to build a rich cultural geography – a deep map, as it were (Bodenhamer et al. 2015) – of the Grand Canyon based on the vision of one of the region's earliest European-American promoters. Peabody offered a way of seeing the Grand Canyon that would help set a visual template for what the Grand Canyon was supposed to look like, both photographically and in person. When this magnificent region became a US National Park in 1919, it is no small coincidence that many of the roads, pathways, and lookout vistas were constructed at the same locations that Peabody embodied and represented decades earlier.

Enchanting the Desert is a web application that offers readers the opportunity to imagine themselves a century before, observing the slideshow exactly as Peabody sold it through his catalogues. At the same time it creatively unpacks the place-based histories of the territories represented in the slideshow. The Grand Canyon is far from a single location but is rather a vast region comprised of over 1,200 toponyms and countless more unnamed places, each a thread of the tapestry that makes the Grand Canyon what it is. Knowing which of these places appeared throughout the slideshow has up to now been impossible.

Building a geography for this series of photographs has been achieved through experimental cartographic techniques and careful user interface design. To map Peabody's camera vision was first and foremost a matter of identifying the exact locations where he set up his tripod, including also the pitch, heading and focal length of his lenses. Bauch and his team achieved this by using a virtual landscape design software called Natural Scene Designer (NSD).[1] Using some textual clues from Peabody's original slideshow narration, the author carefully traversed the virtual Grand Canyon, nudging the location, heading and pitch until the virtual pictorial rendering (Figure 4.5) exactly matched Peabody's photograph (Figure 4.6).

Bauch developed an intricate technique for this process, what he calls photographic georeferencing. Put simply, by visually matching each original photograph with its rendering in the virtual environment, his method works the software backwards, asking it to reveal the latitude, longitude, heading, pitch and other information that must be if the picture looks like this (see Figure 4.7).

Figure 4.5 A pictorial rendering made in 2013 with the virtual landscape design software Natural Scene Designer. It is based on Henry Peabody's 1899 photograph 'Up Grand Canyon, from Moran Point'. (Source: With permission of Nicholas Bauch.)

Figure 4.6 Henry Peabody, 1899, 'Up Grand Canyon, from Moran Point'. (Source: Photograph courtesy of the Huntington Library, San Marino, California.)

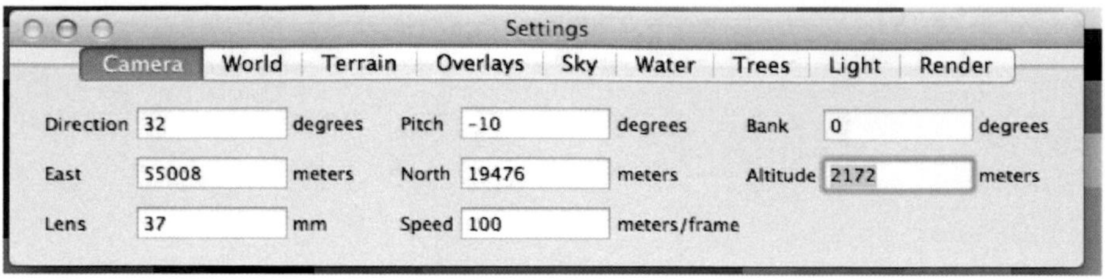

Figure 4.7 Camera information calculated in 2013 by the software Natural Scene Designer for the pictorial rendering in Figure 4.5. (Source: Used with permission of Nicholas Bauch.)

Important to note is that normally NSD is used in the opposite direction, meaning that a user inputs latitude, longitude, etc. – into the fields shown in Figure 4.7 – in search of what the pictorial rendering for that information will look like. This creative 'hack' of the software enabled Bauch and his research team to begin answering the two deceptively simple questions that undergird the entire project. It was, in the end, an attempt to get into the shoes of the photographer, or rather into the landscape of the Grand Canyon as experienced by Peabody.

In the web application that is now in its fourth year of development, readers move through three types of content: the photos, an interactive map and a collection of over eighty essays, the topics of which are anchored to the particular places one visually consumes in the photographs (see Figure 4.8).

The web application is designed so that readers can move among these three elements seamlessly, able to drill down into the details of an essay while never losing sight of the photograph they are reading about or a map showing the point from which the image was originally made. Readers, in other words, always have access to the proverbial trees as well as the more general forest that they make.

Enchanting the Desert is a large undertaking. It has been conceived, written and designed from its inception to exist as a web application, not as an addendum to a printed text and not as an unpublished tool used to make conclusions. The project is the conclusion. It is a new genre of scholarship that uses the medium of the web to convey geographical theses and historical findings. The medium allows for a new type of spatial narrative to flourish, where arguments are not made linearly but are instead made based on where a reader positions him- or herself within the geography created by Peabody's camera vision.

DISCUSSION

Writing history poses distinctive challenges when historians engage in the digital world. One central aspect, highlighted in the examples above, is the

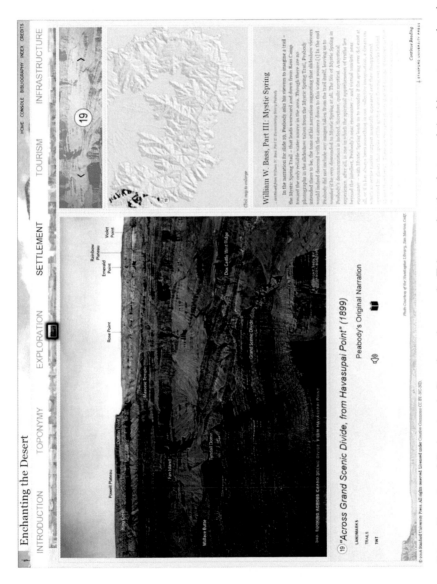

Figure 4.8 One possible configuration of *Enchanting the Desert*'s reader console. Take note that the photograph (and its custom-made colour tint and landmark labels), a map indicating which territories in the photograph are actually visible, and an essay menu are all at the reader's disposal. (Source: Image used with permission from Nicholas Bauch.)

challenge of historical empathy. Understanding people in the past by their own standards means that we need to contextualise the information and try to shift perspectives. There is a challenge to understand the past as a 'foreign country', a place where language and concepts as well as context differ in fundamental ways from our contemporary world (Lowenthal 1985). This cognitive and emotional ability to understand unfamiliar perspectives across time and space, often labelled historical empathy, is a central but also complicated matter in historical studies (Davis et al. 2001). Closeness to primary sources and the environments studied may be a way to overcome temporal and spatial gaps of understanding. In the cases presented in this chapter, researchers use a mixture of traditional and digital methods to better understand the life and circumstances facing people in the past. Visits to the archives have been combined with visits to the places of historical events. In the practice of digital history this connection to historical settings is still important. Materiality may certainly affect our construction of knowledge (Latour 1999) and researchers in digital history may benefit from physical reminders of the complexity of the fragmentary remains behind neat data.

The cases presented consciously avoid tool-driven data fishing; rather they select a limited number of sources aimed at defined research questions. This has been a conscious choice to better be able to answer the research questions and communicate findings in nuanced ways. To get a deeper and empathetic understanding of the trails from Auschwitz and 'walk in the shoes' of the tormented women, Marc J. Masurovsky made the winter walk himself. Nicholas Bauch has made multiple visits to the Grand Canyon to get a better sense of the places captured by Peabody and Zephyr Frank has spent months with handwritten documents in the archives and wandering the neighbourhoods of his study in Rio. The digital cannot replace such tangible experiences. But using digital tools gives us the opportunity to capture richer data from this kind of fieldwork. Images, recordings, notes and other georeferenced data can today be used in the process of revisiting the past in historical scholarship. Digital tools can be used to complement printed material in ways that may help the historian overcome the unreachability of the past so evident when going to the archives (Robinson 2010). Using visualisations makes it possible to organise the information in new ways, for instance linking it to geographical locations and on temporal scales. Digital tools can be used to collect different types of data and to explore relationships in time and space beyond what may be possible in more traditional explorations using pen and paper. Closeness and distance is vital in our understanding of the past and digital tools may help us see things in a larger perspective and also zoom in on selected parts in time and space. Dynamic digital representations can also help the researcher better understand change over time (cf. Griffin et al. 2006). Possibilities to select and analyse temporal and spatial scales in historical material may show patterns hidden in notes and spreadsheets. Visualisations can be very useful when processing data. In the projects described researchers have consciously used digital tools to curate their data and to explore it from different perspectives.

The digital realm offers another major challenge to historians with respect to the critical treatment of sources. To closely scrutinise and interpret accounts from and about the past is pivotal in historical studies. It has been argued that the digital turn makes the humanities too data-driven and oriented towards quantitative methods, losing the values of critical qualitative methods (Fish 2012). If research is led by the accessibility of data, albeit a very large amount and well visualised, it risks being led along the wrong path (Prescott 2013). Digital tools may reconstruct the fragmentary primary sources into clean and neat visualisations and thereby create a distance to the original sources. But, in the examples we have presented above, it is evident how humanistic and critical analysis can be central in historical studies based upon digital material. While each author here begins with the digitisation of some primary documents and or data, they all evaluate the digital representations as they would any other document that falls under the purview of critical examination. In each case, that is, we see how the authors 'meet the digital' part way, never assuming that a digital tool can answer questions without an interpreter.

There are some indications that novice users may lose their awareness of their theoretical position and empathy when using large data sets (Nygren 2014). When facing a large set of data and statistics it may be an instinctive reaction to start sorting the information and quantifying, rather than reflect upon the starting point of your research and critical perspectives and conduct a more interpretive investigation. Close reading of a few documents may perhaps make it easier to hermeneutically scrutinise the information. However, digital tools and material can also be used to closely analyse how smaller fragments fit into a bigger picture. It may even be easier for a historian to keep track of different perspectives when using digital annotations instead of traditional highlighters and marks in margins. When closely scrutinising formulations and coding material there is also a risk that you may spend too much time coding and recoding your data. Thus the risk of getting lost in an abundance of information is followed by a risk of re-reading and re-coding data so many times that your codes and not your research questions become central. Therefore it is necessary in the research process to stay focused on the bigger picture of research aims and theoretical considerations to avoid the 'coding trap' (Gilbert 2002). This is important when using qualitative and quantitative data analysis software, both in the categorisation and analysis. To avoid getting lost in the abundance of digital material and being navigated by the tools we strongly suggest a focus on research questions and the contextual uniqueness of history.

Regarding digital presentations, we need to consider other aspects in the scholarship of digital history. As trained historians and researchers in Digital Humanities you may very well be able to see how representations, in all forms, are always simplifications of a complex reality based upon fragments. This, however, may not be the case of the audience, and the seductive technology makes it more important to show the uncertainties which are so hard to visualise. In digital history the writing of history may be more than creating text. In digital platforms you can create and present multiple interlinked narratives, integrate images, maps, commentary and primary sources in the same field of vision, and curate and shape the reader/user's experience, allowing for a hybrid experience (cf. Thomas III and Ayers 2003). But as a final presentation visualisations need to help the reader/user see behind the seductive cleanliness of data presentations and animations. It is also important to bear in mind how multiple narratives and multi-modal presentations may confuse the reader/user rather than give a richer understanding of the topic. There may be a risk of cognitive overload for readers in hypertext environments (cf. Gerjets and Sheiter 2003). All users need to learn to become critical readers and navigators in multi-modal environments, but digital historians need to understand the audience in somewhat new ways when the digital tool becomes a publishing tool. Digital historians also need to be able to review scholarship in new media if we want to make use of new opportunities and safeguard quality in historical scholarship (Presner 2010; Nygren et al. 2014).

The creation of multi-modal dynamic representation is a new challenge, but it may also be a rewarding one. Working in teams, with diverse skills in programming, database management, cartography and visual storytelling, historians have today at their disposal an expanded toolkit for the exploration, interpretation and presentation of data. Collaborating with designers and across disciplines invites us to construe richer and more nuanced images and understandings of the past. In the case of understanding the intensity of the spread of tuberculosis, the visualisations open up possibilities of interpretations beyond limited notes found in the Sacramento parish records. But it needs to be followed by personal narratives in order to also show the intensity on a personal experiential level. When using visualisations such as those describing the spread of tuberculosis in Rio and people's movements in Budapest, this risks turning human suffering and anxiety into distant dots, but linked to related information and framed in a sensitive way it may be used as a spatial narrative paying attention to the environment and highlighting actions rarely noticed in historical writing. Thus it is central to present and frame the data to help the user empathise with the perspectives of the actors.

Visualisations can also be used to bridge the gap between data and empathetic narration. In the works of Gigliottiet al. (2014) it is evident how dots and maps may become a compassionate illustration of physical personal experiences (see Figure 4.4 above). And in this collaboration, a combination of geography, testimonies and art illustrates the history of people walking the trails of sufferings linked to Auschwitz. The basis for this digital artwork is human experience, historical understanding and creative artwork. This is an interesting interdisciplinary meeting and a collaborative way of grasping the big picture and empathising with the unfathomable events of the Holocaust. This artwork, with its solid basis in empirical data, shows a way to integrate art and science; cartography and hermeneutical interpretation combine to display how historical narratives may be shaped in ways previously inconceivable in historical scholarship.

Enchanting the Desert exemplifies what can be done with digital methods vis-à-vis scholarly communication. By blending the theoretical rigour of cultural geography with the techniques of GIS and the artistry of geovisualisation in a narrative format, Bauch's work extends narrative forms associated with the research monograph into a new terrain of interactive and multiplex narratives. This new spatial narrative is grounded in a mixture of technical applications (GIS, viewshed analysis) and conventional textual interpretations of cultural artefacts. Bauch's work is the pilot project for Stanford University Press's digital monograph publishing initiative, an initiative that is revolutionising how humanities scholars can practise in digital media. The Press peer-reviews and publishes born-digital scholarship under their imprimatur, giving accreditation to digital work just as any regular print book would have. Because of this effort, the gap between what Digital Humanities scholars are making and the established pathways of traditional academic distribution and accreditation is now much smaller. Until now, this gap threatened the very survival of the Digital Humanities because there was no incentive for a group of researchers to spend their time building a digital platform to advance their arguments when there was always the looming pressure to do the 'real work' of publishing.

One way to imagine work within the Digital Humanities is that any given project exists on a continuum between two poles. The first pole is when digital tools are used behind the scenes, when a researcher is scampering for a proverbial notepad on which to scribble out ideas and thoughts and to see what data might look like when graphed, charted or mapped. In this scenario the digital part of doing research is a building block on which interpretation can be layered or from which creative new insights can be gleaned. These insights are then inserted into a textual narrative that – usually – fits with the established publishing model of a journal article or book.

The other pole in how digital tools can be utilised is that they become a medium for communicating research results (i.e. interpretations and insights) in novel ways that allow readers to experience the data on their own terms, within the curation of the author and his or her arguments. At this pole the digital tool becomes a publishing tool introducing a new genre of academic communication. Of course neither of these fictitious poles are ever exactly reached. However – and this is the lesson to be learned – when scholars decide to engage with digital techniques they will inevitably fall somewhere on this continuum, and it would behove them to have a sense of where they are on it.

It is hard for any one person to do this work alone. Collaborating across disciplinary borders with an openness to experiment and learn new things, we can add nuances and dimension to historical studies through digital methods. Collaboration may be a challenge, particularly in traditional humanities departments. Stanford's Center for Spatial and Textual Analysis has experimented with organisational forms that are uncommon in the humanities. To an extent, these forms more closely resemble a scientific research lab, with varied personnel taking on different roles according to domain expertise working in teams and co-authoring digital scholarship. The architecture of the workspace itself can be important inasmuch as it creates a space wherein team members work side-by-side and talk when necessary. Informal, serendipitous encounters in this context are as important as planned meetings. Though the content of the work is digital in nature, the production of the work is very much face-to-face. Working together, borrowing forms of collaborative scholarship from other fields and being attentive to the space of collaboration, we can imagine digital history as an inviting field for scholars across a range of generations and temperaments.

NOTE

1. The Software *Natural Scene Designer* is available for purchase in both PC and Mac formats at: <https://www.naturalgfx.com/>.

REFERENCES

Bodenhamer, D. J., Corrigan, J. and Harris, T. M. (eds) (2010) *The Spatial Humanities: GIS and the Future of Humanities Scholarship*. Bloomington: Indiana University Press.

Bodenhamer, D. J., Corrigan, J. and Harris, T. M. (eds) (2015) *Deep Maps and Spatial Narratives*. Bloomington: Indiana University Press).

Braudel, F. (1949) *La Méditerranée et le monde méditerranéen à l époque de Philippe II*. Paris: Colin.

Cole, T., Giordano, A. and Steiner, E. (2014) 'New Multimedia Publication: Mapping Mobility in the Budapest Ghetto'. Available at: <https://cesta. stanford.edu/2014/06/27/new-multimedia-publication-mapping-mobility-in-the-budapest-ghetto/>.

Davis, O. L., Yeager, E. A. and Foster, S. J. (eds) (2001) *Historical Empathy and Perspective Taking in the Social Studies*. Lanham, MD: Rowman & Littlefield.

Dougherty, J. and Nawrotzki, K. (eds) (2013) *Writing History in the Digital Age*. Ann Arbor: University of Michigan Press.

Drucker, J. (2011) 'Humanities approaches to graphical display', *Digital Humanities Quarterly*, 5: 1.

Ethington, P. J. (2007) 'Placing the past: "groundwork" for a spatial theory of history', *Rethinking History*, 11 (4): 465–93.

Fish, S. (2012) 'Mind your p's and b's: the digital humanities and interpretation', *New York Times*, 23 January. Online at <opinionator.blogs.nytimes.com/2012/01/23/mind-your-ps-and-bs-the-digital-humanities-and-interpretation/#more-118957> (last accessed 15 June 2013).

Gerjets, P. and Scheiter, K. (2003) 'Goal configurations and processing strategies as moderators between instructional design and cognitive load: evidence from hypertext-based instruction', *Educational Psychologist*, 38 (1): 33–41.

Gigliotti, S., Masurovsky, M. J. and Steiner, E. (2014) 'From the camp to the road: representing the evacuations from Auschwitz, January 1945', in A. K. Knowles, T. Cole and A. Giordano (eds) *Geographies of the Holocaust*. Bloomington: Indiana University Press, pp. 192–221.

Gilbert, L. S. (2002) 'Going the distance: "closeness" in qualitative data analysis software', *International Journal of Social Research Methodology*, 5 (3): 215–28.

Griffin, A. L., MacEachren, A. M., Hardisty, F., Steiner E. and Li, B. (2006) 'A comparison of animated maps with static small-multiple maps for visually identifying space-time clusters', *Annals of the Association of American Geographers*, 96 (4): 740–53.

Knowles, A. K., Cole, T. and Giordano, A. (eds) (2014) *Geographies of the Holocaust*. Bloomington: Indiana University Press.

Latour, B. (1999) *Pandora's Hope: Essays on the Reality of Science Studies*. Cambridge, MA: Harvard University Press.

Lefebvre, H. (1974) *La production de l'espace*. Paris: Éditions Anthropos.

Lowenthal, D. (1985) *The Past Is a Foreign Country*. Cambridge: Cambridge University Press.

Mills Kelly, T. (2013) *Teaching History in the Digital Age*. Ann Arbor: University of Michigan Press.

Moretti, F. (2013) *Distant Reading*. London: Verso Books.

Nygren, T. (2014) 'Students writing history using traditional and digital archives', *Human IT*, 12 (3): 78–116.

Nygren, T., Foka, A. and Buckland, P. I. (2014) 'The status quo of digital humanities in Sweden: past, present and future of digital history', *H-Soz-*

Kult, 23 October. Online at< http://www.hsozkult.de/debate/id/diskuss ionen-2402> (last accessed 19 March 2015).

Prescott, A. (2013) 'The deceptions of data'. Online at <digitalriffs.blogspot. com> (last accessed 18 July 2014).

Presner, T. (2010) 'Digital Humanities 2.0: a report on knowledge'. Online at <http://cnx. org/content/m34246/1.6/?format=pdf> (last accessed 20 May 2015).

Robinson, E. (2010) 'Touching the void: affective history and the impossible', *Rethinking History: The Journal of Theory and Practice*, 14 (4): 503–20.

Rosenzweig, R. (2011) *Clio Wired: The Future of the Past in the Digital Age*. New York: Columbia University Press.

Schuurman, N. (2000) 'Trouble in the heartland: GIS and its critics in the 1990s', *Progress in Human Geography*, 24 (4): 569–90.

Shapin, S. (1998) 'Placing the view from nowhere: historical and sociological problems in the location of science', *Transactions of the Institute of British Geographers*, 23 (1): 5–12.

Soja, E. W. (1989) *Postmodern Geographies: The Reassertion of Space in Critical Social Theory*. London: Verso.

Sternfeld, J. (2012) 'Pedagogical principles of digital historiography', in B. D. Hirsch (ed.), *Digital Humanities Pedagogy: Practices, Principles and Politics*. Cambridge: Open Book Publishers, pp. 255–90.

Suri, V. R. (2011) 'The assimilation and use of GIS by historians: a socio-technical interaction networks (STIN) analysis', *International Journal of Humanities and Arts Computing*, 5 (2): 159–88.

Thomas III, W. G. and Ayers, E. L. (2003) 'The differences slavery made: a close analysis of two American communities'. Online at: http://www2. vcdh.virginia.edu/AHR/ (last accessed 10 July 2015).

White, R. (2010) 'What is spatial history?', *Spatial History Project*. Online at <https://web.stanford.edu/group/spatialhistory/cgi-bin/site/pub.php? id=29> (last accessed 20 May 2015).

CHAPTER 5

The Object and the Event: Time-based Digital Simulation and Illusion in the Fine Arts

Stephen Hilyard

> Even though both may look the same on the surface, a digital image
> may be said to differ from its analog counterpart in terms of the
> verifiable past and a possible future. Because of its dependence on an
> 'a priori' real-world referent subject, a photograph by nature refers to
> the past – a viewing experience termed by Roland Barthes as a sense
> of the 'having-been-there'. With the digital image, whose construction
> could potentially be totally fictive, one can claim at most that the event
> represented 'could possibly be'. (Legrady 1995)

To date, the integration of digital tools into fine-art practice has focused on
three modi operandi which may be conveniently identified via typical subject
matters. These are: technology as a 'wonder show' (in which the demonstration of new capabilities is an end in itself); technology as its own subject matter;
and finally art which takes the form of a critique of mass media/commerce/
systems of power. In this chapter I will argue that one particular subset of
capabilities provided by digital media tools has yet to be widely exploited in
the field of fine art, namely the ability to create convincing time-based (i.e.
taking place over time) simulations using 3D modelling and animation software. I will discuss the work of a number of artists currently working with
the simulation capabilities of digital media in this way and position this work
against a description of how, twenty years ago, fine-art photographers were
quick to recognise the relevance of digital simulation techniques to a number
of discourses in their field, something that did not happen until recently in the
field of moving image artwork.

Digital tools allow us to create convincing simulations of our world,
which is to say they allow us to create the kind of cultural objects that we are
accustomed to accepting as evidence of the 'real world' out there. To put this

another way, we might say that the computer is very good at lying. It should be noted that neither the computer nor the camera is inherently truthful or untruthful. The technology complies with the laws of physics and of its own construction. Questions of truth only arise with regard to the way the tools are used and, most importantly, the ways in which the results are interpreted. In the fine-art context the ongoing advances in digital technology provide the artist with a wealth of opportunities to create metaphors which deal with the questions of subjectivity, contingency, mediation via culture and relativism in the context of our lived experience of the world. This is not so much an appeal to the concept of the dissolution of 'reality', in the familiar terms of 'simulacra and simulations' (Baudrillard 1983), rather this is a new way of dealing with the idea that we live in a web of illusion, or at least that our experience of the world is inescapably shaped and delineated by our own minds. While digital tools have been used this way for more than twenty years by artists working with still images, until recently the same level of sophisticated simulation was not being applied to moving images. Paradoxically, although Hollywood has been one of the primary driving forces behind the development of simulation technologies, their use in the fine-arts was initially limited to work within the rather defined field of fine-art photography.

No discussion of simulation in the fine-art context would be complete without first mentioning Jean Baudrillard's foundational text for postmodern critical theory. In Chapter 1 of *Simulacra and Simulations*, 'The Precession of the Simulacra', Baudrillard presents a characteristically enigmatic argument that our culture has reached a point in which simulation *precedes* the real (1983: 1). There is an important distinction here between simulation and representation in that simulation is not involved in the signifier/signified dichotomy. This is because the simulation *is* the thing itself. In fact, Baudrillard claims that simulations constitute our new reality – same as the old reality with the exception that it is reproducible. Baudrillard seems to be describing a form of consciousness that is entirely generated by culture, one which has become more and more divorced from the concrete as the connections within that culture (communication) have become more efficient. If our culture was once a tool which helped us to deal with the world outside, now it has enveloped that world, it has become it, so that the map becomes the territory (Baudrillard 1983: 1). In this chapter I will look at a specific part of this process, one of those connections within our culture: the creation of ever more convincing technological simulations of the real which are presented to us via our senses of vision and hearing. An important aspect of the process is the convincing part. This brings up questions of the authority we award to the content we experience and hints at a possible physiological level of belief which leaves the mind at the mercy of the body.

PHOTOGRAPHS

When digital tools for the manipulation of single images first became available to artists in the early 1990s they immediately became part of a number of ongoing discourses in the field of fine-art photography. I will briefly summarise some of these before presenting some specific cases. One of the most fundamental debates concerned the relative value of the photograph which is 'made' (that is to say an image of a staged scene or an image created by photomontage or manipulation) as opposed to one that is 'found'. A belief in the importance of 'found' photography (and by extension the irrelevance of 'made' photographs) is still widely held by many photographers, particularly photojournalists, and is closely linked to the concept of 'The Decisive Moment'. This term was quoted by Henri Cartier-Bresson (1952a) in the preface to his first book *Images à la Sauvette* and was used as the title for its English translation (1952b). The term is often associated with the tradition of documentary street photography pioneered by Cartier-Bresson which emphasises the photograph as a record of real events and a form of impartial evidence. According to this school of thought the photograph's intervention in the image should be limited to the selection of the precise framing, in time and space, of the real world which will allow the image to reveal the true nature of its subject. According to this view the photographer is a form of hunter who undertakes an almost mystical search for the image, but he does not create it, he merely finds it, acting as a kind of curator of reality. In his preface Cartier-Bresson specifically contrasts his school of photography with 'manufactured or staged photography'. There is a direct connection here to another long-running debate over the photograph as a measure of truth, as a reliable account of a single reality. While followers of the Cartier-Bresson school would argue that it is the role of the photographer/ hunter to go out and capture singular truth, subsequent schools of thought emphasise the manipulated nature of all image making, even via the simple act of prioritising one moment over another, and the multiplicity of potential meanings imminent in any image. The traditionalist view also implies a very specific relationship between the photograph and time, namely that it must be created in a single moment, a point of view not shared by photographers of the 'making' school who wished to escape the tyranny of the single shot. A last question, closely interrelated to those mentioned above, is the relationship between fine-art photography and painting. Can the photographer enjoy the same freedom of interpretation and invention that the painter does? In what ways should the work that a photograph does differ from that of a painting? It can easily be seen that new digital tools, which allowed for sophisticated photomontage and manipulation of images, would be of interest to photographers on the 'making' side of all of these debates.

In 1992 Jeff Wall created a photographic work entitled *Dead Troops Talk (a Vision After an Ambush of a Red Army Patrol, near Moqor, Afghanistan, Winter 1986)*. At the time, Wall was already a major figure in the world of fine-art photography whose work was being shown in museums all over the world. *Dead Troops* is a massive image (approximately 8 feet by 14 feet), on the scale of the history paintings which it self-consciously references. In keeping with the history-painting tradition, it appears to depict the event parenthetically referred to in its title. It presents the viewer with a tableau of separate scenes played out by dead and dying Soviet soldiers against the backdrop of a rocky battleground. In contrast to the tradition of history painting, many of these scenes have an air of macabre comedy. The image contains elements that suggest that it is a document of an event as it happens and we notice the kind of details typically found in documentary photography. A number of Afghan figures, for instance, are only partially visible, cut off by the edge of the frame, while another appears unaware of the camera as he rummages through a bag. And yet this is not a documentary photograph when taken as a whole. In fact this photograph was never 'taken as a whole'. It was digitally assembled from about 100 separate shots made over a period of months in a rented studio near Wall's hometown of Vancouver. Parts of the image which might appear accidental have in fact been very carefully calculated. As well as actors and various background elements, the building blocks of this image included clinically accurate models of disembodied wounds. All of these elements were seamlessly combined using digital technology which had only become available a few years earlier.

Although *Dead Troops* was Wall's first image to use large-scale digital compositing it was not the first complex tableau image that he had created; it came in the middle of a series of works he later referred to as his 'philosophical comedies'. Before *Dead Troops* he created an image with a similar air of gruesome comedy entitled *Vampire's Picnic* which involved no digital assemblage. The scene was staged and lit on an outdoor set and shot as a single take. Following *Dead Troops*, however, Wall created a second image, *A Sudden Gust of Wind (after Hokusai)* which used the new digital workflow. Once again about 100 separate image elements were composited together, in this case to create a modern-day Canadian re-enactment of the eponymous woodcut in which the sky is full of flying papers, leaves (and a hat) that could never have been so perfectly positioned by a single gust of wind. The important point is that the digital tools were not a prerequisite for this body of work, but they did allow Wall to take what he was already doing further. The digital workflow allowed greater control and thus a higher level of realism, which functions to convince the viewer that what they are seeing is 'true'. The same techniques freed the image maker from the dead hand of the 'Decisive Moment'.[1] Now that an image could be assembled from multiple events that occurred at different times, Wall could create images that seemed ever more unlikely, leading the viewer to question whether what she was seeing was even possible. The key to any artwork that makes use of simulation and illusion is the tension between these two qualities – the simultaneous appearance of *truth* (this looks like a real thing) and *impossibility* (this event could never have happened). Digital methodology is clearly not required for this effect and it is not the point. However, it does allow this artistic strategy to be followed to its conclusion. The simultaneous appearance of truth and impossibility is what I refer to as a 'clue', and clues are very important to the functioning of any artwork that deals in simulation and illusion. While users of simulation technologies in commercial fields may assume that verisimilitude is the standard (albeit a changing one) by which their work will be judged, the artist using the same tools finds themselves in a paradoxical position. If an artwork is intended to deal in a poetic and non-verbal way with its subject then it does that by the juxtaposition, by the internal tensions between its parts. In the case of an artist who wants to exploit the conceptual implications of simulation the fact that simulation is taking place is a crucial part of the work which the viewer must to some extent perceive. The poetic effect disappears when the simulation disappears, in other words when it becomes so successful that the viewer no longer realises it is taking place. For this reason the simulation must be successful in some ways but fail in others, and it is the relationship between these parts which makes the point.

Jeff Wall was not the only fine-art photographer who was an early adopter of digital techniques. A number of other prominent photographers also began working this way in the early 1990s, and to varying degrees they also left clues in their work. Probably the most prominent of these was Andreas Gursky. In 1996 he created an image entitled *Atlanta* which left no doubt as to its synthetic origin. Once again this image is made up of details which are convincing and appear to be 'true' within an overall arrangement that is clearly impossible. This was done by merging an image of an architectural interior with its mirror copy. The image thus created appears to depict the interior of a vast atrium delineated by repeating layers of balconies. In keeping with common themes in Gursky's work the architecture is both huge and dehumanising, a man-made sublime. On closer inspection the diminutive figures of a few maids can be seen on the balconies along with the tools of their trade. The perspective within the image is severely controlled to create a composition of perfectly parallel or converging lines. However, the perspective is also clearly impossible, or at least very unlikely, as there are two separate vanishing points, a result of mirroring the original image. Small details, such as the maids and their cleaning carts, however, have been changed or moved around to remove a sense of perfect symmetry and further confuse our reading of the image. Once again we find a tension between the details and the image taken as a whole, between the truth of objects and the impossibility of an event. In this case the building blocks of the image appear to be true – the various architectural elements, the maids and the ash trays and the balcony plants. The impossible event would be the one in which the photographer, standing in for the viewer, stands in front of the scene depicted.

The decades since *Dead Troops* and *Atlanta* were created have not seen a decline in interest in the simulation and illusion among fine-art photographers. In fact these themes have only grown more prominent in the work of young photographers, two of whom I will mention below. This work is created in many different ways, from elaborate landscape models, complete with weather, staged in tanks full of mysterious liquids[2] to complex digital assemblage and manipulation.[3] Scott McFarland, for instance, creates images that continue to worry at the fraught relationship between photography and time. He often makes single images by combining elements from multiple photographs taken at different times. In some cases the clues to this process are quite clear, for instance the series of images entitled *Empire* in which scenes from the botanical gardens of the Huntington Library were created from shots taken at different times of day, giving rise to mismatched shadows across the image. In other images landscape photographs were combined which were shot from the same location in different seasons, for instance *Orchard View with Effects of Seasons (Variation #1)*. Some images from the series *Street View* combine multiple events photographed from the same location; the resulting image is full of believable details. However, the 'event' of the image as a whole contains a few too many apparently simultaneous decisive moments to seem plausible.

Dominic Hawgood is a young photographer only recently graduated from the Royal College of Art. If McFarland's multi-shot composite photographs seem to be informed by the well-established discourse around the photograph and the decisive moment, Hawgood's work seems to be informed by an equally long-running ambivalence concerning the photograph as a record of events, as a measure of truth or as a model of a simple singular idea of history. The subject matter of his work from 2012 to 2015 would seem to fall easily into the tradition of documentary photography – spirituality and ecstatic religion among very specific social groups in the USA and UK. However, his methodology is the very opposite of the documentary tradition in that he photographs carefully orchestrated re-enactments of events. For a body of work entitled *The Conversation*[4] he photographed women speaking in tongues, but arranged for them to re-enact their religious ecstasies alone against deliberately neutral back drops, thus removing any of the context which in a documentary photograph would help to tell us a story. The next body of work[5] took as its subject the rituals of worship in evangelical African churches in London. None of the photographs were made at the actual events; Hawgood directed actors to enact scenes. The clearly staged settings and the typically controlled studio lighting make it clear that these images were not plucked from the real world. We do not know whether these scenes are re-enactments or purely fictional, or a mixture of both. It is not even clear if all of the imagery even originated with real-world physical objects. Hawgood releases very little information about his process, but he has revealed that one of his images, a high-production-value, candy-coloured image of a spray bottle full of holy water, was not created by a camera at all. It is a digital rendering of a 3D digital model, a virtual object (in O'Hagan 2015).

TIME

As we have seen, photographers have been using the sophisticated simulation capabilities of digital tools to question the status of their medium as a measure of truth for more than twenty years. During that time no parallel developments took place among artists working with moving images. While it is true that there are many examples of artists digitally manipulating video during this time they tended to stick to the modernist tradition of lo-fi technique and exhibited little interest in illusionism or the creation of convincing simulations. A good example of this kind of work would be a series of video pieces by Paul Pfeiffer[6] in which he painstakingly removed elements from footage of sporting events by repainting each frame by hand. This process left the ghostly outlines of removed sportsmen clearly visible, creating a strikingly eerie effect. However, there was no attempt here to fool the eye in the way that Wall and Gursky were doing in photographs from the same period. There are no doubt many reasons for this difference, not the least of which would be the technical and financial challenges of creating convincing time-based digital illusions. It would also be true to say that the field of video-art has never shared the particularly medium-specific anxieties that inform the work described above. Whereas photography has always looked to painting as a measure of what it is and is not, the field of video art emerged 150 years later, closely associated with performance art whose measure was taken against all things theatrical. More importantly 'truth' has never been an issue for artists working with moving images the way that it has been for photographers. While the question of whether the (still) camera can lie has been a mainstay of fine-art photography the video/movie camera has never been held to the same standard by the artists who use it or their audience.

The history of moving-image art does include artists who deal in the fantastical, most notably Matthew Barney. Barney's work[7] speaks the language of cinema and makes use of relatively few digital special effects, even in his more recent work. Cinematic works like the films in Barney's *Cremaster* series deal in expressionism, surrealism and above all storytelling. Barney is unashamedly a showman much like the film-makers of Hollywood, albeit with a radically different set of goals and criteria for success. As such he need not be concerned with the reliability of his medium. Perhaps the most important reason that artists working with moving images have not felt the need to explore their medium's responsibility to speak truth can be found in this connection to cinema. We are all comfortable with the idea that moving images are spinning us a yarn, and have been since long before moving-image art became conceivable. The history of photography does not contain a similar tradition of mass-market fiction. The photograph has always stood as either a record of fact or the singular expression of the artist.

The use of time-based digital illusions in the fine arts had to wait for the emergence and maturation of a new field we could loosely describe as digital media. This is a way of making art distinct from the earlier discourses of photography and video-art. Digital media has its own set of preoccupations and a developing history. While artists have been making use of digital technology since the first personal computers became available, the field has seen considerable development in the last eight years or so. It was in 2007 that the first sophisticated examples of time-based digital illusionism began to appear in the art world, a new direction in digital media. The artists I will discuss below create work which does not fit into the triumvirate of 'digital-media types' mentioned above, what I would describe as 'first-wave' digital media art. This new work does not take its own techniques as its subject matter in the way that first-wave digital art often does, or even in the way that photographers do when they question assumptions about the camera and the photograph. This work deals with issues beyond artistic mediums. In this regard it could be seen as a return to an earlier model of the artist as one who deals with human experience in a poetic manner rather than an operator sealed in a closed system of artistic production and commentary. While each of the works deals with its own specific subject matter there are a number of common conceptual threads implied by the use of simulations which they all share. These overarching themes all lead back to the way in which we construct our experience of the world and the importance of our shared culture to that process. Subjectivity, contingency and relativism in the context of our lived experience of the world are the hallmarks of the new reality described by Baudrillard. The ever more sophisticated digital tools created by the games and movies industries were not created to explore these ideas but it almost seems as if they were.

The software used to create the work that I will be discussing here is time-based and deals with 3D digital models which can be animated or controlled in real time. This is an important distinction from the more manageable non-time-based 2D image manipulation used in the field of fine-art photography. While digital manipulation of images is most often achieved by combining elements from multiple photographs this new work generates synthetic imagery by rendering digital models in virtual space. The final output takes the form of moving images and sound, presented in various ways, rendered to fixed video sequences, or rendered in real-time 'performances' which may span decades. In the same way that Barney can co-opt the methodology of cinema while maintaining a radically separate set of priorities, the artists described below are repurposing tools created by the games and movie industries towards their own ends.

Before discussing specific artworks I would like to evoke a concept that originates in the world of commercial illusionism which will be helpful when thinking about the work. The term 'Uncanny Valley'[8] was coined to describe an experience any consumer of contemporary media will be familiar with. The term is most often applied to humans but is applicable to any living creature that is intended to be sympathetic. It is closely related to the explanation of the uncanny presented in Ernst Jentsch's (1906) seminal chapter 'On the Psychology of the Uncanny' which includes a number of examples involving confusion between the living and/or inanimate status of an object (examples include a corpse, a zombie, an automaton). It originated in the field of robotics but has become most relevant in the fields of digital animation and special effects. It may be depicted by imagining a graph whose horizontal axis represents how realistic a reproduction of the human form is, from 0 per cent (for instance an industrial robot) to 100 per cent (a real human), while the vertical axis indicates a typical viewer's level of comfort or 'familiarity' with a likeness. The graph delineates a steady increase in positive emotional response as the likenesses increase in realism. However, in the small region just before 100 per cent realism is achieved the viewer's response will drop drastically, before jumping back up for the 100 per cent realistic likeness (see Figure 5.1). This dip in the graph is the Uncanny Valley. It corresponds to simulations of the human that are almost perfect but not quite there. In the field of robotics this effect was observed when attempts were made to create convincing humanoid robots complete with simulated facial features, skin and hair. The result was creepy rather than sympathetic.

The Uncanny Valley has been a bugbear for the entertainment industry whenever it has attempted to replace human actors with totally convincing digital simulations. A case in point would be the 2001 animated movie *Final Fantasy – Spirits Within*, the second in a series of four movies based on the successful video game franchise. This was the first attempt to create a completely photorealistic CGI (computer-generated imagery) feature film in which everything was digitally generated, including the actors. In part this was a technical feat intended to gain attention by pushing the limits of the technology available. It was also seen as a prototype for future film production. The movie's lead character, Aki Ross, was designed to be a digital actress who would go on to become a 'star' in her own right. The thinking was that the production company would then be able to cast her in future movies and

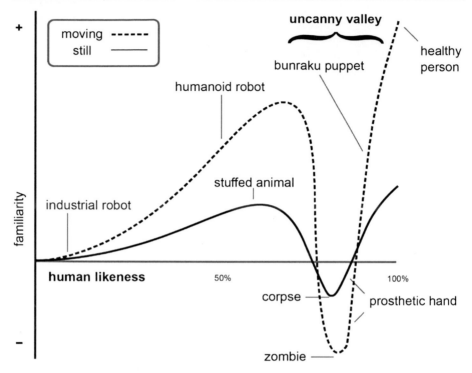

Figure 5.1 The Uncanny Valley. (Source: Jasia Reichardt (1978) *Robots: Fact, Fiction, and Prediction.* London: Thames & Hudson.)

games, developing her career like a particularly malleable flesh-and-blood actress. Unfortunately Aki's acting career never went any further. Although all the digital humans in the movie were meticulously simulated, as well as being voiced and motion-captured from A-list actors, the final result fell afoul of the Uncanny Valley. They were just short of being totally convincing, which left them being merely creepy. *Final Fantasy – Spirits Within* was a box office flop. Subsequent movies in the *Final Fantasy* franchise ditched the realistic digital actors and returned to a more anime-inspired look. Most movies that have attempted to create fully digital actors have suffered a similar fate (for instance *Polar Express* (2004), *Beowulf* (2007)). On the other hand successful digital actors have tended to be non-human (for instance the blue skinned Na'vi of *Avatar* (2009) or Gollum from *Lord of the Rings* (2001, 2002, 2003)).

While the Uncanny Valley is a place to be avoided at all costs for those making commercial use of digital simulation, in the fine-art context it becomes a useful path to understanding the new work that is being created with digital media. While most works do not attempt to simulate human beings, there is a lingering sense of the uncanny about all of it. The tension between the simultaneously familiar (and believably 'real') and the unfamiliar (synthetic) that is at the heart of the uncanny experience is what draws attention to the underlying conceptual themes of the artwork. It also functions as the kind of clue without which this artwork would not function. An artwork involving a totally successful simulation can no longer incorporate the implications of that simulation into its conceptual mechanism; it might as well be real. We will also see that, as with the photographic work discussed earlier, the frisson between the familiar and the strange, between the real and the impossible, exists between the parts and the whole. The artist creates a world that is locally familiar but globally strange, made up of objects that we can easily understand and believe in which are taking part in events we cannot easily place in our lived experience of the world. Both the photographers described above and the digital media artists I am about to discuss take advantage of an apparent double standard in the ways that our minds attribute authority. Apparently the events depicted in a scene are held to a higher standard than the objects which make up the scene. It seems that the event is perceived at the level of the social, hence it is susceptible to reason. The event is assessed by a process which includes the clues left by the artist as to the event's synthetic nature, therefore it is open to suspicion. On the other hand the object belongs to a much older category: it is pre-social, a thing-of-the-senses. Our minds cannot help but believe our eyes when it comes to objects. We are able to simultaneously disbelieve in an event while believing in the objects which make it up because the event is intellectually understood while the object is assimilated at a physiological level which we cannot escape. This contradiction and the tensions it creates in the viewer are at the core of any artwork based on simulation and illusion. This is what makes this work so fascinating and attractive, in the manner of the miniature train set landscape or the fish-tank diorama, while retaining the disturbing undertones of the uncanny, in the manner of the ventriloquist's dummy or the waxwork museum.

THE WORK

In 2007 I created a video piece entitled *One Life*[9] (see Figure 5.2), part of a trilogy dealing with love in three different forms. In the case of *One Life* the subject was love in the context of family. The viewer is presented with a panoramic view of impossibly profuse apple blossom. During the course of the video the camera moves through a landscape consisting entirely of clouds of white flowers and occupied by a large family of bees. At first the bees behave naturally, wandering around lazily and feeding on the blossom. However, as the camera moves into the forest of blossom their behaviour becomes less and less normal. The bees start to form dramatic lines and swarms, delineating increasingly complex curves and arabesques. Their performance climaxes with

Figure 5.2 *One Life*, Stephen Hilyard, HD video animation, 6:39 min., 2007. (Source: Courtesy of the artist.)

a dance in which the swarm creates a series of mysterious figures and knot patterns. This takes place against a flowery back drop that has become similarly excessive, arranging itself into a completely symmetrical stage for their performance. The soundtrack of *One Life* consists primarily of the sounds of the bees themselves. Behind the steady murmur of the feeding bees can be heard a second set of muffled conversations, the sound of dialogue from daytime television soap operas apparently playing in an adjacent room. The sections of dialogue all make reference to various family relationships and conflicts, a key theme in the genre. The dialogue is mostly too muffled to be intelligible, but the original backing music of the scenes can be heard. According to the conventions of the soap opera form, music only plays at time of conflict or high drama – only sections of dialogue that included background music were sampled for the piece. Additional music was added from a collection of generic 'suspense and drama' soundtracks, creating a marked tension between the sun-drenched beauty of the white blossoms and the increasingly menacing audio world the viewer finds herself in.

One Life was created using a hybrid workflow combining 2.5D animation of images of real blossom with 3D animated bees. While the blossom is in fact just flat images spaced out in 3D virtual space, like flats on a stage, the camera movement is limited in a way which conceals this and creates a convincing sense of 3D space. Similarly the bees are small enough and detailed enough to be convincing individually. The viewer experiences a collection of believable parts that are brought together into a whole that is increasingly strange and in this case sinister. While the individual boughs of blossom are convincing (they are details of real trees), they have been combined into an array that is clearly impossibly symmetrical as well as almost overwhelmingly profuse. The bees begin the video as softly murmuring clichés of a pleasant summer's day but their manoeuvrings soon take on an air of menace while hermetic meaning is hinted at by their formations.

Beyond its specific subject matter *One Life* incorporates a conceptual thread which runs through all my work. This could be summarised as an exploration and celebration of the profound in its various forms. Central to this project is the recognition that everything we believe and understand about profundity is a cultural construct. Such concepts as beauty, love or the sublime are not absolutes but constructions (not to say accidents) of history. My contention is that this does not cheapen such concepts in any way, it merely makes them more human. The ideals we project onto the world around us are good examples of such constructs. An example of this would be our association of wilderness landscapes with such concepts as liberty, spiritual fulfilment or natural order. These associations are in fact quite recent additions to western culture. A common strategy in my work is to use digital simulation techniques to exaggerate such ideals to the point where they become visible, creating a metaphor for the process of projection. In the case of *One Life* the ideal of beauty and of the garden as a place of serenity and refuge are presented to the viewer in a way which soon becomes excessive. The blossom which was at first beautiful becomes suffocating. The bees transform from passive details within the scene into an active collective. The details remain familiar but the event which is the swarm has become strange. While the piece begins by presenting the garden as an exaggerated case of our ideal of 'the beautiful' by the climax this has transformed into 'the sublime' in which danger and beauty are combined for elevated effect. In all my artwork the goal is to create a certain level of discomfort in the viewer caused by unresolved internal contradictions. The viewer is encouraged to pay attention as she attempts to resolve these contradictions. In the process she creates meaning. However, this is a riddle with no answer so the viewer never arrives at a comfortable solution. *One Life* is a good example of the way that digital simulation technologies allow me to create a level of cognitive dissonance by presenting a document of the world in which believable (and hence 'real') objects are taking part in an impossible event. This is the same contradiction at the heart of an experience of the uncanny, as described by Jentsch, in which a scene or object is simultaneously familiar and strange. This has proved to be a valuable strategy for an artist who is fundamentally preoccupied with the constructed nature of experience, one that has been used on a number of other pieces.[10]

Jonathan Monaghan[11] began creating artwork using 3D digital animation software in 2007 while still an undergraduate student training for a technical career in the entertainment industry. After finishing his degree he made the unusual choice to apply his technical skills to a career as a fine artist rather than following his peers into the industry. He has gone on to create an extensive body of video artwork using the sophisticated simulation techniques developed by the movie and video-game industries. He is an artist who grew up in the world of digital simulation as first a consumer and then a creator of content. In an email conversation,[12] Monaghan states: 'My first artistic interests were not traditional painters, sculptors, or even video artists, but video game designers and science fiction movies.' Although games and movies were what first inspired Monaghan, he has taken the techniques and visual language of these commercial forms and repurposed them to very different ends. His work deals with the history of power structures within our society, but it does not take the familiar form of 'institutional critique' artworks.[13] His videos are gorgeous and kitsch extravaganzas of architecture and materialism. They seem to revel in their own excess while simultaneously creating a pervasive air of the uncanny. In this world a giant mutant penguin consumes its own young while merged with the architecture of a gothic cathedral. We watch the decadent relics of France's *ancien régime* explode in disco–hued slow motion in the dead zone of a generic capitalist cubicle farm. In an excerpt from a recent article Monaghan describes his work:

Orchestrated in a virtual computer space, my works act more as windows into another world, another dimension, a kind of alternate reality. This world is fantastical and bizarre, but parallels our own, where imagery of power, wealth, and authority are conflated with consumerism, science fiction, ancient mythologies, and historical works of art.[14]

The above mentioned penguin appears in 2009's *French Penguin*. Over the course of the video the camera moves through a gothic cathedral which has lost its roof. There are a number of queasily biological elements integrated into the architecture which breathe and flex. The camera moves along the ambulatory before turning the corner into the apse to reveal an altarpiece that has been hybridised with a giant emperor penguin. Rather than guarding an egg between its feet, the penguin gives birth to a monstrous flesh-blob child with a black cross growing out of its head. The penguin parent promptly eats its young and returns to its original somnolent state.

Monaghan's interest in the history of power and privilege has led him to borrow imagery for *French Penguin* from the later days of the French monarchy and the revolution that deposed it. He refers to these quotations as evocations of 'tragic or perilous decadence'.[15] The piece *Dauphin 007* (2011) (see Figure 5.3) is another good example of this, combining the story of the prince, as personified by a lion, with hi-tech medical equipment (another recurring theme). The young prince/cub is born, along with his crown, from a highly detailed gothic facade which once again incorporates a number of biological elements. Before he can assume his crown it is stolen by a black eagle. The crown is hovering overhead once more when the lion prince walks into a glossy plastic MRI scanner which is also a guillotine. His head is removed and flies away leaving his hollow and headless body hooked up to an IV drip. The black eagle returns to torment him before we see him expire in a white heaven, dwarfed by a maniacal rotating chandelier of medical equipment.

The associations between historical power structures and those of the present day are brought to mind by *Office* (2013) (see Figure 5.4), which focuses on a mysterious object in a familiar office environment. It appears to consist of a fragment of baroque architectural ornament complete with painted vignettes and marble busts of the rich and powerful of eighteenth-century France. As the camera rotates around the object we see a series of shiny plastic structures alternating with the antique statuary. These seem to be modelled on the MRI scanner which first appeared in *Dauphin 007*, but they also have a sci-fi feel as they include cryptic control panels and glowing pinstripes. As the camera continues to orbit the mysterious object the statues of the great men of another age explode slowly into a myriad of fragments, revealing interiors that glow with vibrant pastel colours.

Monaghan's strategy, as stated above, is to create a 'parallel world' in order

Figure 5.3 *Dauphin 007*, Jonathan Monaghan, HD video animation, 3:10 min., 2011. (Source: Courtesy of the artist.)

Figure 5.4 *Office*, Jonathan Monaghan, custom video animation, 4:32 min., 2013. (Source: Courtesy of the artist.)

to explore the real world. Digital simulation allows him to choreograph objects which do not belong together into impossible events. The processes of history are made visible by the collision of objects and environments from different times, a metaphor for the constant conversation between the past and the present that goes on within any culture. The 3D digital environment allows him to create facsimiles of hybrid luxury objects with such a high level of finish and precision that they become parodies of our timeless obsession with bling. It is all here, from the excesses of baroque architecture to the expensive materials and stripped down lines of high modernist interiors, from the Fabergé egg to the glossy and opaque surfaces of the latest Apple device. This kind of software allows the artist to create anything she can imagine – in fact her imagination is the only limit. In Monaghan's case this allows him to create constant confusion between the organic and the inorganic, between the living and the dead. An air of the uncanny prevails as architecture sprouts fleshy appendages and orifices or a galloping stag is rendered in highly polished gold. Monaghan's animals sprout buildings and his buildings give birth to animals. The work is replete with the kind of 'riddle without solution' mentioned above, drawing the viewer into a conversation with the imagery without ever offering an answer. The power of these effects depends on the realism of the individual parts in contrast to the absurdity of the situations they find themselves in, something only made possible by the digital environment that Monaghan chooses to work in.

Alex McLeod[16] is a digital media artist who began working with 3D digital animation software in 2007. His work adds a second layer of simulation – he creates very realistic simulations of what appear to be artificial scenes created by a model-maker using real materials.

> When I began building these worlds I wanted to work with the idea of interconnected matter and life cycles. Rather than portraying a realistic looking tree I used ones that were obviously fake, but tried to make them look like what they were made from was real.[17]

These simulations of representations take the form of complex dioramas or model landscapes, seemingly made from shiny plastic, cast resin, string, balsa wood and paint. They appear to be very real solid objects, but they are clearly making no attempt to simulate real landscapes; rather, they imply an overactive model-maker, maybe a whimsical child, compulsively building imaginary worlds. Certain tropes appear repeatedly, for instance a simplistic cloud form made up of intersecting shiny plastic spheres, always depicted hanging from strings.[18] This format doubles down on the process of constructing a personal reality from the whole cloth of one's hopes, needs and fears – this is a simulation of a fabrication. A good example of this way of working is a piece entitled

Frozen Cascade (see Figure 5.5). As is the case with many of McLeod's works, this piece appears as both a still image and an animated video. The still image presents the 'hero shot' of a landscape diorama of indeterminate scale. The animated version takes us for a tour of the diorama as the camera flies smoothly between mountains built of transparent resin and under white plastic clouds. The same clear resin forms a body of water surrounded by a forest of pines trees which are merely stacks of green plastic cones, some in a mirrored Mylar finish. A number of elevated boardwalks have been made from balsa wood, leading up to a detailed model of a sailing ship apparently wrecked on a simply sculpted alabaster rock. There is a rainbow made of grey, white and chromed plastic. On closer inspection a balsa wood wishing-well can be found in the corner of the scene. The atmosphere is both cheerful and claustrophobic.

Although McLeod's work has incorporated a variety of scenic genres, from natural landscapes to urban scenes, they are consistently presented as digital simulations of simplified real-world models. These dioramas appear to be very real objects made from recognisable materials. While McLeod created these simulations they imply a second creator – if these dioramas exist (and they appear very solid) then they must have been made by someone. They are packed with an overwhelming amount of detail, the viewer is led to consider the backstory of this fictional modeller and her mania for making. They appear to be miniatures, the camera's point of view allows us an omnipotent god's-eye view and brings to mind all the attractions of miniaturised worlds from train sets to bonsai trees. The tension in this work is created by choices the artist has made with regard to lighting and materials. The lighting is very realistic, using sophisticated rendering techniques to give a highly effective sense of solidity to the scenes. By contrast the materials from which the various objects are made remain implausibly perfect. There are a variety of methods which allow an artist working with 3D models to mimic the kind of imperfections, wear and dirt that we see on objects all around us. In fact this kind of detail remains the 'holy grail' of digital rendering which strives for total realism. Complex multi-layered materials are often created in which various properties are controlled by images or algorithms which have been customised to match the topography of the object. McLeod has not used any of these techniques, and we are left with an apparently real object that seems to be made from impossibly perfect materials, in fact an inversion of the other work cited in this chapter in which believable parts make up an impossible whole. Once again the viewer must grapple with a riddle with no solution and the shadowy figure of the second maker it implies.

The last artist I will discuss is John Gerrard,[19] and once again the year 2007 appears to be pivotal. His work is unusual as it involves real-time rendering of digital models by a game engine. This is a piece of software that is used to create the visual experience of a video game. Up to this point all the time-

Figure 5.5 *Frozen Cascade*, Alex McLeod, HD video animation w/print, 2:19 min. / 40" × 60", 2010. (Source: Courtesy of the artist.)

based work that I have discussed was created by rendering digital sources into a fixed video sequence, a process which is often very slow and resource-intensive. Once created the content of the video is also fixed. By contrast, a game engine will render digital assets quickly enough to show motion in 'real time' as a player interacts with a game or while the contents of the virtual world are being controlled by programming. An example of the latter would be the AI controlled non-player characters in a video game. Because images must be rendered very quickly real-time rendering is much more challenging for the software and hardware than simply frame-rendering to video. It also requires very rigorous control of resources (polygon counts of models, image sizes in materials, etc.[20]). The advantage of real-time rendering is that the experience may be interactive, as it is in a video game, or it may be controlled by software. Gerrard creates real-time rendered video installations which are software controlled. This allows him to create moving-image artworks which unfold over durations measured in decades rather than minutes. His early work[21] took its imagery from the dustbowl landscape of Texas and Oklahoma and the infrastructure of the industrial farming which takes place there. His earliest real-time rendered works appeared in 2007. One year later he created *Oil Stick Work (Angelo Martinez/Richfield, Kansas) 2008*. In a simple yet stunningly effective choice, Gerrard created a moving-image artwork with a duration of thirty years. The software is programmed to create an environment synchronised with the real world, in which the sun rises and sets and nothing takes place during the hours of darkness. During the day the camera is focused on a large silver metal industrial barn structure with adjacent silos and outbuildings located on an empty plain. Six days a week a simulated character named Angelo Martinez emerges from the barn at dawn and works until dusk, painting the walls black with a small oil stick crayon. Each day he completes about a square metre. He is scheduled to complete the task thirty years after he started. As the piece has progressed over the years since 2008 Martinez has brought scaffolding and ladders out of the barn as needed. In a particularly brilliant act of curation *Oil Stick Work* was installed for a full year in a London Tube station.[22] One can imagine regular commuters checking in with the piece day after day, keeping track of their fellow worker's painfully slow progress towards the completion of a futile task.

Gerrard has gone on to create an extensive body of work using real-time video rendering, often creating artworks of extreme duration. This work deals with a wide range of subject matter, from a recreation of a disused school in Cuba to an examination of the real-world infrastructure of the Internet. He refers to these works as 'simulations' rather than using more familiar terms like 'video installation'. In terms of the visual experience of this work there are clear parallels with other work described in this chapter. We are being presented with a simulation of the kind of evidence we are accustomed to accept as proof of events in the 'real world', in this case video. The parts are convincing while the event remains implausible. However, when we consider the way this work was created we find simulation on a deeper level, that of the actual mechanics of reality. Gerrard creates worlds which have a life of their own with their own rules and limitations embedded in the programming which controls them. In the case of *Oil Stick Work* the program contains instructions about each step in the process, the equipment required and how it will be deployed, but none of this code will be enacted until the process is allowed to run its course. While the instructions and rules are predetermined, specific events do not have to be. Unlike traditional animation that is locked in place by key-frames,[23] this kind of 'procedural' animation is the result of the interplay between the various parts of the coding, often creating unpredictable and complex behaviours that could not have been anticipated by its creators. This procedural approach can be applied in many ways in the 3D digital environment, from generating the 2D pattern of a tiger skin to controlling a complex animation of AI characters. Typically an artist creating content procedurally creates rules which give her control over the general features of the end result – she could tell you that this will create a pattern of tiger stripes or these AI characters will take part in a game and one of them will win. However, the artist has no control over specific details, she could not tell you exactly where a particular stripe will occur or which AI character will be the winner. Defining an extreme duration for Angelo Martinez's encoded performance is merely an elegant way of drawing attention to the profoundly hermetic nature of this life, at once hopelessly predetermined on the large scale yet unknowable locally.

CONCLUSION

The key to any artwork that makes use of simulation and illusion is the tension between the simultaneous appearance of truth and impossibility. In the context of fine art a completely successful simulation may do no conceptual work and is useless. This is why clues are such a vital part of all the artworks that I have described, whether it is the double perspective in Gursky's *Atlanta*, the impossibly perfect materials of McLeod's dioramas or a fantastical creature embedded in Monaghan's apparently real architecture. In the frame of reference of any particular artwork the tension is generated between the parts and the whole, between the truth of objects and the implausibility of the events they are taking part in. It appears that our minds perform a form of 'double-think' which allows them to continue believing in objects which have been presented in situations that are clearly suspect. It is important to note that none of the artworks described here are attempting to simulate a full sensory experience of the world. These simulations take the form of the kind of documents we are accustomed to accepting as evidence of the real world somewhere 'out there'. As such they function based on the authority that we grant them. We have been ascribing authority to accounts of the world beyond our senses since language first developed. Our authorising habits and standards are fluid and have been changed by each new form of document, from the hand-made image through the written word to the mechanically made moving image with sound. As our tastes become more sophisticated illusions that once seemed convincing now fail to impress. When looking at the ways in which recent technological advances have changed our authorising habits what is most striking is the degree to which they have not changed them. It seems surprising that anyone with even the most cursory experience of popular culture would believe in anything they see on a screen anymore, but it seems that, on a visceral level at least, we cannot help ourselves. In fact a vast entertainment industry of special effects movies and games is dependent on the fact that emotionally we cannot help but believe our eyes, even when intellectually we know we are being fooled. Similarly the artwork discussed in this chapter relies on the fact that we cannot help but believe in the objects being presented even though they are taking part in events which we cannot believe in. I do not think that this speaks to some vestigial belief in a single reliable reality 'out there', I believe this is taking place at a physiological level. While the earliest digital simulations in the field of photography marked anxieties about the medium itself, this new work should turn our attention to the bodies which are experiencing simulation and the complex ways in which the mind ascribes authority to the senses.

The developments in time-based simulation in the fine arts I have described here are part of an ongoing process. In the future, artists will be able to make use of increasingly complex sensory simulations, from 3D stereographic imagery to various forms of virtual reality experiences. It seems an open question whether the paradoxical relationship between the object and the event will remain available to the artists of the future as a conceptual gambit. As the minds of future art viewers continue to be shaped by their own cultural production will they reach a point at which the intellect triumphs and it becomes impossible to convince anyone of anything? On the other hand the physiological integration of senses and mind may withstand the most sophisticated levels of simulation, providing artists with an expanding field in which to exploit this paradox in the pursuit of some form of poetry.

NOTES

1. The term 'The Decisive Moment' was quoted by Henri Cartier-Bresson in the preface to his first book and was used as the title for the English translation. The term is often associated with the tradition of documentary

street photography which Cartier-Bresson pioneered which emphasises the photograph as a record of real events and a form of impartial evidence. According to this school of thought the photograph's intervention in the image should be limited to the selection of the precise framing, in time and space, of the real world which will allow the image to reveal the true nature of its subject.

2. See landscape images by Kim Keever available at <http://kimkeever. com/> (last accessed 29 July 2015).

3. See work by Simen Johan available at: http://www.simenjohan.com/ (last accessed 29 July 2015).

4. See <http://dominichawgood.com/the-conversation> (last accessed 29 July 2015).

5. See <http://dominichawgood.com/under-the-influence> (last accessed 29 July 2015).

6. See *Fragment of a Crucifixion (After Francis Bacon)*, video loop, Paul Pfeiffer, 1999, also *Three Studies at the Base of a Crucifixion* (2001), *The Long Count I, II & III* (2000–1).

7. Matthew Barney's cinematic artworks include the *Cremaster Cycle*, five feature-length movies, 1994 to 2002; *Drawing Restraint 9*, feature length movie, 2005; *River of Fundament*, feature length movie, 2014.

8. See Masahiro Mori (1970) 'Bukimi No Tani (The Uncanny Valley)', Energy; also: Jasia Reichardt (1978), Robots: Fact, Fiction, and Prediction. London: Thames & Hudson, pp. 26–7.

9. Available at <http://stephenhilyard.com/gall_ol.htm>.

10. In the case of *Always (2007)* (<http://stephenhilyard.com/gall_alw. htm>) this involved a realistic simulation of a cloud dancing a very unnatural dance to the melody of a love song. *Morning Glory (2008)* (<http:// stephenhilyard.com/gall_mg.htm>) takes the viewer on a fantastical journey into a flower which leads to a 3D landscape hidden in a decorative plate by Wedgwood.

11. <http://www.jonathanmonaghan.com> (last accessed 2 August 2015).

12. E-mail conversation between Jonathan Monaghan and the author (30 April 2015 to 15 May 2015).

13. See artworks by Fred Wilson, Hans Haake, Michael Asher, Jenny Holzer and Barbara Kruger, among others.

14. Jonathan Monaghan (2014) 'Jonathan Monaghan: man without a movie camera', in Crystal Bridges Museum of American Art blog, 23 September 2014, available at <http://crystalbridges.org/blog/jonathan-monaghan-man-without-movie-camera/> (last accessed 2 August 2015).

15. E-mail conversation between Jonathan Monaghan and the author (30 April 2015 to 15 May 2015).

16. <http://alxclub.com> (last accessed 2 August 2015).

17. E-mail conversation between Alex McLeod and the author (30 April 2015 to 6 July 2015).
18. For example, the following pieces: *Clouds* (<http://alxclub.com/video/113166838>), *Jolly Ranch* (<http://alxclub.com/print/jolly_ranch.jpg>), *Prismatic Planes* (<http://alxclub.com/video/27382821>), *Blue Wall* (<http://alxclub.com/print/blue_wall.jpg>) and many others.
19. <http://www.johngerrard.net> (last accessed 2 August 2015).
20. Game engines which render in real time utilise polygonal 3D digital models in which curved surfaces are approximated by flat facets with three or four edges. The appearance of these models is controlled by materials which use 2D image data to control the colours of the different parts of the model, as well as other material properties like transparency.
21. See John Gerrard (2007) *Animated Scene (Oil Field)*, *Dust Storm (Manter, Kansas) 2007*, *Dust Storm (Dalhart, Texas) 2007*, simulations, at <http://www.johngerrard.net>.
22. This work was displayed at Canary Wharf Tube Station from 28 March 2010 to 28 March 2011. See <http://www.viewlondon.co.uk/whatson/oil-stick-work-london-article-9469.html> for details (last accessed 6 August 2015).
23. Keyframe animation is the digital equivalent of tradition hand-drawn animation in which 'key' images or poses are drawn which, spaced out in time, define the final motion of the image. The intervening frames are later created to span between these keyframes. In the digital context properties are defined by the user at points in time, for instance the location of an object, leaving the software to create the transition between the two different states.

REFERENCES

Barney, M. (1994–2002) *Cremaster Cycle*, five feature-length movies.
Baudrillard, J. (1981) *Simulacres et Simulation*. Paris: Éditions Galilée.
Baudrillard, J. (1983) *Simulations*. New York: Semiotext(e).
Cartier-Bresson, H. (1952a) *Images à la Sauvette*. Paris: Editions Verve.
Cartier-Bresson, H. (1952b) *The Decisive Moment*. New York: Simon & Schuster.
Gerrard, J. (2008) *Oil Stick Work (Angelo Martinez/Richfield, Kansas) 2008*, online at <http://www.johngerrard.net/oil-stick-work.html> (last accessed 19 August 2015).
Gursky, A. (1996) *Atlanta*, Cibachrome print.
Jentsch, E. (1906) 'On the psychology of the uncanny', in *Psychiatrisch-Neurologische Wochenschrift*, 8.22 (25 August), pp. 195–8 and 8.23 (1 September), pp. 203–5.

Legrady, G. (1995) 'Image, language, and belief in synthesis', in H. Amelunxen (ed.), *Photography after Photography: Memory and Representation in the Digital Age*. Munich: G+B Arts, pp. 88–91.

McFarland, S. (2006a) *Empire*, series of inkjet prints.

McFarland, S. (2006b) *Orchard View with Effects of Seasons (Variation #1)*, digital C print.

McFarland, S. (2012) *Street View*, series of inkjet prints.

McLeod, A. (2010) *Frozen Cascade*, HD video animation 2:19 minutes and print 40" × 60".

O'Hagan, S. (2015) 'In raptures: Dominic Hawgood photographs the evangelical experience', *Guardian*, 20 February, online at <http://www.theguardian.com/artanddesign/2015/feb/20/dominic-hawgood-under-the-influence-evangelical-african-churches-london> (last accessed 19 August 2015).

Pfeiffer, P. (1999) *Fragment of a Crucifixion (After Francis Bacon)*, video loop.

Reichardt, J. (1978) *Robots: Fact, Fiction, and Prediction*. London: Thames & Hudson, pp. 26–7.

Sakakibara, Motonori (2001) *Final Fantasy – Spirits Within*, animated feature film, dir. Hironobu Sakaguchi.

Wall, J. (1991) *Vampire's Picnic*, transparency in light-box.

Wall, J. (1992) *Dead Troops Talk (a Vision After an Ambush of a Red Army Patrol, near Moqor, Afghanistan, Winter 1986)*, transparency in light-box.

Wall, J. (1993) *A Sudden Gust of Wind (after Hokusai)*, transparency in light-box.

CHAPTER 6

Data Visualisation and the Humanities

Lisa Otty and Tara Thomson

Visualisation has always been a key to understanding: thought has never constrained itself to just one modality. We extend our minds through diagrams, organise our thoughts in maps, tables and charts (Card et al. 1999). Drawing is intimately intertwined with writing as stories evoke pictures and lines become letters and words. 'Without drawing I feel myself but half invested in language,' wrote Samuel Taylor Coleridge (Piper 2012: 69). Many of our most celebrated writers – from Johann Wolfgang von Goethe to Jack Kerouac – drew up complex charts to plot their works. 'Synopsis was a key antecedent to narration,' as Andrew Piper has remarked; 'the visualisation of writing is an essential step in the creative process' (ibid.). As readers we construct mental images too, using our visual imaginary to help us to grasp meaning (Gambrell and Jawitz 1993). Knowing that his stories would come alive when readers could orient themselves in his imaginative space, Robert Louis Stevenson commissioned a map to accompany the 1883 publication of *Treasure Island*. In *The Life and Opinions of Tristram Shandy, Gentleman* (1759), Laurence Sterne punctuates one of his digressionary tales with the rococo flourish of a line, as a character waves his cane. Curlicuing around the page, it represents the expressive force of the movement, reminding us of the limitations of language and the intuitive force of the visual: seeing is believing, as the saying goes. As such examples show, visualisation is not new to the humanities; it has long been a means to make the invisible visible, to help us imagine events, understand relationships, open out new panoramas, immerse ourselves in other worlds.

In the age of information, visualisation practices have taken on a new urgency and importance: computational culture generates complex data at speeds and scales unimaginable even a few decades ago. Much of the data that is gathered today is also dynamic, generated, for example, through harvesting social media sites, with new data streaming in every second and older data being continually reshaped and refined. Such 'big data' requires new technologies of interpretation, new modes of processing that can reveal the significance and relevance it may contain. This is where visualisation can come into its own, as a means to sort through and manage information, enabling its analysis and interpretation, and allowing researchers to identify patterns and anomalies. It is within this context – as the complexity of our data sets has increased, and as the design of effective and elegant visualisations has come to rely on increasingly specialised statistical and programming skills – that 'data visualisation' as a research field in itself has begun to gain traction. The parameters of this emergent field are still very much open to debate.[1] Some, for example, seek to distinguish between scientific data visualisation and information visualisation on the basis of the data they use, reserving the former for visualisations of purely numerical data and the latter for visualisations that convey non-numerical information such as relationships or locations. Others use them synonymously and draw distinctions between visualisation, as a means of discovering structures, and information design, as the expression of data that already has a clear structure. As one pioneer in the field has rather derisively puts it, 'the purpose of computing is insight, not pictures' (Hamming 1973). In these terms, the success of a visualisation comes down only to whether it reveals new significance and patterns that were previously obscure.

The assumptions that underpin these discussions – with their repeated alignment of visualisation with science and quantitative data, coupled with an apparent disdain for 'design' and aesthetics – can be troubling from a humanistic perspective. The idea that visualisation can transparently reveal patterns lodged within data relies on a notion of methodological neutrality and unbiased observation that is problematic and deeply at odds with the hermeneutic theories that motivate the humanities. Indeed, in a recent *Digital Humanities Quarterly* article, Johanna Drucker has suggested that visualisations may be 'a kind of intellectual Trojan horse' through which the humanities are in danger of uncritically importing and adopting the epistemological biases of the sciences (2011: para. 1). 'So naturalized are the Google maps and bar charts generated from spread sheets', she writes, 'that they pass as unquestioned representations of "what is"' (ibid.). This rhetorical force has also been explored in the work of sociologist Bruno Latour, who positions visualisation and the research paper as the crucial tools of science 'in action' (1986, 1987). Latour has argued that visualisations work in the same way as research papers to validate constructions, to reify them as 'evidence', and by circulating this evidence as widely as possible, to make these constructions appear as if they were 'fact'. The concept of 'data' is crucial to this process: 'Data pass themselves off as mere descriptions of a priori conditions,' writes Drucker:

Rendering *observation* (the act of creating a statistical, empirical, or subjective account or image) as if it were *the same as the phenomena observed* collapses the critical distance between the phenomenal world and its interpretation, undoing the basis of interpretation on which humanistic knowledge production is based. (Drucker 2011: para. 1)

Framing visualisation as a neutral process of revealing patterns in data, in other words, comes dangerously close to positioning it as something remote from humanistic enquiry, which takes as its subject the very layers of representations and constructions that such a claim obscures.

Today the humanities are being encouraged to 'dig into data', as the call for the Arts and Humanities Research Council's (AHRC) recent high-profile funding initiative put it, and as scholars in the humanities have responded to this call, they have also begun to question the assumptions inherent in the term: while Lisa Gitleman and others have reminded us that 'raw data is an oxymoron' (2013), Drucker has argued that we should reconceive data as a *capta*, 'taken not given, constructed as an interpretation of the phenomenal world, not inherent in it' (2011: para. 8). Even the applicability of the term to the traditional objects of humanistic study has been questioned: many humanists resist the reduction of texts, images, books, articles, interviews, recordings, bibliographies, manuscripts and other such objects of study to 'data'. What is at stake in doing so is illustrated in a delightfully facetious lecture by Kurt Vonnegut (2007: 23–38). In 'Here is a Lesson in Creative Writing' Vonnegut maps the plot lines of well-known stories and novels, assigning the diegetic events to their value on a scale between 'good' and 'bad'. The reduction to such pointedly subjective categories cannot fail to remind us that the parameters by which we organise information are already interpretations. The joke is that no one knows what 'good' and 'bad' really are: as Vonnegut concludes, they shift according to perspective, from one character to another, and from one moment to another. Mobilising what Drucker calls 'the *representational* force of the visualization as a "picture" of "data"' (2011: para. 12) in order to undercut it, Vonnegut makes a case for the complexity, ambiguity and richness of narrative and positions this against scientific reductionism. He articulates the challenge to which humanists are now beginning to respond: can modes of visualisation be created that can take proper account of the richness and complexity of the material we study? Can we create visualisations that respect subjective insight and facilitate the critical distance crucial to humanistic interpretation?[2]

An approach that recognises both the underlying dataset and the visualisation itself as cultural constructions must necessarily concern itself with the processes of creation: the method of acquiring that data; the decisions taken in parsing and filtering; the methods by which the visualisation's parameters were determined; the design choices. Formal and aesthetic qualities are not afterthoughts but crucial components of the rhetorical statement that a visualisation makes. Only by explicitly thinking through the implications of these decisions and choices at each stage can we come to understand what Tanya Clement calls 'the layering of representations of representations that make up the digital methodologies we use' (Clement: para. 39). In practice this means being attentive not only to the data and the visualisation itself, but also to the tools used, the context around the presentation and the effects that are created. It requires recognition that, as Marian Dörk and her colleagues have recently argued, 'visualizations are always situated and particular to the assumptions of their designer as well as the context of the viewer' (Dörk et al. 2013). In their article, 'Critical Info-Viz: Exploring the Politics of Visualisation', Dörk et al. propose attending to four principles during creation and interpretation as the starting point of a critical approach to visualisation: disclosure, plurality, contingency, empowerment. Disclosure involves making data and information on decisions and choices explicit and available to viewers in order to expose the position of the author and enable viewers to challenge assumptions and methods. The principle of plurality encourages design that can accommodate multiple perspectives and enable plural interpretations. Contingency acknowledges the situation of the viewer and demands flexible visualisations that different viewers can relate to according to their own situation. Finally, the principle of empowerment suggests that, rather than presenting viewers with a picture of 'what is', visualisations can be created in ways that are dynamic and interactive and linked to other social objects and contexts in ways that encourage critical interpretation and facilitate independent conclusions. 'The principles of disclosure and plurality largely address insight by promoting comprehensible representations, while contingency and empowerment are guiding principles towards impact through flexible interactions and empowering experiences' (Dörk et al. 2013: para. 52). Approached with these kinds of principles in mind, visualisation in its various forms can be a powerful tool for both exploration and communication within the humanities. Visualisations can stimulate thinking, generate new perspectives and operate as analytical tools that generate insights (and pictures!). They can also challenge humanists to consider new approaches and to explore the opportunities, challenges and specific demands of data at scale. The humanistic imperative to the kinds of critical principles which Dörk et al. propose, moreover, promises to move the field towards a more nuanced and sophisticated use of the medium which has the potential to benefit practitioners not only in the Digital Humanities, but also in the fields of computer science and information design.

There are several good introductory texts to programming languages and environments, written by those with expertise in these fields, and visualisations can be created in many ways and with various different tools. Rather than focusing on the use of any single technology or method (which may well be superseded by the time this book is published), in the next section we discuss the key processes involved in creating visualisations. In the final section of the chapter, we will provide a more in-depth case study focused on a large literary historical project that involved collaboration with computer scientists to create bespoke visualisations. The resources required for such a project may not be available to many scholars, particularly in the early career stage, but we hope that our discussion will offer useful insights applicable to projects of varying scales.

PROCESSES AND PRINCIPLES

The various processes that go into creating visualisations have been sketched out by several practitioners. As early as 1999, Stuart Card and his co-authors developed a basic reference model describing the transformation of data into visual forms. Firstly, raw data is transformed into data tables, which include metadata. In other words, raw data is organised – which may mean refining, filtering or curating – and documented. Once prepared, data tables are then transformed into visual structures: here the researcher identifies the most appropriate visual forms in which to represent the data, such as bar charts, graphs or scatter plots, and creates these. Then, different views of the structures are introduced through view transformations which specify graphical parameters: for example, we may use features such as colour, transparency or size to signify qualities such as quantity, density or date of origin, and then enable viewers to filter according to these parameters. Finally, human interaction intervenes into each of these transformations (Card et al. 1999: 17).

In *Visualising Data* (2008),[3] a useful introduction to working with the Java-based programming environment *Processing*, Ben Fry adopts a more task-focused model based on the actions of acquiring (getting the data), parsing (analysing the data you have acquired), filtering and mining (separating out the data you actually need), representing (choosing a visual form), refining (designing it effectively) and interacting (facilitating users to engage with the data in various ways) (2008: 5). As Fry points out, these actions are neither as discrete nor as sequential as the list makes them appear: some might happen simultaneously, some might be skipped according to the data and project, some might be repeated or revisited at different points during the project. However, they provide a convenient vocabulary and framework through which to consider the particular challenges of humanities visualisations.

More recently still, Bill Ferster (2012) has proposed a more conceptual scaffold built around the acronym ASSERT:

Ask a question
Search for information
Structure the information
Envision the answer
Represent the visualisation
Tell a story

Designed to encompass and expand upon earlier models, Ferster's ASSERT framework puts the creation of visualisations into more recognisably humanistic terms. 'Story-telling is one of the primary ways we make sense of the world,' Ferster writes. 'A good visualisation answers a question using primary source evidence to tell a story' (Ferster 2012: 41). Indeed, as he frames the process, the parallel to familiar and more conventional research processes seems clear: beginning with a question, searching for answers, creating a narrative which elaborates those answers and engages readers.

Figures 6.1 and 6.2 are visualisations created as part of the AHRC-funded Poetry Beyond Text: Vision, Text and Cognition project, which ran between 2009 and 2011.[4] Bringing together a multi-disciplinary team of researchers in cognitive psychology, literary studies, film and visual art, the project aimed to investigate how reading strategies affect perception, interpretation and perceived aesthetic value. Among a range of critical, empirical and digital methodologies, one of the approaches we took was to visualise the process of reading using digital eye-tracking machines. This involves cameras being calibrated to readers' pupils in order to track fixation points and durations and measure saccades, the tiny jumps the eye makes as it moves from fixation to fixation. Figure 6.1 is a map of these fixations, plotting them and labelling them numerically in chronological order. Figure 6.2 is a heat map, a type of visualisation which represents the density of fixations through the use of colour: the deep red areas were those that sustained the highest number of fixations, shading off through yellow into the green areas which represent low fixation areas. Using these two images as our key examples, we shall talk through the process of creating and sharing these visualisations following Ferster's ASSERT model, and paying particular attention to the critical principles outlined by Dörk et al.

The Poetry Beyond Text project team were interested in the reception of formally experimental writing, in how multi-modal genres such as concrete poetry, text art and artists' books were read and understood in relation to the more conventional categories of 'literature' and 'visual art'. Taking into account that perceptions and judgements can shift over time and with experience, we sought to explore the reception of such works with different groups of 'co-researchers' (students, artists, poets) over an extended period. This is reflected in the project's overarching research questions:

Figure 6.1 Fixation chart of a page from David Bellingham's *Fresh Fruit and Tables* (The Changing Room Gallery, Stirling 2008). (Source: Poetry Beyond Text Project, University of Dundee and University of Kent.)

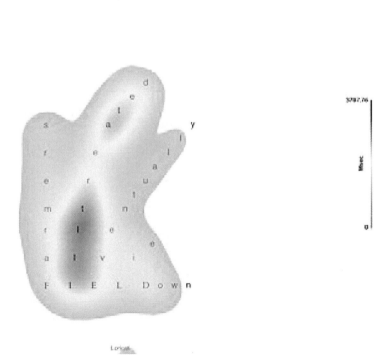

Figure 6.2 Heat map of Jim Carruth's poem 'Field' from *Cowpit Yowe* (Ludovic Press, 2008). (Source: Poetry Beyond Text Project, University of Dundee and University of Kent.)

1. When artworks combine textual and visual elements, how do the modes of attention specific to reading text and viewing images interact and modify each other?
2. What factors determine whether the combination of textual and visual elements in such works enriches or limits their meaning and aesthetic value?
3. How are evaluative and interpretive responses to such works affected by the development of enhanced reflective awareness about the processes involved?
4. How can critical and psychological models of perception and aesthetic experience inform and be informed by the creation of new works of art?

As well as analysing reported accounts of reading experiences and other forms of reflective response, we wanted a mechanism to help us gain insight into the private and ephemeral process of reading as it happens. We needed to find a way to make the invisible visible, to bring a subjective experience or cognitive process into objective view.

Used primarily in cognitive psychology, eye-tracking has been used to establish typical patterns of eye movements for reading text and looking at pictures, as well as models of the cognitive processes reflected by such behaviour. We hoped to adapt this method to explore the relationship *between* reading and looking: our approach was exploratory in this respect, as we were interested in what patterns might arise from the process. How long would people look at a specific part of the work? In what order would they read words and images? How would layout affect established reading patterns such as left–right, top–bottom? More broadly, we wanted to use the resulting visualisations to open up discussion and reflection on the ways in which co-researchers' varied reading strategies influenced their subsequent assessments of interest, meaning and aesthetic value. Gathering the information for visualisation took considerable effort: each co-researcher had to visit a laboratory several times over the course of a few months, and spend up to an hour at a time in front of a screen and camera, with their head carefully positioned on a chin rest. Presenting an image file of a single page on the reader's screen, the eye-tracking machine captured vast amounts of numerical data from the calibrated camera, identifying the screen location of each fixation as well as sequence and duration. Recalling the principle of disclosure, it is worth pointing out that this process in itself is likely to have introduced biases: reading does not normally take place under such physical restraint and this may well have contributed to the reader's behavioural patterns. It is easy to imagine, for example, that co-researchers may have read either more slowly as they were aware of being watched or more quickly as a result of wishing to move their heads.

As the Poetry Beyond Text example suggests, the process of acquiring data, or 'searching for information' in Ferster's terms, can be a complex and time-consuming process. For humanists, there is often an initial process of quantifying their question through identifying interesting numerical data (prices, amounts and transactions) or aspects of interest (the density of connections in historical networks, points on maps, quantities of books published and so on). Where acquisition can be quite easy, through the use of application program interfaces (APIs) to download bulk data from social media platforms for example, or through the reuse of data sets created by others, working with extant data or within a set of parameters defined by others can also introduce elements that need consideration: restructuring, cleansing and refining the data to the extent that is appropriate to a specific research question is likely to involve considerable thought and effort.

The ways in which data is gathered and constructed will affect how it can be parsed, filtered and mined; these processes in turn will affect how it is presented. Parsing and filtering ensure that the data is in a logical format and that this format is clean or consistent enough to produce reliable results. For the Poetry Beyond Text visualisations, our data was parsed automatically by the eye-tracking machine and then human intervention was required to exclude badly calibrated recordings and other misleading anomalies, and to produce specific subsets focused on areas of interest. However, depending on the nature and scale of the data and the project, the processes involved here may vary quite dramatically. It may be possible to do quite a bit automatically but as we will see in the next section, as we discuss the Palimpsest project, in order to construct the kind of high-quality, bespoke data that many humanities projects require, there is often a significant element of human curation. Preparing data well – taking care to ensure that it is gathered consistently and effectively parsed and filtered – is vital to ensuring that any results that analysis yields are as reliable as possible: time spent on well-conceived and considered data preparation and curation is seldom wasted, as it means that mining is more effective, patterns and results can emerge more clearly, and realising significant results is more likely.

Once data has been gathered, parsed and refined, the initial step towards design is the choice of a visual representation. As Ben Fry suggests, this is

a lynchpin that informs the single most important decision in a visualization project and can make you rethink earlier stages. How you choose to represent the data can influence the very first step (what data you acquire) and [. . .] what particular pieces you extract. (Fry 2008: 9)

Different choices of visualisation forms have different affordances and different strengths. If a visualisation is to present the relationship between part and whole (for example, the composition of a group by nationality, age or gender) then a simple bar chart or pie chart is an obvious choice. If, however, it is intended to enable comparison of differences in number, then a bar chart makes this far easier as the size of rectangular columns can be gauged more easily than the size of irregular segments. If continuous data is of interest (for example, fluctuations in the numbers of members of a group over its lifetime) then a line graph would be more appropriate. Histograms can be useful in identifying composition, or location and density, across a large body of data, or scatter plots for correlations between two quantitative dimensions. Each of these simple forms requires different data, structured in a particular and different way.

For the Poetry Beyond Text project the choice of layout and other design parameters was restricted by the proprietary software used. For conventionally trained humanists without high-level programming skills, such 'off-the-shelf' software packages can be great resources when chosen carefully and used appropriately.[5] However, such software can introduce biases and ideologies inherent in their algorithms and visualisation syntax. Looking at the heat map (Figure 6.2), the eye-tracker software presents areas that sustained significant fixations as red, a colour that has a strong metaphorical association with heat: it is easy to imagine then that the red areas are the subject of a burning intensity, and to register this as an indication of interest. While this may sometimes be the case, it is not necessarily so. For example, in Figure 6.2, it seems more likely that the repeated fixation stems from a visual confusion between two similarly shaped letters at a crucial point in the visual structure of the poem, demanding a change in the direction of reading. Such conceptual metaphors need to be grasped and approached with caution as they can have profound consequences for interpretation.

The representation of a visualisation, in Ferster's scheme, is the point at which design comes to the fore. Design can have a huge impact on whether a visualisation successfully communicates. The difference between Figures 6.1 and 6.2 is a case in point. Even looking at a very simple data set, with a limited number of fixations, it is really quite difficult to get a lot of information out of the fixation map (Figure 6.1): there is an excess of detail, including the numerical ordering of the fixation points, and too little visual contrast between the light blue fixation points and the white background. The visual field is further confused by the fact that all the points are the same colour, so differentiating between them is difficult. In contrast the heat map, though considerably less detailed, is easy to interpret with its conventional and highly differentiated colour scheme.

The success of the visualisation comes down to a combination of graphic design and human perception. Information can be coded through more automatically processed codes such as visual conventions and colour (see Card et al. 1999: 30). As many commentators have shown, most notably Edward Tufte, poor design can make information difficult to access, have serious

Figure 6.3 Stroop test (originally described in 1935 by J. Ridley Stoop in 'Studies of Interference in Serial Verbal Reactions', *Journal of Experimental Psychology*, 18 (6): 643–62). (Source: the authors.)

consequences and can confuse and even completely mislead viewers. The Stroop effect, a well-known psychology experiment conducted in the 1930s, provides a good example of the cognitive dissonance that poor design can create. Experimenters gave readers two sets of words and found that, when given a list in which the names of colours were printed in ink of another colour (Figure 6.3, left), readers found it more difficult to name the colour of the word due to interference. When words were printed in the same colour as the colour named (Figure 6.3, right), readers were significantly quicker in identifying the colour of the ink.

Psychologists of perception have given many more such examples: in his 1923 essay on 'Laws of Organization in Perceptual Forms', gestalt psychologist Max Wertheimer argued that certain principles of visual perception could be deduced (1938: 71–88). Perhaps the strongest codes are spatial: position and relative position. Wertheimer identified a principle of proximity, which dictates that objects positioned near one another will appear to belong in a group, and a principle of similarity, which dictates that objects that appear the same in terms of size, colour or other visual cues, will also appear related. For example, in Figure 6.4, it seems natural to see abc (downwards, starting top left), def, ghi and so on as groups, whereas it is quite difficult to conceive of the pattern c, bf, aei, dhl, etc. as a grouping.

a	d	g	j	m	p	s
b	e	h	k	n	q	t
c	f	i	l	o	r	u

Figure 6.4 Visual groupings after Wertheimer's original drawings: example 1. (Source: The authors.)

a d g   j m p s
b e h k n   q t
c f i   l   o   r u

Figure 6.5 Visual groupings after Wertheimer's original drawings: example 2. (Source: The authors.)

```
*   *   *   *   *   *   *

*   *   *   *   *   *   *

*   *   *   *   *   *   *
```

Figure 6.6 Visual groupings after Wertheimer's original drawings: example 3. (Source: The authors.)

In Figure 6.5, however, this natural grouping is disrupted by the similarity of b, e, h, etc. denoted by the colour red, making their relation seem intrinsically apparent.

This suggests that badly grouped information, information selected and arranged by ill-defined criteria or poorly distinguished differences, can easily confuse and disengage viewers. This is clearly what is at issue in Figure 6.1, where all of the fixation points are represented by blue circles and it is therefore difficult to perceive any order or significance in the layout. In an effective visualisation, groups should be clearly demarcated and visual contrasts should be made quite strongly. A third principle of repetition is demonstrated in Figure 6.6, where a pattern that has been established is broken, disrupting the sense of visual groupings on both the vertical and horizontal axes.

The graph in Figure 6.7 shows how ignoring such visual principles can lead beyond dissonance to deception. It depicts the number of people signing up to a class over the course of ten years.

The line depicted suggests a downward trend based on the most recent numbers; however, this is because that final data point actually represents enrolments in a six-month period rather than the twelve-month period that each previous point had represented: extrapolating from these figures, the trend in fact looks likely to continue upward for the year 2010. The design is misleading because it breaks the visual principles of similarity and repetition and groups substantively different data sets together. Although Gestalt psychology is out of fashion now, the visual principles that Wertheimer and his peers deduced have been enormously influential and remain foundational to design today.[6]

'Tell a story' is the final stage of Ferster's conceptual scaffold, reminding us that as situated and contextual objects visualisations serve rhetorical pur-

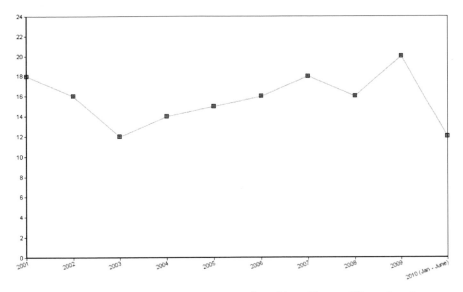

Figure 6.7 Graph showing misleading representation of data. (Source: The authors.)

poses and offer exciting and innovative means to engage viewers. As Ferster puts it, 'this innovative medium has the potential for sustaining a meaningful virtual dialogue between scholars and their audience, using data as the liaison' (2012: 3). While the Poetry Beyond Text visualisations were not designed for use beyond the project, they were also used in a series of feedback loops in which the participants were invited to examine and reflect on their readings and the visualisations together. The interest that the visualisations generated – as images/objects rather than as evidence – among the readers with whom we were working and among audiences at conferences and other venues was unforeseen but striking. Offering a unique window into the private, subjective cognitive processes that go on when an individual is reading, they stimulated extensive discussion among the co-researchers who had helped to create them and among the broader research and creative communities around the project. Co-researchers, fascinated by their own tracking images, attempted to offer explanations for their tiny and subconscious eye movements, and were provoked to reconsider their responses to works they were looking at. Seeing that they had moved quickly over sections of the poem, for example, or focused on a particular section, they reflected on their own reading behaviour and how it inflected interpretation, often changing their evaluation of the poem in the process. Others, including the poets and visual artists working as part of the project, analysed the visualisations as a group to identify aspects of layout that could potentially disrupt the reading process or the relation to images that facilitated specific interpretations or foci. Finally, alongside all of the works to which they responded and the responses they provoked, the visualisations were added into a publicly accessible digital archive housed in the Scottish Poetry Library and designed to make the research materials generated by the Poetry Beyond Text project publicly accessible in the long term. While the visualisations themselves were relatively simple and static, the narratives that grew up around them were plural, diverse, dynamic and complex. Each visualisation told a micro-story about one person's engagement with a textual work; as a sequence they became part of a larger narrative, a story revealing how such formally experimental works play with, disrupt and manipulate the cognitive conventions of reading.[7]

The creation of stories or narratives is one of the primary ways in which we make sense of our experiences and encounters (Gershon and Page 2001). While the kinds of static visualisations discussed thus far in this chapter have long been used to support narrative construction, as Edward Segel and Jeffrey Heer have pointed out, 'an emerging class of visualizations attempts to combine narratives with interactive graphics. Storytellers, especially online journalists, are increasingly integrating complex visualizations into their narratives' (2010: 1139). Such 'data stories' break traditional narrative conventions in important ways and recall the dynamic between what Roland Barthes (1975) famously termed *readerly* and *writerly* texts. Where traditional *readerly* narratives are typically author-controlled and linear, the *writerly* text overturns the dichotomy between reader and author, positioning the reader as writer taking an active role in the construction of narrative and meaning. Similarly, as Segel and Heer write, 'tours through visualized data similarly can be organized in a linear sequence, [but] they can also be interactive, inviting verification, new questions, and alternative explanations' (2010: 1139) and can thus be considered to operate on 'a spectrum of author-driven and reader-driven approaches':

> A purely author-driven approach has a strict linear path through the visualization, relies heavily on messaging, and includes no interactivity [. . .] A purely reader-driven approach has no prescribed ordering of images, no messaging, and a high degree of interactivity [. . .] A reader-driven approach supports tasks such as data diagnostics, pattern discovery, and hypothesis formation. (Segel and Heer 2010: 1147)

Most current visualisation tools focus on exploration and analysis, leaving the creation of narrative context to the reader (Segel and Heer 2010). While they can be contextualised by their authors, for example with the disclosure of information about their creation or by their presentation in specific narrative contexts, they do not enable the kinds of rich and dynamic creations that can support either author-led storytelling or empower reader-led discovery. This has been a key ambition in the development of more recent web-integrated and humanities-led tools, such as Voyant[8] and Palladio,[9] as well as presentation environments such as Omeka[10] and Tableau[11] which facilitate the publication of interactive and dynamic graphics such as maps and timelines.

Such reader-driven or *writerly* visualisations have the potential to introduce pluralistic design and facilitate multiple interpretations. They enable consideration of the situatedness of the viewer and, allowing a choice of additional or alternative forms, facilitate filtering, mining and exploration of the data in various ways. This approach speaks to the critical principles of Dörk et al., allowing viewers to adapt the experience to their own interests and take writerly control of the level of information they are presented with. Viewpoint controls and an ability to interactively filter, mine and visualise the information that is most directly relevant or of interest to their own contexts and the narratives they wish to construct can empower viewers to create their own stories.

A CASE STUDY IN HUMANITIES VISUALISATION: THE PALIMPSEST PROJECT

The Palimpsest project ran between 2014 and 2015 and was funded by the AHRC as part of the aforementioned 'digging into data' scheme. Its multidisciplinary team included researchers in literary studies and informatics, with specialists in text mining, geoparsing, information visualisation and human–computer interaction.[12] The project was designed with visualisation already in mind: it aimed to create a suite of interactive visualisations of Edinburgh's literary cityscape, using an extensive data set of literary texts. Building on findings from a prototype developed in 2012,[13] the project team aimed to gather a more expansive data set by mining several large collections of digitised text for works set in Edinburgh.[14] We wanted to create a cumulative model of literary Edinburgh that captured as large a selection of narrative works as our workflow and timescale might allow. We envisioned two visualisation outputs through which end users could explore our database: an interactive map of Edinburgh, featuring narrative extracts set in locations around the city (see Figures 6.8 and 6.9), and a complementary mobile application that would allow users to move through the city's narrative history *in situ* (see Figure 6.10). The suite of visualisations was released online under the name *Lit Long: Edinburgh*.[15] Rather than using off-the-shelf software, the team developed these tools specifically for the Palimpsest project;[16] however, many of their features draw on familiar visualisations, such as Google Maps, GPS navigation, word clouds and histograms. While the resources required to develop a visualisation project like this may not be available to all researchers, the processes and principles discussed here are widely applicable to visualisation projects of any scale or scope.

As can be seen from Figures 6.8 and 6.9, these public outputs are highly complex visualisations, presenting a large amount of literary content and

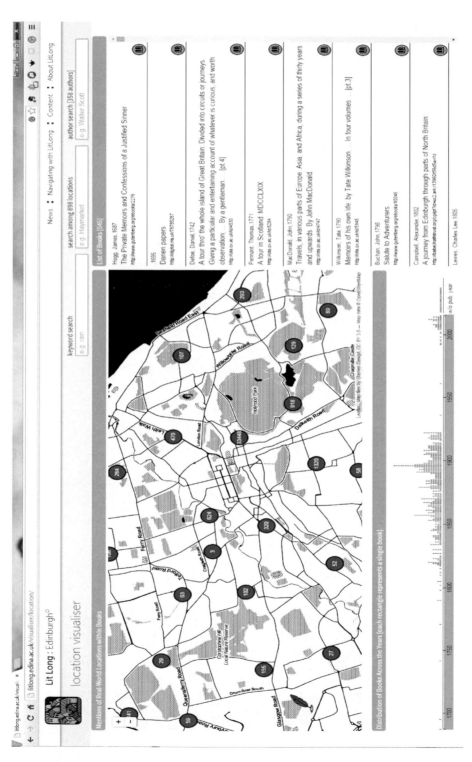

Figure 6.8 The *Lit Long: Edinburgh* location visualiser: a 'bird's eye view' of literary Edinburgh. (Source: Palimpsest Project, University of Edinburgh and University of St Andrews.)

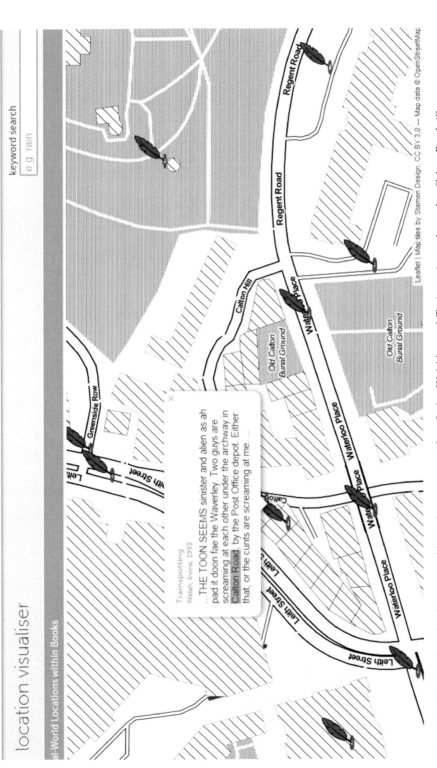

Figure 6.9 The location visualiser zoomed in to show an extract from Irvine Welsh's novel *Trainspotting* geolocated to Calton Road. (Source: Palimpsest Project, University of Edinburgh and University of St Andrews.)

metadata that correlate in ways that might be difficult for a reader to fully grasp from just browsing the data tables. The bird's eye view of Figure 6.8 demonstrates the potential of visualisation, providing an overview of the full data set that geolocates narrative extracts throughout the city. Situating all of the extracts on the map synchronously enables intertextual discoveries: users can see how a particular location has been described in various texts across several centuries, all at once, and can interpret these coincidences of location independently. This also demonstrates the significance of the title Palimpsest, which means a space (literally a piece of paper or parchment) which has been inscribed again and again over time, and thus contains layers of signification. Palimpsestual mapping has recently attracted the interest of scholars wishing to visualise literature and literary history.[17]

Overlaid on the *Lit Long* map, the main interactive features are clusters of location pins, represented as bubbles, each containing a number. The array of clusters communicates the density of place-name mentions in the literature, while the numbers represent the number of individual textual extracts pinned to each location or area. Users can click on a cluster to reveal a cloud of keywords associated with each location, giving an overall sense of how a particular location has been described. As users zoom in on the map (a design feature with which most users of online maps are familiar), clusters disperse into increasingly precise locations until the closest street-level view is reached and individual pins containing textual extracts become visible (Figure 6.9). As such, this tool offers multiple perspectives on representations of Edinburgh in literature, ranging from a broad, historical view to a more focused view of individual narratives. The clustering and dispersal mechanism represents a design choice made in response to the large Palimpsest data set; however, while it may not be familiar to most users, we concluded through extensive testing that as one engages with the familiar zoom feature, the behaviour of the clusters renders their meaning apparent. Users are further empowered to filter the data by author, book title, place name or keyword. If someone is interested, for instance, in how Sir Walter Scott used the city in his narrative works, or in how descriptions of the Canongate have changed over time, or in a map of locations named in Muriel Spark's *The Prime of Miss Jean Brodie*, he or she can easily filter the data in order to visualise only these representations. As such, data interpretation is not prescriptive and plural interpretations are enabled by user-driven viewing parameters. These features empower users to explore the data and shape their own stories about its significance.

The mobile application (see Figure 6.10) presents yet another way for users to explore the database. The app can enable discovery, presenting textual extracts pinned to the user's current location, or it can be used to curate a tour of locations filtered by either author, title or keyword.

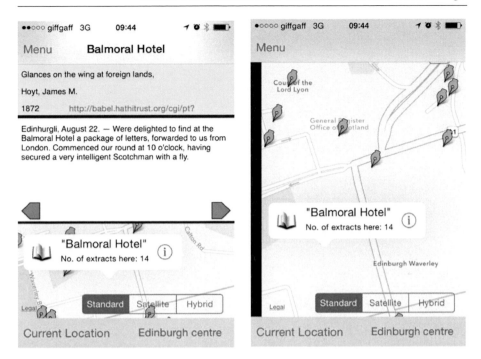

Figure 6.10 (a) and (b) The *Lit Long: Edinburgh* mobile app.
(Source: Palimpsest Project, University of Edinburgh and University of St Andrews.)

In Figure 6.10, the image on the right shows the navigational view, which centres on the user's current location; the image on the left shows the extract view, in which users can scroll through narrative extracts about their current location. The mobile app enables users to explore the city's literary history by reading about the very places through which they are currently moving. This is where contingency comes into play most clearly: while the data set may not be changing *per se*, the visualisation takes into account the situatedness of the viewer, allowing users to explore the data from their particular vantage point.

As suggested earlier, a visualisation does not begin with data but with questions. The Palimpsest research questions were:

1. What kind of Edinburgh cityscape emerges from the geo-referenced machine reading of a very large data set of literary texts which reference and draw on the city's topography?
2. How does such a cityscape compare, differ from and supplement conventional or standard readings of Edinburgh's literary topography?
3. How can text mining and computational linguistic analysis techniques be refined through input, curation and feedback from literary scholars in order to better support their needs?

4. What mapping and visualisation techniques will allow intuitive and illuminating representations of, and encounters with, the literary cityscape both for scholars and for a wider range of extra-academic users?

These research questions were designed with the end visualisations already in mind. Knowing that we were working toward the development of interactive maps guided our workflow design and shaped our approach to gathering and filtering data. These questions capture many of the key processes and principles involved in creating visualisations: they set a suitable method for gathering and structuring data; they envision the results and plan toward visual representation; they consider audience and user interaction; they take a humanistic approach to computational processes (input and refining); and they ultimately aim to 'tell a story' from the resulting visualisations, as Ferster suggests. What this makes clear is the critical importance, for effective visualisation, of knowing your data.

At the time of the *Lit Long* launch, the project database contained over 47,000 narrative extracts from 550 unique texts which were pinned to over 1,600 place names in and around the city of Edinburgh. While the final data set may seem large, it was acquired through machine reading of digitised collections totalling over 380,000 texts. To this end, a bespoke gazetteer of Edinburgh place names was compiled using Open Street Maps, historic maps, guides to literary landmarks and ad hoc additions to account for colloquial and historical namings of Edinburgh locations. After using the gazetteer to search the collections for mentions of Edinburgh, and after applying filters to deprioritise ambiguous place names, over 33,000 works were added to the data set for further filtering. At this stage, human curation was required to arrive at a data set that met our literary critical criteria: we were looking for 'Edinburgh-centric' works involving significant Edinburgh settings, which either belonged to a recognisably literary genre, such as the novel or short story, or had strong narrative or locodescriptive components – both memoirs and travel journals, for example, were included.

As literary scholars, we did not have the technical expertise to manage the data set in its table form. As such, another visualisation tool was developed to aid this stage of human curation. With our input regarding a useful structure for the data (including title, author, date, list of Edinburgh place names and associated snippets, and Library of Congress codes where available), the team's visualisation experts developed an annotation tool, the interface pictured in Figure 6.11.[18]

The Palimpsest annotation tool was a highly interactive visualisation, empowering us as end users to make informed decisions, curate the data set by humanistic standards and annotate the data with useful comments. These annotations, for example, later enabled us to weed out duplicate works and

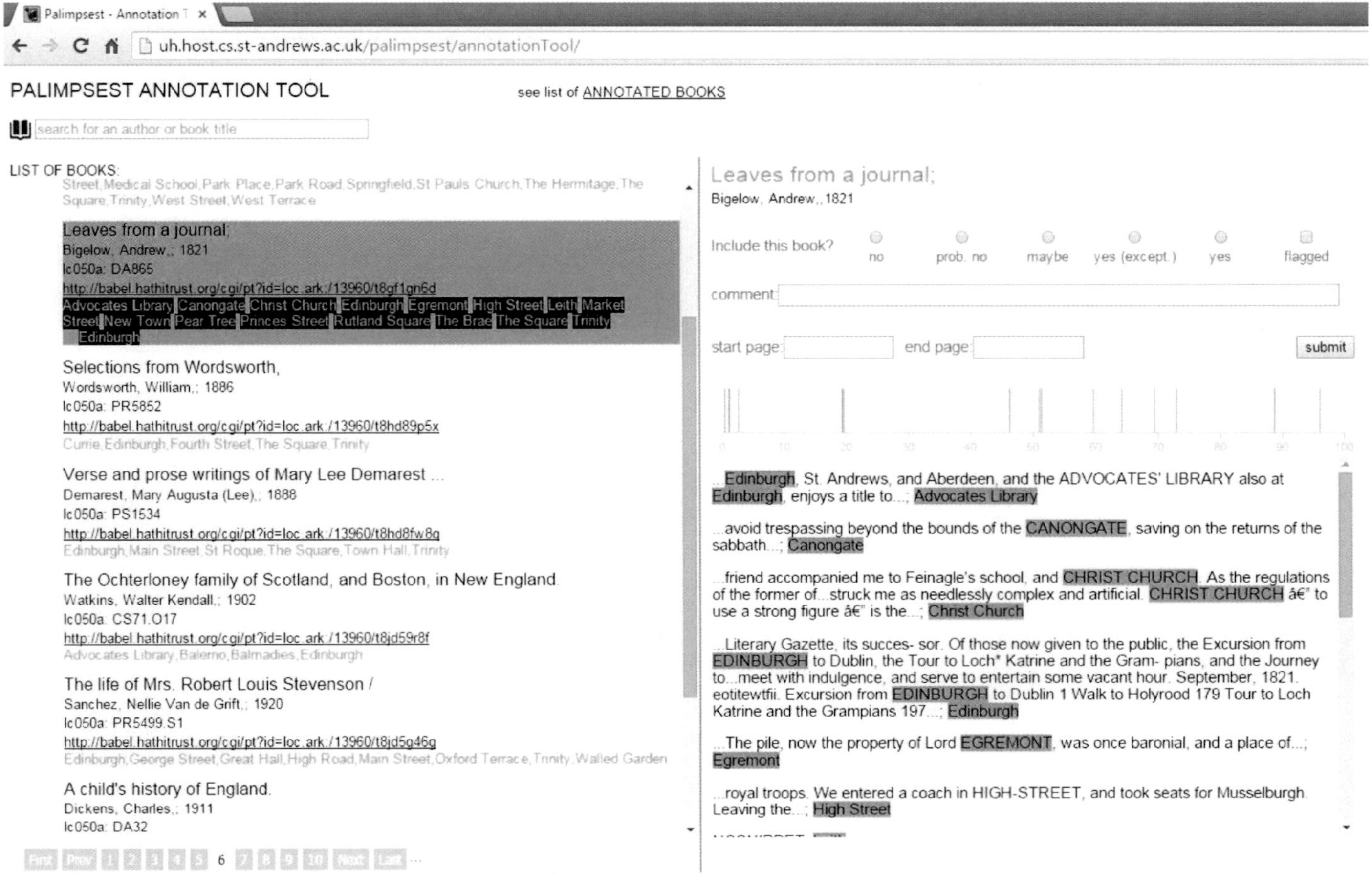

Figure 6.11 The Palimpsest annotation tool. (Source: Palimpsest Project, University of Edinburgh and University of St Andrews.)

make informed editorial decisions about copy texts. This visualisation was not designed for public presentation, but was intended as a tool for facilitating workflow and generating ideas. For instance, it was through the annotation tool that we were able to identify the aforementioned ambiguous place names that were filtered out of the data set. As this process makes clear, the acquisition, restructuring and refining of data was not an easy set of tasks and, as in the Poetry Beyond Text example, involved considerable thought and effort, potentially much more than a map visualisation might imply.

This process of data collection and curation highlights the importance of disclosure and transparency. Given Drucker's claim that maps can appear as 'unquestioned representations of "what is"' (2011: para. 1), that is the propensity of a map to appear as naturalised or complete, it was essential that we clarified the limits of our data. While the collections that we text-mined were some of the largest digital collections of text in the world, they still do not contain all literary works set in Edinburgh, as not all literature has been digitised. Furthermore, our selection of copyrighted works was limited to what our time and resources enabled us to negotiate with authors and publishers. These limits are acknowledged on the *Lit Long* website, which hosts the project visualisations, to give readers a clear indication that the visualisations necessarily tell an incomplete story. While users can filter certain parameters, there are limits to those functions as well. Certain fields of enquiry cannot be represented in the visualisation, such as author gender, as these were not included in the metadata attached to the data we acquired. Similarly, some fields of interest such as publication date cannot be visualised properly as they are inconsistently applied in the various source collections' metadata. While limits such as these are not disclosed on the website, our aim is to discuss them in forthcoming publications about the project.

It is also essential with visualisation projects to be transparent about the assumptions underlying our chosen models, as mentioned earlier. One glaring assumption about maps is that they represent the topographical facts of the world. If the *Lit Long* map says the Parliament building is at the east end of the Canongate, then it must in fact be so. However, Edinburgh's Parliament was once in a different location and the textual extracts from that period referring to the Parliament are erroneously pinned to the building's current location. This leads us to the most problematic aspect of mapping literature: imaginative, fictional or narrative spaces, even if they have real-world referents, are not real spaces. How, for instance, can we map imaginative and historical relationships of a narrator to a place? Take Sir Walter Scott's words, from *Chronicles of the Canongate*: 'We will not descend to notice the claims of mere upstart districts, called Old New Town and New New Town, not to mention the favourite Moray Place, which is the newest New Town of all' (1827: 2). This extract is pinned three times to Edinburgh's New Town on the *Lit Long* map, but Scott's deployment of 'new town' in this sentence is at once literal, playful, facetious, colloquial and historically situated, while not specifically referring to Edinburgh's real New Town. In another example, generalised data is often imprecisely specified: in the case of *Lit Long*, descriptions of 'Edinburgh' itself are pinned to a random central location that happens to be situated in Edinburgh's Old Town. This perpetuates the perception that Edinburgh's Old Town is its literary and imaginative centre when, in fact, many locations outside of the Old Town have a rich narrative history as well. These are all examples of issues that arise when seemingly objective methods of data visualisation meet humanistic enquiry.

This brings us back to where we began – the importance of taking a critical approach to visualisation. Ultimately, the visualisations generated in the projects discussed here are useful, interesting and aesthetically stimulating, but they are not sufficient ends in themselves. Visualisations need to address a research question: in every case, your research question will shape how you collect, parse and filter data and the choices you make in how it is visualised. In humanities study, the critical work occurs when we draw arguments from the visualised data, when we 'tell a story', the final step in Ferster's ASSERT model. These critical interventions can and should extend beyond the data itself, though, to tell a story about the processes outlined through this chapter. We must consider how we reconcile the conflicts that arise in rendering humanistic content as 'data', and how data visualisation can work effectively together with humanistic models of enquiry. Some problems cannot be reconciled, yet they can also lead to productive insights, such as that described above regarding the 'accidental' specification of generalised data. The ethical dimension of using visualisation in humanities research demands that we be transparent about how we, as researchers, are positioned *vis-à-vis* our data. This is one way in which visualisation shares key principles with more traditional research methods, as criticism works toward a discourse which is more open and less anxious to protect itself against inconsistency.

NOTES

1. For readers interested in the definition of terms around visualisation, Lev Manovich provides a useful discussion in his 2010 article 'What is Visualization?' Available at <http://manovich.net/content/04-projects/063-what-is-visualization/61_article_2010.pdf> (last accessed 10 August 2015).
2. See, for example, the Palladio suite of tools developed by researchers at Stanford University at <http://www.palladio.designhumanities.org>; or C. Plaisant et al. (2006) 'Exploring erotics in Emily Dickinson's

correspondence with text mining and visual interfaces', *Proc. of the 6th ACM/IEEE-CS Joint Conference on Digital Libraries*, pp. 141–50.

3. Fry's *Visualising Data: Exploring and Explaining Data with the Processing Environment* (2008) is a useful introductory text supplemented by a series of online tutorials available at <https://processing.org/> (last accessed 10 August 2015).

4. Poetry Beyond Text: Vision, Text and Cognition was led by Professor Andrew Roberts of the University of Dundee and funded by the Arts and Humanities Research Council. The project team comprised Andrew Roberts, Martin Fischer, Mary Modeen, Lisa Otty, Anna Schaffner, Ulrich Wegner and Kim Knowles. More information about the project is available at <http://www.poetrybeyondtext.org/> (last accessed 10 August 2015).

5. There are many visualisation tools available. Beginners might wish to try the following, all of which are freely available online: for network graphs, Nodexl (Excel plugin, available at <http://nodexl.codeplex.com> (last accessed 10 August 2015)) and Gephi (available at <http://gephi.github.io> (last accessed 10 August 2015)); see also Many Eyes (available at <http://www-969.ibm.com/software/analytics/manyeyes> (last accessed 10 August 2015), Voyant (available at <http://voyant-tools.org> (last accessed 10 August 2015)) and Palladio (available at <http://palladio.designhumanities.org> (last accessed 10 August 2015)) for an array of text mining and visualisation tools.

6. Gestalt principles of perception form the basis of Rudolf Arnheim's highly influential 1954 book *Art and Visual Perception: A Psychology of the Creative Eye*. Oakland: University of California Press. They are also the basis of Robin Williams' helpful 2003 guide to visual design, which we recommend for those developing visualisations: *The Non-Designers Design Book*. San Francisco: Peachpit Press.

7. For discussion of the project's findings regarding reading see Andrew Roberts et al. (2013) 'Space and pattern in linear and postlinear poetry: empirical and theoretical approaches', *European Journal of English Studies*, 17 (1): 23–40, and Anna Schaffner et al. (2012) 'Reading space in visual poetry: new cognitive perspectives', *Writing Technologies*, 4 (1): 75–106, available at <http://www.ntu.ac.uk/writing_technologies/index.html> (last accessed 10 August 2015).

8. See note 5 for details.

9. See note 5 for details.

10. Omeka is a free, open-source platform which enables the creation of online exhibitions and web collections. Available at <http://www.omeka.org> (last accessed 10 August 2015).

11. Tableau is a free online platform for creating visualisations. Available at <https://public.tableau.com> (last accessed 10 August 2015).

12. The Palimpsest team was led by Principal Investigator, Professor James Loxley (University of Edinburgh). The Co-Investigators were Professor Jon Oberlander (University of Edinburgh), Professor Aaron Quigley (SACHI research group, University of St Andrews) and James Reid (EDINA, University of Edinburgh); the research and development team included Beatrice Alex (University of Edinburgh), Miranda Anderson (University of Edinburgh), Ian Fieldhouse (EDINA), Claire Grover (University of Edinburgh), David Harris-Birtill (SACHI, University of St Andrews), Uta Hinrichs (SACHI, University of St Andrews), Nicola Osborne (EDINA), Lisa Otty (University of Edinburgh) and Tara Thomson (University of Edinburgh). Further details about individual roles on the project can be found at <http://litlong.org/about-litlong/team/ (last accessed 10 August 2015).

13. The Palimpsest prototype was a small, mobile-friendly website featuring extracts from literary texts set in Edinburgh. As proof of concept, the prototype demonstrated how a map visualisation might enable users to discover the city's rich literary heritage, whether they were engaging with the full data set or a set filtered according to their interests. The database of extracts was curated manually, and was limited to 200 textual extracts from well known literary works; for greater scope, the methodology for the larger project discussed here was substantially modified. The Palimpsest prototype team was led by James Loxley and Miranda Anderson (University of Edinburgh). Further details and a view of the tool are available at http://palimpsest-eng.appspot.com> (last accessed 10 August 2015).

14. The collections searched included the Hathi Trust Digital Library, the National Library of Scotland's Licensed Digital Collections, the University of Oxford Text Archive, the British Library Digital Collections and Project Gutenberg. As these collections only contain material out of copyright, we also included over 40 unique works by several contemporary authors, with their permission and the permission of their publishers.

15. James Loxley, Beatrice Alex, Miranda Anderson, David Harris-Birtill, Claire Grover, Uta Hinrichs, Jon Oberlander, Lisa Otty, Aaron Quigley, James Reid and Tara Thomson. *Lit Long: Edinburgh* [online]. Available at <http://litlong.org/> (last accessed 10 August 2015), interactive web resource and archive.

16. The Palimpsest project tools and data are open source and available for use by anyone who might wish to replicate the project for another location. These can be accessed via GitHub at <https://github.com/LitPalimpsest> (last accessed 10 August 2015). There are also several off-the-shelf mapping and geolocation applications for use in Humanities research, including Neatline (free Omeka plugin, available at <http://

omeka.org/add-ons/plugins/neatline> (last accessed 10 August 2015), Hypercities (free, available at <http://hypercities.ats.ucla.edu> (last accessed 10 August 2015), Unlock (free, available at <http://edina.ac.uk/unlock> (last accessed 10 August 2015) and ArcGIS (proprietary software, available at <https://www.arcgis.com> (last accessed 10 August 2015).

17. See, for instance, Shelley Fisher Fishkin (2011) '"Deep Maps": a brief for digital palimpsest mapping projects', *Journal of Transnational American Studies* [online], 3 (2): n.p. Available at <https://escholarship.org/uc/item/92v100to> (last accessed 10 August 2015) and Karen Elizabeth Bishop (2011) 'The propositional logic of mapping transnational American studies – a response to '"Deep Maps": a brief for digital palimpsest mapping projects', *Journal of Transnational American Studies* [online], 3 (2): n.p. Available at <https://escholarship.org/uc/item/90r5479j> (last accessed 10 August 2015).

18. Online interfaces can appear as highly naturalised environments, but as Drucker reminds us, all interfaces are data visualisations that prescribe the way we interact with information. For further discussion, see Johanna Drucker (2011) 'Humanities approaches to interface theory', *Culture Machine* [online] 12: 1–20. Available at <http://www.culturemachine. net/index.php/cm/issue/view/23poet> (last accessed 10 August 2015).

REFERENCES

Barthes, Roland (1975) *S/Z*, trans. Richard Miller. London: Cape.
Card, Stuart K., Mackinlay, Jock D. and Shneiderman, Ben (eds) (1999) *Readings in Information Visualization: Using Vision to Think*. San Francisco: Morgan Kaufmann.
Clement, Tanya (2013–15) 'Text analysis, data mining, and visualizations in literary scholarship', in Kenneth Price and Ray Siemens (eds), *Literary Studies in the Digital Age: An Evolving Anthology* [online] (MLA Commons), n.p. <https://dlsanthology.commons.mla.org/text-analysis-data-mining-and-visualizations-in-literary-scholarship/> (last accessed 10 August 2015)
Dörk, Marian, Collins, Christopher, Feng, Patrick and Carpendale, Sheelagh (2013) 'Critical InfoVis: exploring the politics of visualization', *CHI 2013 Extended Abstracts*, 27 April – 2 May, Paris, n.p.
Drucker, Johanna (2011) 'Humanities approaches to graphical display', *DHQ: Digital Humanities Quarterly*, 5 (1): n.p.
Ferster, Bill (2012) *Interactive Visualization: Insight Through Inquiry*. Cambridge, MA: MIT Press.
Fry, Ben (2008) *Visualising Data: Exploring and Explaining Data with the Processing Environment*. Sebastopol, CA: O'Reilly Media.

Gambrell, Linda B. and Jawitz, Paula Brooks (1993) 'Mental imagery, text illustrations, and children's story comprehension and recall', *Reading Research Quarterly*, 28 (3): 265–73.

Gershon, N. and Page, W. (2001) 'What storytelling can do for information visualization', *ACM*, 44 (8): 31–7.

Gitleman, Lisa (ed.) (2013) *'Raw Data' Is an Oxymoron*. Cambridge, MA: MIT Press.

Hamming, Richard (1973) *Numerical Analysis for Scientists and Engineers*. New York: McGraw-Hill.

Latour, Bruno (1986) 'Visualisation and cognition: thinking with eyes and hands', in H. Kuklick (ed.), *Knowledge and Society: Studies in the Sociology of Culture Past and Present*, *Vol. 6*. Greenwich, CT: Jai Press, pp. 1–40.

Latour, Bruno (1987) *Science in Action: How to Follow Scientists and Engineers through Society*. Cambridge, MA: Harvard University Press.

Piper, Andrew (2012) *Book Was There: Reading in Electronic Times*. Chicago: University of Chicago Press.

Scott, Walter (1827) *Chronicles of the Canongate: Second Series*, Vol. 1. Philadelphia: Carey, Lea, & Carey.

Segel, Edward and Heer, Jeffrey (2010) 'Narrative visualisation: telling stories with data', *TVCG*, 16 (6): 1139–48.

Vonnegut, Kurt (2007) 'Here is a lesson in creative writing', in Kurt Vonnegut, *A Man without a Country*. London: Bloomsbury, pp. 23–38.

Wertheimer, Max (1923/1938) 'Laws of organization in perceptual forms', W. Ellis (trans.), in *A Source Book of Gestalt Psychology*. London: Routledge & Kegan Paul, pp. 71–88.

CHAPTER 7

Curating Mary Digitally: Digital Methodologies and Representations of Medieval Material Culture

Cecilia Lindhé, Ann-Catrine Eriksson, Jim Robertsson and Mattis Lindmark

> Medieval objects were offered to the senses, their rich surfaces teasing the desire to touch, to smell, to taste and to experience them in space. Treated as art, displayed in clinical and transparent glass cages, they lose their wider sensorial dimension and submit to our regime of the eye. The textured surfaces, flattened by the even electric lights, deflate to reveal a dead, immobile, taxidermized image. (Pentcheva 2010: 1)

'Medieval objects were offered to the senses, their rich surfaces teasing the desire to touch, to smell, to taste and to experience them in space,' writes Bissera V. Pentcheva in the epigraph above.[1] But when devotional objects, which originally were used in cult and liturgy, are displayed in glass cages, published as photographs in books or in digital collections, they lose their wider sensorial dimension. Crucial aspects of the objects' material and aesthetic qualities are obscured in these kinds of remediation.[2] For example, certain digital collections of medieval materiality reproduce a post-romantic notion of aesthetics, remediate the logic of print technology[3] and use linear perspective in their display.[4] One result is that the images are presented as objective replicas that emphasise a fixed single appearance and are reimagined in a snapshot of an 'original' condition. These types of remediation limit our view of medieval representation, argues Martin Foys, who writes that: 'In modern representation, the power of print culture joins with that of perspective to re-render medieval objects as singular, static and unified' (2009: 169). Foys argues that in the early modern period a shift took place where previous notions of space as a category used to classify sensory experiences changed to another kind of category: the mathematical attempt to precisely calculate and classify space. This is connected to the concept of perspective and its rise during the Renaissance dominates the ways in which we re-produce space. Naturally, perspective did not inform the production of medieval art in the way it does most modern forms of visual expression. However, according to Foys, it usually governs how modern audiences interpret and value early medieval objects (2009: 168).

What kind of knowledge about medieval Madonna sculptures do the inter-faces – such as the book page, the museum display or the web page – express?[5] Is it possible to use an experimental digital interface to shed new light on the medieval conception of the Virgin Mary? Is it possible to heighten the performativity of the medieval images and to capture their changing multi-sensous appearances? Is it possible to put forward the medieval view that these objects had an agency of their own, and emphasise their performativity rather than their mimetic or historic qualities only?[6] Is it possible to focus on the interaction between object and subject, between a Madonna and a viewer, and thus perhaps unfold Mary's performance in a physical space?

These are the questions that were explored in the cross-disciplinary research project *Imitatio Mariae: The Virgin Mary as a Virtuous Model in Medieval Sweden*[7] and which will be addressed in this chapter, with a special focus on the project's methodological work. The project examined (represen-tations of) the Virgin Mary as a role model for lay people during the Swedish Middle Ages (1100–1500). We focused on a selection of scenes and stories from the life of Mary, and how they are depicted in the interplay between motifs in Old Swedish texts and visual representations such as mural paint-ings and Madonna sculptures.[8] One part of the project is also to convey how a digital multi-modal environment – which facilitates the interplay between screens, bodies' movements, and different sound and light images – can act as a critical lens through which to view contemporary conceptions of medieval material culture. One important methodological task has been to investigate how an advanced digital and location-specific infrastructure can establish a critical approach to humanistic knowledge production. In an effort to offer an alternative to the concentration on text-based meaning,[9] production and reception, we decided not only to write articles but also to construct a digital interactive installation (using high-resolution screens, sensors, directional sound and light) and a web-based archive that in their form problematise the representation of the image of the Virgin Mary. The aim of these digital projects is not to try to recreate medieval lay people's experience of interacting with these objects, but rather to problematise different re-mediations of the Virgin Mary's journey from cult object to art object. We have tried to capture the power to transform the viewer from observer to participant and further to emphasise the performativity of these objects. One point of departure was that medieval devotional objects were meant to be physically experienced and that touch, sound, movement and even smell and taste formed a crucial part of encountering and relating to them. The installations and the archive not only orchestrate the Swedish medieval church as a multi-modal and performative space, but as Matt Ratto describes the methodology of critical making, it is a model set up to challenge the division between theory and material practice in humanities research.[10]

As N. Katherine Hayles (2012), and before her Marshall McLuhan and others, has pointed out, the remediation and organisation of knowledge shapes our thoughts and actions. This is an awareness that we translated into practice in order to imagine new modes of organisation and thought and to ask new research questions where an experimental digital interface was used as a lens. Consequently, we tried not only to bridge or to problematise the gap between material and conceptual exploration, but also to think critically about knowledge production within the humanities. In this chapter we explore the iterative or dialogic movement from the original conceptualisation of the project to building the first prototypes, and then highlight the new questions and concepts prompted by the prototypes. Or, in other words, the journey from performing traditional scholarship – such as writing articles and performing iconographic and hermeneutical analyses of visual media – to creating a scientific installation that both functions as a vehicle for research and a novel way to present research results.

THE INSTALLATIONS: RHETORICAL THEORY

For the project we collected circa five thousand photographs and video recordings from close to one hundred medieval parish churches from the regions of Östergötland, Uppland and Gotland. The photographs show various scenes from the life of the Virgin Mary depicted on a great variety of material such as wall paintings, baptismal fonts, altar screens, wooden Madonna sculptures, reliefs, even a stone bench. The initial aim was to use the photographs to create tools that facilitated the research process and the project's aim to study the interplay between text and image. We also wanted to emphasise and activate not only the visual, but multiple senses in an interplay between the spectator and the images. Lots of work has already been done on the ocularity of the later Middle Ages with its emphasis on seeing and visuality,[11] but existing digital tools and related models often convey conventions of knowledge as primarily visual, running the risk of neglecting other sensory features.[12] Further, digital projects often stress the mimetic qualities – their fidelity to what they are taken to represent – of the visual reconstruction.[13] For us, it was crucial to avoid a representational approach to vision and not to create immersion or illusion through such photorealistic simulations, partially because we wanted to underline the constructedness of the image of the Virgin Mary and partially because we wanted the interface to expose and support the activity of interpretation and not only to display information. Consequently, instead of placing our material in 3D reconstructions of particular church interiors, immersive virtual reality environments such as the CAVE or digitised archives reminiscent of print culture, we decided to use the photographs in a multiple screens environment.

Church spaces, the liturgy and religious practice have of course changed considerably since the Middle Ages and records of liturgical practice are rare in Sweden. We do not know how people moved in a church during services or private visits, what all the possible interactions between people and visual objects could have been or how the liminal experiences of heaven and earth were staged.[14] Theology professor Alf Härdelin (2005) describes the church building and its interiors as 'an open window' to the spiritual world; the medieval church interior was a material space where one could use the human senses to pierce through materiality and experience the heavenly realm (Härdelin 2005: 9–11). In this pursuit, medieval aesthetics, images and architecture were meant to *do* something with their audiences, not just represent or portray (Carruthers 2013: 15).[15]

The project was affiliated to HUMlab, a Digital Humanities laboratory at Umeå University. Early on we decided to use the unique infrastructure of the lab space (Figure 7.1), including ten screens arranged in a circle (two 65" and one 70" touch screen, seven 52" screens) and one rear projection screen (170"). Connected to the screenscape is an interaction technology system, together with various forms of sensors and cameras, sound and a flexible light ceiling that creates special effects, shapes and images on the lighting plane as well as projecting different colours.

Rather than using the representational qualities of this space, we wanted to explore its performative potentials. At the same time it was also important to create research tools that could be used by the project members, such as juxtaposing images from different churches and zooming in on details otherwise difficult to perceive.

The first installation piece, *The Magnifier*, was developed for the 170" high-resolution, back-projected screen. The user can choose between several different thumbnails and with the aid of a pointer move the image, as well as zoom in and out of the photographs. Due to the high-resolution screen, it is possible to zoom in on paintings on ceilings and in other areas that could be difficult to reach but it is also possible to simulate the distance at which churchgoers experienced these images. The second prototype, *The Digiti*, allows the user to juxtapose image and medieval manuscripts on a 70" touchscreen. Several thumbnails are available at the top of the screen and it is possible to compare two images at a time by using touch. These two installations have mainly been developed by, and used as tools for, the project members, since they make

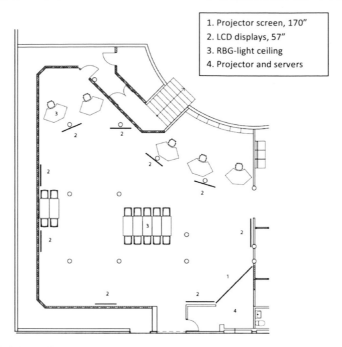

1. Projector screen, 170"
2. LCD displays, 57"
3. RBG-light ceiling
4. Projector and servers

Figure 7.1 HUMlab. (Source: Robertsson (2011: 9).)

possible the juxtaposition of images as well as the magnifying of details in paintings. However, two installations are more experimental in their formats. In *The Calendarium*, a Madonna with child functions as the basis for an exploration of different Madonnas. With the aid of a pointer the participant has to find different spaces in the digital image that contain other Madonnas in smaller variants. This piece is also a useful research tool that makes possible the juxtaposition of Madonnas in different styles, from different locations and times. But also, and perhaps more importantly, it is how the images are found that is crucial here. When a new, previously hidden Madonna becomes visible, the search patterns in the image are connected to the light in the ceiling that changes colour depending on which image one finds. This puts emphasis on the fact that it is not the artwork as authentic historical object that is most important, but rather the aesthetic object as a field of potential, as a process. Again, this is aligned with the aim of putting more attention to acts of producing rather than displaying a finished form of representation and simulation. And in *The Sensorium*, depending on a body's movement towards the screen, images from Saint Bridget's Vadstena abbey emerge. The sensorium registers the movement of a body that approaches the screen and triggers new images; when the altar piece is shown *Ave Maria* is heard being sung in one of the churches. Also, the light in the room changes continually in relation to the body's movements toward the screen. It emphasises several senses such as sight, sound and touch.

Building is often seen as a core activity within the digital humanities.[16] However, in *Speclab* Johanna Drucker (2009: xi) writes that digital environments often seem to be designed according to a hierarchical relationship between technological tools and humanities tools, where the former methods have been granted greater authority: 'Computational methods rooted in formal logic tend to be granted more authority in this dialogue (between computational technology and the humanities) than methods grounded in aesthetic and subjective judgment.' Considering this, we tried to invert this power relation by building the installations around core humanities concepts; they are based on the rhetorical notions of *memoria, ductus* and *ekphrasis*. *Memoria* was the rhetorical faculty of memory based on the placement of allegorical images within constructed mental architectures such as a building or a landscape, thus stressing the importance of linking spatiality to memory images.[17] In her *Book of Memory*, Mary Carruthers (2011) describes *memoria* as a conceptual motor for the organisation and motivation of thought for the medieval writers and states in an earlier text that: 'One may conveniently think of this activity in spatial terms, as if memories have been stored in a variety of places and must be called together in a common place where we can become aware of them, where we can "see" them again and know them in the present' (Carruthers and Ziolokowski 2002: 1). The goal of *memoria*, then, was not to repeat previously stored material, as we often use the term today. Rather, it was about 'creative thought' and, according to Mary Carruthers, it is 'crucial to understand [. . .] that what is important to for example early pilgrims is not the site as an authentic, validated historical object [. . .] What is authentic and *real* about the sites is the *memory-work*, the thinking to which they gave clues' (Carruthers 1998: 42; emphasis in original). This means that the sites, such as a temple or a city, and in this case the digital installations, are supposed to trigger imagination and creativity through embodied and sensorial interaction. Within our project we used *memoria* in the broad, classical and medieval cognitive sense of thinking and categorising. Monastic *memoria* was an art of image making – to the mind's eye – that was performed in close connection to existing images and actual words that 'someone had seen or read or heard – or smelled or tasted or touched, for multiple senses . . . were cultivated in the monastic craft of remembering' (Carruthers 1998: 10).[18] Central to this way of thinking is not how truthfully the images represent but rather their 'cognitive utility', that is if they can be used as sites upon which it is possible to build or invent new content, such as thought or prayer (Carruthers 1998: 72).

Related to medieval views on materiality and agency is the rhetorical concept *ductus*. This is the second concept we based the installations on. It can be translated as 'directed motion' and it analyses the experience of artistic form as an ongoing, dynamic process rather than as the examination of a static or completed object. *Ductus* is also about performance and process, or the journeying through a work of art rather than examining a static or completed object (Carruthers 2010: 198). The interactive installations take *ductus* as a condition for navigating the Swedish medieval church space in digital environments and aim to move from the church presented as text to an experience of the church space.[19]

The third concept, *ekphrasis*, is defined by the assumption of a live audience; it emphasises immediacy and the impact on the listener. When an orator spoke about a place, a monument or an event unseen or unfamiliar to the audience he was supposed to use details to create a visual image 'in the mind's eye' of the listeners. A defining feature of the rhetorical *ekphrasis* was not just an effective use of verbal description, but also immediacy and immersion through the senses. In *Progymnasmata*, Hermogenes describes *ekphrasis* as an expression that brings about sight through sound: 'Virtues (*aretai*) of an ecphrasis are, most of all, clarity (*saphêneia*) and vividness (*enargeia*); for the expression should almost create seeing through hearing' (35). The auditory dimension of *ekphrasis* has been lost in the modern definition but was of course an important element in the rhetorical situation.[20] And in the same text Theon writes that 'Ekphrasis is a descriptive (*periegematikos*) speech which brings (literally "leads") the thing shown vividly before the eyes' (Webb 2009: 51). *Periegematikos* is an adjective that equals the speaker with a *guide* showing the listener around the sight – 'shows its audience around, gives it a tour' (Webb 2009: 54). Quintilian also discusses how a visual impression generated by *enargeia* 'makes us seem not so much to narrate as to exhibit the actual scene while our emotions will be no less actively stirred than if we were present at the actual occurrence' (Quintilian 1953: 6.2.32). Thus, in a successful *ekphrasis*, the scene is not so much narrated as exhibited and Ruth Webb (2009) describes the rhetorical situation as a theatre or exhibition: 'Drawn as they are from different domains, these metaphors all suggest slightly different relationships between speaker, addressee and referent: the subject matter may be "brought" into the presence of the audience (speaker as theatrical producer), or the audience may be "led around" the subject (speaker as tour guide)' (54–5).

Interactive installations and virtual reality art have evolved from and in relation to architecture, sculpture and performance and these artworks are realised in virtual spheres that generate tangible spatial experiences. However, Hellenistic visual art and poetry also created modes of viewing in order to involve and integrate viewers and readers, visually as well as spatially, into compositions (see Wands 2007; Zanker 2003: 27). In our installations emphasis was moved from the problem of representing a visual object to the user's bodily interaction with an environment, where *ductus* was the guiding principle for establishing *memoria* and *ekphrasis* in relation to the medieval images.

We deployed digital interfaces to direct attention to physical interaction and to the materiality of the work, and thus encourage a rediscovery of a bodily/ tactile and multi-sensory experience in relation also to non-digital artefacts; the interactive installations were used to strengthen sensation and highlight that vision is an embodied and multi-sensous activity (Pentcheva 2010: 26).[21] Whereas viewers in front of a screen watching a 3D model or browsing through an archive of images are usually expected to be immersed by what is happening on the single screen, our installations foreground the space between the viewer and the multiple screens. This awareness of space brings focus to acts of producing instead of to a finished product and by trying to avoid photorealistic immersive simulations also help us call attention to the constructedness of knowledge: of ambiguity, uncertainty and lack of singularity or fixity. It is by examining and orchestrating these spaces – *loci* – as a space that emphasises materiality, physical interaction and the multi-sensory experience that the user can experience the medieval objects in a novel way.

THE ARCHIVE: METHOD AND WORKING PROCESS

More traditional approaches to visual media include iconography, iconology and semiotics, but we wanted to shift the emphasis away from meaning, from representational and mimetic qualities, toward the way that these objects could perform in a space. We favoured material sensations instead, and by tracing the rhetorical operations of these objects we tried to emphasise how medieval images could affect and persuade their viewers through an appeal to the senses, or in other words we wanted to put forward the view that devotional sculptures have an ability to elicit tactile and auditive as well as visual responses to their materiality.[22] The prototypes were built in close collaboration between computer technicians and scholars in an effort to destabilise the kind of hierarchical relationship of which Drucker (2009) writes, and further to extend knowledge and skills in the relevant technical areas as well as within the field of conceptual exploration.

Method-wise, in order to establish a productive relationship between medieval and digital materialities, the project could be described as oscillating between a number of positions: between theory and practice; between critical making and text/image analysis; between programming and rhetoric. Moreover, it is an example of a very distinctive form of collaboration between humanities scholars and computer technicians, where the scholar introduces rhetorical concepts to the programmers, who in turn develop the digital platforms, but in a constant dialogue. The methods that we used are inspired by critical making, which could be described as a combination of creative physical and conceptual exploration in order not only to bridge the gap between the physical and the conceptual, but also to encourage a critical perspective on humanistic knowledge production in a digital age (Ratto 2011). Both the development and use of these research methods and tools require a combination of expertise that is not easy to find among humanities researchers. Further, finding people that are open and willing to experiment both within and beyond their own fields is also necessary in a project such as this.

The first stage of the working process mainly comprised its conceptualisation: finding the theoretical and rhetorical starting points and identifying the technological conditions and possibilities. It was crucial that the researchers did not order a specific model nor that the computer technicians presented a set model of their own, but that the first prototypes were created in an iterative, open and flexible dialogue. The second phase, when the first prototypes had been built, involved a process of reconfiguration, conversation and reflection. We made changes to the prototypes and discussed in what way the rhetorical concepts were staged, we explored different possibilities, and, most importantly, we discussed how the prototypes could critique and extend relevant rhetorical concepts and models. Or, in other words, we analysed medieval material culture through the installations.[23] Eventually, the working process showed how interpretation is rethought through the encounter with computational methods and that computational methods are rethought through the encounter with humanistic modes of knowing. Several ideas, problems and questions arose, but two were especially interesting to us. Firstly, it became clear that tools and interfaces communicate ideas: they both produce and transmit knowledge. And, secondly, in combination with our initial aim not to create a finished model (or a mimetic representation of, for example, a church interior), we wanted to investigate whether it would be possible to create a critical visualisation that showed the different stages of the research process. These queries resulted in the idea of a web-based archive where the logic of the site-specific installation would be implemented. The archive (that currently only exists as a prototype) consists of a 3D model of the HUMlab space where the aim is that the user can walk around and experience the installations, either as simulations or real-time events (Figure 7.2).[24] The walls in the room are transparent which make it possible to discern all the photographs that constitute the installations. This was important, as we wanted both to make the user aware of the whole of the archive as well as to highlight the working process behind the installations.

As part of the second phase, when we were discussing the prototypes and concepts, it also became clear that the combination of rhetorical analysis and interaction technology created immediacy. The concept of immediacy draws on Hans Ulrich Gumbrecht's (2004) analysis of medieval culture as a particularly strong culture of presence. In *The Production of Presence: What Meaning Cannot Convey*, Gumbrecht writes that the humanities, for too long, have

Figure 7.2 The archive. (Source: Mattis Lindmark.)

taken the relation to the literary text, or the art object, for granted. He argues that there is an implicit distance in the hermeneutical analytical practice, a searching for meaning and a distance between the subject and the object, and that this essentially Cartesian dualism has prevented us from discussing what art and literature also do: communicate immediacy and presence, or moments of intensity (Gumbrecht 2004: viii).[25] We wanted the archive to communicate these moments of intensity, which is why it is also possible to leave the simulation of the HUMlab space and enter an open area where it will be possible to explore all the images of the archive (Figure 7.3).

Here, we avoided traditional metadata tagging, such as age, creator, etc. Instead, the images are tagged with the Virgin Mary's emotions (such as sorrow and joy), and it will be possible to follow and juxtapose details such as the Virgin Mary's hand on Jesus' dead body or Elizabeth and Mary embracing during the visitation from different parish churches. This archive is not for searching for a single piece to be closely read, but rather to explore, experience and reflect on the presence and intensity of these objects. Further, we wanted to develop an interface that does not conceal the decisions and processes on which it was based and we tried to be analytical about the relationship between the archival base and what the archive stores. This could be described as a practice that arose from the combination of conceptualising and building. It forms a critique of an archive organised according to linear time and further problematises how medieval materiality and medieval space have been represented previously in print and in online open collections. So, instead of adapting to an interface that merely presents a collection of photographs, we tried to design scholarly tools that in their form revise, question and describe the formative stages of the research process.

The medieval past exists through intermediates, of which some are written works while others are visual. One aim of the installations and the archive described here was to explore the limits that print culture has imposed upon the pre-print, and then to explore how an experimental digital interface based on rhetoric could provide opportunities to lift those critical limits. Johanna Drucker (2014) argues for the need and importance of digital interfaces that incorporate humanistic principles in their organisation and she calls for 'humanist computer languages, interpretative interfaces, and information systems that can tolerate inconsistency among types of knowledge representation, classification, fluid ontologies, and navigation' (178). And one way, according to Drucker, is to let the interface express a content model that comes from critical study, editing, bibliography or other traditions rooted in the appreciation of and engagement with cultural materials. Another way could be to use rhetoric as a conceptual foundation for digital installations, as we have done in the *Imitatio Marie* project. Digital interactive installations foreground the significance of space and architecture in a similar sense to how ancient

Figure 7.3 The archive 2. (Source: Mattis Lindmark.)

rhetoric was based on its performance in particular (public) spaces – such as the agora and the stage – or as Mary Carruthers (2010: 2) argues: 'The heart of rhetoric, as of all art, lies in its performance; it proffers both visual spectacle and verbal dance to an audience which is not passive but an actor in the whole experience, like the chorus in a drama.' The combination of rhetoric and interaction technology can suggest new modes of critique and, not least, create an understanding of the ways in which medieval material culture remains in a continuous process of reformulation, reinterpretation and repurposing.

ACKNOWLEDGEMENTS

We would like to thank Jonas Ingvarsson for comments and feedback.

NOTES

1. Roughly speaking, there exist two different views on medieval culture and the senses. One states that the Middle Ages were a culture of high sensual intensity and the other that it was a time of sensual starvation (Gumbrecht 2008: 1–10).

2. It is worth noting in this context that what remains in Sweden of, for example, medieval Madonna sculptures are those that survived the Reformation and were not burned or hidden in attics, barns or bell towers. Today some of these objects have been brought back to the (still Protestant) churches where they are no longer used in cult and liturgy but rather as art objects. The result is that when Catholic images are presented in this way it creates distance and objectification. For a discussion about how vision could interpose a distance between subject and object, see Jay (1994); Grosz (1990: 38). For a critique of this view of vision see Biernoff (2002: esp. 88 ff.).

3. Digital media is an outgrowth of print culture. We do not argue for a sharp break between print and digital culture. Further, it is important to stress that print technology, or any medium for that matter, does not have one singular and particular logic but rather many different logics that are contrasted through time and dependent on specific histories of printing. For a recent critical discussion on the concept of print culture, see Gitelman (2014: 8). Marshall McLuhan (1962) used the term 'print culture' in *The Gutenberg Galaxy: The Making of Typographic Man*. This concept was both criticised and broadened by Elizabeth L. Eisenstein (1993). Further, while Eisenstein contrasted print culture to scribal culture, Walter Ong (1982) made a distinction between print and oral cultures.

4. The digital collections that we refer to are, for example, the Swedish Historical Museum's digital collection: see <http://mis.historiska.se/mis/sok/start.asp>. See also Lindhé (2015).

5. The concept of interface will be discussed further below, but we follow Johanna Drucker's (2014: 152) definition of interface as 'an ambivalent, persuasive space that could provoke interpretation, behaviours, actions, and that involve humanistic theory'. Further, '[a]esthetic dimensions and imaginative vision make interface a space of being and dwelling, not a realm of control panels and instruments only existing to be put at the service of something else' (Drucker 2014: 152).

6. See, for example, medieval historian Caroline Walker Bynum (2011) who writes that: 'Throughout the Middle Ages, matter was defined – and explored – as the locus of change' (25); 'The physicality we encounter in devotional objects (often in their combination of colors, depth of relief, textures, and materials) reflects and results from the fact that they are not so much naturalistic (that is mimetic) depictions as disclosures of the sacred through material substance' (41).

7. See the project's website: <https://imitatiomariae.wordpress.com>.

8. The Swedish Middle Ages are normally set at the period after the Viking Times, around 1000 AD. However, the churches and objects studied in this project are from 1100–1500 approximately. Sweden was not a nation state then, but the processes that had started at this point did lead to the creation of a Swedish kingdom. See, for example, Härdelin (2005: 13).

9. Jerome McGann (2001: xi) writes that we 'think in textual codes'. In *How We Think* N. Katherine Hayles (2012: 1) also discusses how we think through, with and alongside media, and that humanistic enquiry still is 'formed by print, nurtured by print, and enabled and constrained by print'.

10. See Ratto (2011: 252–60); Ratto et al. (2014).

11. See, for example, Hamburger (1997); Biernoff (2002); Kessler (2004); Holly (1996).

12. The emphasis on sight in Western cultural practices is well documented. See, for example, Paterson (2007), Classen (1993), Jay (1993), Crary (1990).

13. For example, in archaeology, 'media artifacts produced with the aid of technology are most often evaluated according to their degree of correspondence with what they represent, their mimetic qualities' (Shanks and Webmoor 2013: 88).

14. Even if there are written manuals and theological teachings on how to move, behave and understand space, we still have to speculate to what extent this was actually practised by lay people and whether there existed local variations etc. (see Haight 2004: 282–3; Latourette 1975: esp. ch. 2).

15. The important question was: 'What is it doing (and what is it asking us to do)?'
16. See, for example, Arthur and Bode (2014); Burdick et al. (2012); Somerson and Hermano (2013).
17. See Carruthers (1998, 2011: 9), Yates (2006), Quintilian (XI.Ii. *sqq.*).
18. For the difference between monastic *memoria* and pagan rhetorical practice, see Carruthers (1998: 7 ff.).
19. Compare 'The aim of this essay is to move from the cathedral as text to the cathedral as experience [. . .].' See Crossley (2010: 214).
20. For a discussion about the difference between ancient and modern ekphrasis, see, for example, Webb (2009) and Lindhé (2013).
21. Our project is not the first effort to write about the multi-sensous in relation to the experience of religious imagery. For example, Williamson (2013) argues that historians and art historians increasingly go beyond the visual to address the impact of the other physical senses (pp. 33–4).
22. The concept of 'matter', in this context, concerns not so much the matter of the objects, as focused in Caroline Walker Bynum's *Christian Materiality* (2011), but rather in the human sensations, and how human senses respond and create responses from the objects.
23. At this stage, Jim Robertsson, who, while working with the prototypes also wrote a thesis on the subject, performed a user test that added to our discussions (see Robertsson 2011).
24. The prototype for the archive is programmed in Maya and Unity. See the short film of the first prototype at <https://www.youtube.com/watch?v=WB6hEmUhUfc>.
25. Gumbrecht further writes:

> The word 'presence' does not refer (at least not mainly refer) to a temporal but to a spatial relationship to the world and its objects. Something that is present is supposed to be tangible for human hands, which implies that, conversely, it can have an immediate impact on human bodies. 'Production', then, is used according to the meaning of its etymological root (i.e. Latin *producere*) that refers to the act of 'bringing forth' an object in space. Presence effects appeal to the senses and the 'production of presence' points to all kinds of events and processes in which the impact that 'present' objects have on human bodies is being initiated or intensified. (Gumbrecht 2004: xiii)

REFERENCES

Arthur, P. L. and K. Bode (eds) (2014) *Advancing Digital Humanities: Research, Methods, Theories*. London: Palgrave Macmillan.

Biernoff, S. (2002) *Sight and Embodiment in the Middle Ages*. London: Palgrave Macmillan.

Burdick, A., Drucker, J., Lunenfeld, P. et al. (2012) *Digital Humanities*. Cambridge, MA: MIT Press.

Carruthers, M. (1998) *The Craft of Thought. Meditation, Rhetoric, and the Making of Images 400–1200*. Cambridge: Cambridge University Press.

Carruthers, M. (2010) 'Editor's introduction', in M. Carruthers (ed.), *Rhetoric Beyond Words: Delight and Persuasion in the Arts of the Middle Ages*. Cambridge: Cambridge University Press, pp. 1–13.

Carruthers, M. (2011 [1990]) *The Book of Memory: A Study of Memory in Medieval Culture*. Cambridge: Cambridge University Press.

Carruthers, M. (2013) *The Experience of Beauty in the Middle Ages*. Oxford: Oxford University Press.

Carruthers, M. and Ziolokowski, J. M. (2002) 'General introduction', in M. Carruthers and J. M. Ziolokowski (eds), *The Medieval Craft of Memory. An Anthology of Texts and Pictures*. Philadelphia: University of Pennsylvania Press, pp. 1–31.

Classen, C. (1993) *Worlds of Senses: Exploring the Senses in History and Across Cultures*. London: Routledge.

Crary, J. (1990) *Techniques of the Observer: On Vision and Modernity in the Nineteenth Century*. Cambridge, MA: MIT Press.

Crossley, P. (2010) 'Ductus and memoria: Chartres Cathedral and the workings of rhetoric', in M. Carruthers (ed.), *Rhetoric Beyond Words: Delight and Persuasion in the Arts of the Middle Ages*. Cambridge: Cambridge University Press, pp. 214–49.

Drucker, J. (2009) *Speclab: Digital Aesthetics and Projects in Speculative Computing*. Chicago: University of Chicago Press.

Drucker, J. (2014) *Graphesis: Visual Forms of Knowledge Production*. Cambridge, MA: Harvard University Press.

Eisenstein, E. L. (2009 [1993]) *The Printing Press as an Agent of Change: Communications and Cultural Transformations in Early-Modern Europe*. Cambridge: Cambridge University Press.

Foys, M. ([2007] 2009) *Virtually Anglo-Saxon: Old Media, New Media, and Early Medieval Studies in the Late Age of Print*. Gainesville: University of Florida Press.

Gitelman, G. (2014) *Paper Knowledge. Toward a Media History of Documents*. Durham, NC: Duke University Press.

Grosz, E. (1990) *Jacques Lacan: A Feminist Introduction*. London: Routledge.

Gumbrecht, H. U. (2004) *The Production of Presence: What Meaning Cannot Convey*. Stanford, CA: Stanford University Press.

Gumbrecht, H. U. (2008) 'Erudite fascination and cultural energies: how much can we know about the medieval senses?', in S. G. Nichols, A. Kablitz and A. Calhoun (eds), *Rethinking the Medieval Senses. Heritage/Fascinations/Frames*. Baltimore: Johns Hopkins University Press, pp. 1–10.

Haight, R. (2004) *Christian Community in History: Historical Ecclesiology*, Vol. I. New York: Continuum.

Hamburger, J. (1997) *The Visual Culture of a Medieval Convent*. Berkeley: University of California Press.

Härdelin, A. (2005) *Världen som yta och fönster: Spiritualitet i medeltidens Sverige* [*The World as Surface and Window. Spirituality During the Swedish Middle Ages*]. Stockholm: Sällskapet Runica et Medievala.

Hayles, N. K. (2012) *How We Think: Digital Media and Contemporary Technogenesis*. Chicago: University of Chicago Press.

Hermogenes (2003) *Progymnasmata: Greek Textbooks of Prose Composition*, trans. into English with Intro. and Notes by G. A. Kennedy. Atlanta: Society of Biblical Literature, pp. 73–88. Available at: <https://books.google.co.uk/books?id=21ka6pWJ-pkC&printsec=frontcover#v=onepage&q&f=false>.

Holly, M. A. (1996) *Past Looking: Historical Imagination and the Rhetoric of the Image*. Ithaca, NY: Cornell University Press.

Jay, M. (1993) *Downcast Eyes: The Denigration of Vision in Twentieth-Century French Thought*. Berkeley: University of California Press.

Jay, M. (1994) *Downcast Eyes*. Berkeley: University of California Press.

Kessler, H. L. (2004) *Seeing Medieval Art*. Peterborough, Ont.: Broadview Press.

Latourette, K. S. (1975) *A History of Christianity: Beginning to 1500*, Vol. I. New York: Harper Collins.

Lindhé, C. (2013) 'A visual sense is born in the fingertips: towards a digital ekphrasis', *Digital Humanities Quarterly*, 7 (1), at <http://digitalhumanities.org/dhq/vol/7/1/000161/000161.html>.

Lindhé, C. (2015) 'Medieval materiality through the digital lens', in D. T. Goldberg and P. Svensson (eds), *Between Humanities and the Digital*. Cambridge, MA: MIT Press, pp. 193–204.

McGann, J. J. (2001) *Radiant Textuality: Literature after the World Wide Web*. New York: Palgrave.

McLuhan, M. (1962) *The Gutenberg Galaxy: The Making of Typographic Man*. Toronto: University of Toronto Press.

Ong, W. (1982) *Orality and Literacy: The Technologizing of the Word*. London: Routledge.

Paterson, M. (2007) *The Sense of Touch: Haptics, Affects and Technologies*. Oxford: Berg.

Pentcheva, B. V. (2010) *The Sensual Icon: Space, Ritual and the Senses in Byzantium*. University Park: Pennsylvania State University Press.

Quintilian (1953) *Institutio Oratoria*, trans. H. E. Butler. Cambridge, MA: Harvard University Press, XI.Ii. *sqq*.

Ratto, M. (2011) 'Critical making: conceptual and material studies in technology and social life', *Information Society*, 27: 252–60.

Ratto, M., Wylie, S. A. and Jalbert, K. (2014) 'Introduction to the Special Forum on Critical Making as Research Program', *Information Society*, 30 (2): 85–95.

Robertsson, J. (2011) 'Via Maria: A Visual and Interactive Presentation of Medieval Artifacts'. Unpublished undergraduate thesis, Department of Applied Physics and Electronics, Umeå University.

Shanks, M. and Webmoor, T. (2013) 'A political economy of visual media in archaeology', in S. Bonde and S. Houston (eds), *Re-Presenting the Past: Archaeology Through Text and Image*. Oxford: Oxbow Books.

Somerson, R. and Hermano, L. M. (2013) *The Art of Critical Making: Rhode Island School of Design on Creative Practice*. Hoboken, NJ: John Wiley & Sons.

Walker Bynum, C. (2011) *Christian Materiality. An Essay on Religion in Late Medieval Europe*. New York: Zone Books.

Wands, B. (2007) *Art of the Digital Age*. London: Thames & Hudson.

Webb, R. (2009) *Ekphrasis, Imagination, and Persuasion in Ancient Rhetorical Theory and Practice*. Farnham: Ashgate.

Williamson, B. (2013) 'Sensory experience in medieval devotion: sound and vision, invisibility and silence', *Speculum*, 88 (1): 1–43.

Yates, F. A. ([1966] 2006) *The Art of Memory*. London: Pimlico.

Zanker, G. (2003) *Modes of Viewing in Hellenistic Poetry and Art*. Madison: University of Wisconsin Press.

CHAPTER 8

Raising Language Awareness Using Digital Media: Methods for Revealing Linguistic Stereotyping

Mats Deutschmann, Anders Steinvall and Anna Lagerström

INTRODUCTION

Whether we are aware of it or not, language is at the heart of the mechanisms leading to stereotyping and inequality. It is one of the major factors that we evaluate when we meet others, and it has long been demonstrated that individuals are judged in terms of intellect and other character traits on the basis of their language output (e.g. Cavallaro and Ng 2009; Fuertes et al. 2012; Deutschmann et al. 2011). We also adapt our own language to fit underlying norms and preconceived social stereotypes when we communicate with others. In this way, we help to shape individuals through the way we treat them linguistically. Social identity expressed through language is consequently something that is renegotiated during every meeting between humans (Crawford 1995). An awareness of such mechanisms is especially important for teachers and other professionals working in the context of human contact.

In most language courses aimed at student teachers of various levels, students are given a theoretical overview of research on aspects related to identity (gender, ethnicity, social class, etc.) and language. But however well intended, there is a real danger that research focused on identifying differences also strengthens stereotypes. Further, there is a risk that such theoretical knowledge remains just that: creating the link between so-called *factual knowledge* – for example, theoretical frameworks and previous studies – and *internalised knowledge* applicable in our everyday lives is especially challenging. This is particularly true in the domain of language, where metalinguistic knowledge ideally should be translated into professional language practice, a key skill for anyone working with human interaction.

This chapter describes experiments conducted in 2011, where we used digital media to manipulate identity variables such as gender, with the aim of developing and exploring experiential pedagogic approaches for raising socio-linguistic language awareness about conceived identity-related phenomena in language. We will also describe the planned second phase of this work, RAVE, where we aim to develop further our models to produce more systematically tested methods for exposing and combating linguistic stereotyping. We think that this is an important step in better equipping teachers to judge learners on their individual merits rather than on the preconceived ideas of the group they happen to belong to. Indeed, such awareness is important for any profession related to human contact (health care, the police, law and so on).

PREVIOUS RESEARCH

Stereotyping and language

Not only does stereotyping, based on various social categories such as gender, age, social class, ethnicity, sexuality or regional affiliation, serve to simplify how people perceive and process information about individuals (Talbot 2003: 468), it also builds up expectations of how they are supposed to act. People can choose to ignore such expectations, but they still have to relate to them in their interactions with others (Talbot 2003: 472). Stereotyping is further complicated by what is often referred to as *intersectionality*. Many researchers argue (e.g. Gutierrez et al. 2012) that aspects of identity such as gender cannot be analysed in isolation. Negative stereotypes related to different social catego-ries often interact so that the total effect is greater than the sum of individual factors/aspects. In this way, working–class black women, for example, may be particularly stereotyped.

Studies have shown that stereotypes and prejudices related to race (e.g. Slaughter-Defoe 2012) and gender (e.g. Abrams and Rutland 2008), for example, are established at a very early age and, once learnt, they tend to resist change (Killen and Levy 2008), even when evidence fails to support them or points to the contrary (Sherman et al. 2005). Language is a key element in this bias. According to Collins and Clement (2012: 377), 'language can be concep-tualised as a lens that directs and distorts cognition'. In spite of social efforts in reducing different forms of prejudice, stereotyping and implicit beliefs remain embedded in language, thereby maintaining hierarchical status relations between groups by distorting people's perceptions in very subtle ways that they may not even be explicitly aware of. Classic examples of such distortions include gendered implications when generic meaning is intended, leading to interpretations that exclude the other sex (e.g. Bojarska 2013).

Language is also an important attribute of identity, a signal that draws attention and makes salient certain aspects of the social context. Experiments using so-called matched guise techniques (Lambert et al. 1960), whereby a certain language output is manipulated for regional and/or national accents, have shown that attitudes towards the speaker will be influenced by her/his accent (e.g. Cavallaro and Ng 2009) and language has in fact been shown to be a stronger stimulus for social categorisation than visual cues such as skin colour (Rakić et al. 2011). Given this close link between language and identity, it becomes an important factor in the definition of boundaries between in- and out-groups.

Stereotyping and language in learning situations

Outcomes related to democratic values, identity and communication are clearly defined in all professional degrees of education in the Outcomes section of the Swedish Higher Education Ordinance (Universitets- och högskolerådet 2011: Annex 2). Such outcomes include the ability of teachers at all levels to: 'demonstrate the capacity to respect, communicate and instil a gender equal and equal rights perspective in educational processes'; and to 'demonstrate self-knowledge and a capacity for empathy' in this work. Equipping student teachers with such skills presents a real challenge in higher education.

In this pursuit, it is not enough to have explicit knowledge of the mechanisms involved in stereotyping; people's explicit attitudes and intentions, and the influence on their actions and judgements of inbuilt mind-sets, so-called implicit stereotyping, do not always match (e.g. Collins et al. 2009). It is thus especially important for teachers to possess insights into how they themselves are affected by stereotyping structures and how they may inadvertently contribute to these. This motivates a shift of focus from what language differences exist between different social groupings, to what *beliefs* exist about the language behaviour of different social groupings and how these affect us (Edlund et al. 2007).

With specific reference to gender, studies have shown that gendered expectations affect how we experience real events in various learning contexts (Sunderland 2000). For example, it is well documented that schoolteachers, regardless of gender, tend to give more attention to male than to female students (Sunderland 2000; Chen and Rao 2011), even when they think that they are being more attentive to the female students (Sunderland 2000: 160). A problematised view, however, shows that even if boys get more attention, girls get attention of higher quality, partly due to prejudiced expectations (Sunderland 2004).

Gender stereotypes also influence students' perception of teachers. Abel and Meltzer (2007) were able to show that students evaluated a text more positively when they thought that a male teacher had written it and this type of differential evaluation has been shown in a number of other studies (Goodwin and Stevens 1996; Centra and Gaubatz 2000). Further, both male and female teachers are more likely to receive better evaluations if they fit gender stereotypes than if they deviate from them (e.g. Basow 1995; Deutschmann et al. 2011).

Social class and language in learning situations has also been a topic of frequent investigation and debate ever since the proposal of the influential *Code Theory* in the early 1970s (Bernstein 1971). Although heavily criticised and accused of being 'filtered through a strong bias against all forms of working-class behaviour' (Labov 1972), Bernstein's work has inspired many studies that have demonstrated that working-class learners are linguistically disadvantaged in education (e.g. Littlejohn 2002; Atherton 2013). The language of education is typically based on the middle-class sociolect. Individuals who do not adhere to the Standard risk being unfairly judged as less intelligent on the basis of their language. According to Littlejohn (2002), this is yet another illustration of how the assumptions of a certain social group are shaped on the basis of their language output. Numerous studies over the past few decades have reported that standard accents are perceived more favourably than non-standard accents and here non-native and ethnic accents, in particular, are disfavoured (Edwards 1999; Lippi Green 1997; Lindemann 2003, 2005; Fuertes et al. 2012).

Such tendencies have also been confirmed in educational contexts. Boyd (2003), for example, was able to demonstrate that non-native speaking teachers in Sweden were ranked low for teacher suitability by a panel of headmasters and pupils on the basis of their accents, although they were highly competent on other linguistic variables such as precision and variation of vocabulary, grammatical correctness and fluency, and had good track records with many years of teaching experience. Accent discrimination has also been widely reported affecting graduate students and instructors at college campuses in the UK and the USA (Bresnahan et al. 2002; Kavas and Kavas 2008), and similar prejudices seem to be operating on the judgement of learners' performance. Collins et al. (2009), for example, were able to show that teachers translated descriptions of academic performance into lower grades when the student was identified as black. Negative stereotyping has also been noted with regard to LGBTQ students (Crumpacker and Vander Haegen 1987). In summary, there is little doubt that linguistic behaviours associated with different social groupings play an important part in how we are judged and in how we perceive others.

CASE DESCRIPTIONS

The four cases described below were conducted in 2011 under the project ASSIS (A Second Step in Second Life), a project funded by Umeå University, with the aim to use the affordances offered by virtual worlds in order to raise gender awareness among language teacher trainees and also to allow students to discuss gender issues in an international context. In the project, we worked in *Second Life* (hereafter SL), a 3D virtual-world environment that is built up by its users who communicate through *avatars* (virtual representations of themselves). When students and teachers are represented by their 3D online aliases, unique opportunities for experimenting with identity open up (Warburton 2009) as participants may choose to be represented by an avatar with, for example, a different race or gender than their usual identification. An added advantage of this method in language teaching is that the anonymity afforded by the environment can reduce anxiety and make quiet students feel more inclined to speak, thereby promoting communication and collaboration (Chester and Gwynne 1998; Hawisher and Selfe 1992). There is also the possibility in SL to alter your voice by changing it to a higher (more female) or lower (more male) pitch – so-called voice-morphing. Combining this with the choice of an appropriate avatar produces a convincing illusion, allowing males, for examples, to act through female avatars. In all of the cases described below, we used the voice-morphing tool that is available in SL in packages consisting of five voices (feminine packages, masculine packages and so on) from 'Voice Island' – a location in SL searchable in the internal search engine. Once purchased, the voice morph can be activated at the click of a button. You then have the option to activate one of the five voice morphs provided in the package (see Figure 8.1 below).[1]

Matched-guise experiment

In our first experiment we explored the matched-guise technique using the possibilities that virtual worlds offer for gender manipulation. The original study (see Lambert et al. 1960) investigated how Canadian listeners' attitudes were affected by the language of the speaker. Four bilinguals would read the same text in both English and French. These recordings were then played to respondents or 'judges', who were asked to evaluate the speakers on personal characteristics. Of course the 'judges' did not know that the same people were speaking in the two languages. The study showed that the person reading was evaluated differently depending on which language was used. Since then the technique has been used and developed in a number of studies investigating different attitudes to language output such as national and regional accents (Giles and Powesland 1975; Young 2003; Cavarallo and Ng 2009). While

Figure 8.1 Voice morph options in package 'Feminine 2'. (Source: The authors.)

comparisons of gender effects on evaluations of different dialects have been studied previously (see Andrews 2003), to the best of our knowledge, no study has explored this technique in virtual worlds and the unique opportunities that they afford the experimenter with regard to gender.

Our experiment was set up in a Master's course at a Swedish university with four female students from Sweden, Iran, South Africa and China. They were recorded in SL reading a short text using their real voices and female avatars. We then used female-to-male voice morphing and male avatars to record the same students reading the same texts as 'males'. Approximately fifty outside 'judges' were asked to evaluate the avatars using a seven-point Likert scale. Essentially following the methodology and trait inventory of Cavallaro and Ng (2009), the traits were 'hardworking', 'intelligent', 'ambitious', 'confident', 'trustworthy', 'considerate', 'kind', 'honest', 'caring', 'likeable' and 'funny'. One obvious difference compared to previous studies was that the 'judges' could see an avatar. Because the appearance of the avatar could affect the evaluation, the students were asked to keep their two avatars as 'neutral' as possible in relation to one another.

Based on the results of Andrews' study (2003) where male voices were evaluated higher than their female counterparts on all traits, our hypothesis was that male avatars would be evaluated higher especially on prestige attributes such as 'intelligence', 'confidence' and 'hardworking'. Our hypothesis was refuted. In fact, the female avatars were evaluated higher on *all* characteristics. However, statistically significant differences were only found (t-test, $p \leq 0.05$) for one avatar and for three characteristics ('confident', 'intelligent' and 'kind'). The most feasible explanation for these results was that the poor and artificial quality of the female-to-male voice morphs influenced the 'judges' leading to higher evaluations of the un-morphed female voices. We find it unlikely that the avatar appearances produced this outcome since most of the avatars, male and female, were of rather neutral appearance.

Students' gender-bending

In the second experiment conducted under the project we gave students the opportunity to gender morph to experience if there was any difference in the way that they were treated in conversations when acting as a different sex. The setting for this second experiment was a Master's course in socio-linguistics where the students were to discuss gender and language matters in a cross-cultural setting with peers from Chile. All participants could choose to gender morph or not, and perhaps because almost all students were female and the female-to-male morphs had proved themselves of poor quality, only one person decided to use this option. Unfortunately, she was far from convincing as the voice sounded artificial, but nevertheless she maintained that the experience was 'extremely liberating' but 'quite psychologically disturbing' since she was taken aback by how differently she was treated and she became unsure how to respond in this new situation.

In retrospect, the main problems with this model are the ethical dilemmas it presents. Firstly, we do not know how students may react when they enter the role of the opposite sex. Some students may find this extremely disturbing (for a number of reasons) and the experience may trigger psychological processes over which we have little control. A second dilemma is the fact that interlocutors may say or do things they would otherwise not if they knew the true identity of the conversational partner. People may, for example, disclose secrets or make flirtatious approaches, all of which can cause considerable embarrassment and place students in difficult positions. With all this in mind, we hesitate to propose this approach and instead recommend more controlled models where the educators themselves take on the gender morphed roles.

Evaluation of teacher assistant(s)

Study design

In the third experiment, we used voice morphing in SL to study if gender stereotypes influenced students' perception of teacher performance. The pedagogic aim was to raise teacher trainee students' awareness of this issue.

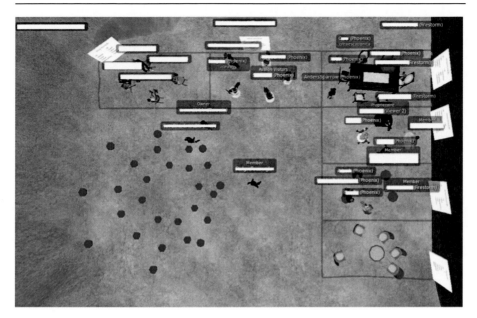

Figure 8.2 Aerial view of sound parcels used for group discussions. Each red rectangle here represents an area that is sound insulated from the rest of the environment. The students could thus sit in smaller groups and converse without being disturbed by others. (Source: The authors.)

The setting was a course in socio-linguistics on the subject of gender attended by thirty-four third-year EFL (English as Foreign Language) teacher trainees. The students were to conduct two case discussions on the topic of gender in the classroom in SL, and would be joined by outside 'expert peers' (active language teachers and researchers). Two workshops with group discussions in SL were designed especially for the study. The workshops took place in SL, and each workshop was held twice, once for student group A (discussion groups A1–A5) and once for student group B (discussion groups B1–B5), this in order to create smaller student groups and thereby enable more teacher–student interaction. Each group was assigned their own 'sound parcel' (see Figure 8.2) or space. The creation of these sound parcels allowed students to talk privately without being disturbed by noise from other groups.

During each workshop various 'expert peers' helped to facilitate the students' group discussions as avatars in SL. The 'expert peers' were primarily teachers and/or researchers active in language teaching in SL, recruited using online networks such as the SLED-list (Second Life in Education). The rationale behind this was that one of our goals was to give the students an opportunity to discuss issues with educators from different cultural backgrounds.

In order to test the students' prejudices about male and female stereotypes,

Figure 8.3 The two teacher assistant avatars, Rory (left) and Rico (right). (Source: The authors.)

one teacher (male) used voice morphing to create two 'fake' avatars, a woman (Rory) and a man (Rico), who served as teacher assistants during the group discussions in SL. The physical appearance of Rory and Rico in SL were kept neutral but obviously female/male. They both wore jeans and shirts, Rory had long red hair and Rico short brown hair (see Figure 8.3). During the study, the students were not aware of the fact that the avatars in fact were the same person but with his voice morphed to a higher (Rory) or lower (Rico) pitch.

In the experiment, Rory and Rico took turns walking around in SL to interact with each of the five student discussion groups (groups A1–A5 and B1–B5) during the two hours the workshops lasted for. After the group discussions the students were asked to evaluate Rory and Rico's performances as teachers in an online questionnaire using Surveymonkey (<http://www.surveymonkey.net>). Here the students were asked to rate Rory and Rico on a scale from one to six (where six represented total agreement with the statement) in relation to nine statements. The statements included Rory and Rico's performances in facilitating discussion, addressing female vs. male students, and listening vs. talking too much themselves (see Table 8.1 for full statements used in the questionnaire). At a final meeting the students were also asked to rate how likeable and intelligent they thought Rory and Rico were. The students' ratings of Rory and Rico in the questionnaire were analysed using a two-tailed t-test.

In order to compare the students' ratings of Rory and Rico with actual performance data, the group discussions were recorded in SL (using the software Screenflow), with the informed consent of the students. The recorded mate-

Table 8.1 The nine statements used in the questionnaire to evaluate Rory and Rico.

1. Overall, Rory/Rico was skilful at her/his job of facilitating the discussion.
2. Rory/Rico addressed male and female avatars equally.
3. Rory/Rico paid more attention to male avatars than female avatars.
4. Rory/Rico paid more attention to female avatars than male avatars.
5. Rory/Rico took over the conversation rather than helping us to engage in discussion.
6. Rory/Rico was good at getting us all to speak without taking too much space herself.
7. Rory/Rico was interested in what I had to say.
8. Rory/Rico had an open mind and listened to all views presented.
9. Rory/Rico had set opinions, which she/he tried to impose on us.

rial was then used to quantify Rory and Rico's performances by counting the number of times that Rory and Rico respectively addressed female or male students (or expert peers), said something to facilitate the students' discussion or 'took over the conversation' by talking about their own opinions or experience. It was also noted whether Rory and Rico spoke to a female or male student or to the discussion group in general. Phrases were considered as 'facilitating discussion' if they directly encouraged a specific student or the student group in general to speak. This category included both questions (e.g. 'What are your thoughts on that?' or 'What statement are you working on?'), and encouraging remarks (e.g. 'That's interesting!' or 'Go on!'). The recordings were also analysed with reference to instances when Rory and Rico 'took over the conversation' and included incidents when Rory or Rico shared examples, experiences or opinions in a relatively lengthy manner that was not directly related to the discussion tasks, even if they were relevant to the discussed topic. Note in this context that the categories in Table 8.1 are broad and there was a real risk for interpretation bias. However, since the same person did all the counting for this study the relative personal bias would be similar for both Rory and Rico.

After the two workshops and the evaluations were completed the design was revealed to the students, that is that Rory and Rico had been one of their teachers using voice morphing, and the group results from the ratings of Rico and Rory were shown. This information was then used as the starting point for a reflective discussion on attitudes, language and gender.

Results

The results of interest here are how the observed conversational performance of Rory and Rico compared with the students' perception of their former performance. In both workshops, Rory and Rico directed proportionally more questions at female students than male students. This difference was marginal for Rory in Workshop 1, however (see Table 8.2). With regards to facilitating the discussions, Rico produced marginally more facilitators than

Table 8.2 Observed conversational behaviour Rory/Rico.

	Workshop 1 (group A+B)				Workshop 2 (group A+B)			
	Female	Male	All	Total	Female	Male	All	Total
No. participants (%)	28 (67%)	14 (33%)		42 (100%)	29 (67%)	14 (33%)		43 (100%)
Utterances directed at males or females (Rory)	33 (72%)	13 (28%)		46 (100%)	21 (84%)	4 (16%)		25 (100%)
Utterances directed at males or females (Rico)	34 (81%)	8 (19%)		42 (100%)	53 (80%)	13 (20%)		66 (100%)
Facilitation directed at males/females/all (Rory)	24 (63%)	4 (11%)	10 (26%)	38 (100%)	12 (36%)	4 (12%)	17 (52%)	33 (100%)
Facilitation directed at males/females/all (Rico)	14 (36%)	11 (28%)	14 (36%)	39 (100%)	18 (43%)	9 (21%)	15 (36%)	42 (100%)
Rory 'took over' (times)			3				0	
Rico 'took over' (times)			6				6	

Rory (39 vs. 38 for Workshop 1 and 42 vs. 33 for Workshop 2). Rory directed a proportionally greater part of her facilitators to female students in Workshop 1, and Rico directed a proportionally greater part of his facilitators to male students in Workshop 1.

In Workshop 2, there was no difference in the proportion of facilitators directed at males and females. Note also that several facilitating remarks were directed at the group as a whole. Finally it should be noted that Rico 'took over the conversation' on more occasions than did Rory (12 vs. 3 times).

There were several inconsistencies between the observed and student-perceived performance of Rory and Rico (see Table 8.3). When reading the results, note that students were asked to rate performance on a scale from 1 to 6, where 6 meant that they strongly agreed with the statement. For full statements see Table 8.1. Average ratings for Rory and Rico were compared using a two-tailed t-test (n.s. = not significant).

The students rated Rico significantly higher than Rory for facilitating discussion (Workshop 2), giving both males and females more attention (Workshop 1) and for making students speak. This result was unexpected as studies show that female teachers are more likely to be rated high for promoting discussion and giving students attention (Bachen et al. 1999). However, data from the sound recordings showed that Rico indeed facilitated discussion more, meaning that the students were not influenced by gender stereotypes in this case. Rory was rated significantly higher than Rico for addressing male and female students equally (Workshop 1), for 'taking over conversation' (Workshop 2) and for 'listening with interest' (Workshop 1). It is well established that teachers tend to address male students more frequently than female students (Sunderland 2000). However, the sound recordings showed that, contrary to this, and to many students' perceptions, Rory and Rico both addressed proportionally more female students. Similarly, contrary to the evaluations, the sound recordings showed that Rico, not Rory, took over conversation more. It is possible that as we expect this kind of behaviour from male but not female teachers this may have affected perceptions.

The final three statements were not directly linked to the sound recording data and as a result lack this controlling factor. Nevertheless, this data contains arguably the most obvious example of gender stereotyping in this study, i.e. that women are better listeners. That Rory was rated higher for being interested in what the students said (Workshop 1) is consistent with previous studies: female teachers are often considered to have a better personal connection with the students (Bachen et al. 2009), are perceived to be better listeners (Centra and Gaubatz 2000) and are considered to give more time and personal attention than their male counterparts (Bennett 1982). In contrast the students thought that Rico 'listened with a more open mind' than did Rory.

Table 8.3 Student ratings of the performance of Rory and Rico.

Statement	Workshop 1 (groups A+B)				Workshop 2 (groups A+B)			
	Students	Average rating		t-test	Students	Average rating		t-test
	n	Rory	Rico	p	n	Rory	Rico	p
1. Good facilitator	27	4.48	4.63	ns	23	4.48	4.78	0.016
2. Addressed males/females equally	25	5.28	4.92	0.001	21	5.10	5.10	ns
3. More attention to males	25	1.40	1.72	0.003	21	1.43	1.38	ns
4. More attention to females	25	1.36	1.72	0.009	21	1.57	1.43	ns
5. Took over the conversation	26	2.23	2.12	ns	20	2.30	2.00	0.030
6. Made students speak	26	3.77	4.15	0.001	20	4.25	4.60	0.015
7. Interested in what I said	25	4.76	4.40	0.004	21	4.76	4.62	ns
8. Listened with open mind	26	4.65	4.65	ns	20	4.75	5.15	0.002
9. Tried to impose his/her views	25	1.68	1.76	ns	20	1.60	1.80	ns

The literature does not list 'open mind' as a male (or female) trait, and we do not know what caused the students to rate Rico higher here. Possibly, to have an open mind is connected with being professional, a trait associated with male teachers according to Sprague and Massoni (2005), but further studies are needed to explore this hypothesis. The statement 'Rory/Rico had set opinions which he/she tried to impose on us' was pretty strong and not compliant with the teacher's teaching style, which explains the low ratings for both Rory and Rico in this statement. In summary, the results from the study are complex but at least partly suggest that the students were influenced by gender stereotypes in their evaluation in that Rory was rated higher for being interested in what the students said, for example.

The main purpose of this experiment, however, was not to evaluate differences in perception per se, but rather to expose them and raise awareness of language and stereotyping issues. After the experiment, the design was revealed during a debriefing, with the aim of using the data as a starting point for discussions on gender stereotypes in the classroom and how these had influenced the students' perceptions. Unfortunately, there were too many distractions during the experiment drawing students' attention from the aim and our students felt that the full intended impact of the experiment as a language-raising activity was not realised. There were several reasons for this: Rory and Rico spent very little time with each group since 'they' had to interact with all groups; the additional variable of an outside discussion partner took much attention; and finally students were focusing on the content since they had to write two graded reports. Many students claimed that they did not get a lasting impression of Rory and Rico, whose presence they experienced as peripheral. We thus conclude that while our results were partly in line with what we had expected, they did not cause the 'aha-effect' we had hoped for. Letting morphed assistants take part during the entire discussion with each group would be a way around this problem.

The lecture model

During the project we were invited by one of our colleagues (Kristy Jauregi at Utrecht University, Holland) to give an online lecture on virtual worlds to her Master's students in Intercultural Communication studying a course on multi-lingualism and mediation. In the course, topics such as culture, identity, stereotypes and the competences of the intercultural speaker and mediator are central. With the aim of demonstrating virtual world identity construction in a practical way, the online lecture, which was formally framed as a talk in SL on virtual worlds by a Swedish lecturer and his two PhD students (see Figure 8.4), was projected to two groups of students (thirty-six in all) in a lecture theatre.

In reality, the lecturer and the PhD students were the same person

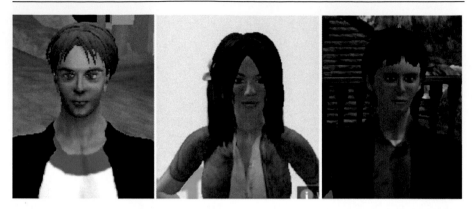

Figure 8.4 The male lecturer character (left) with his female PhD student (middle) and male PhD student (right). (Source: The authors.)

working from two computers using three avatars, with his un-morphed voice representing the lecturer, a female voice-morph representing the female PhD student and a voice-morph which made his voice deeper representing the male PhD student. During the presentation the lecturer introduced the subject of virtual worlds after which he handed over to 'his PhD students' and logged out. In the first trial, they then each gave a twenty-minute talk about virtual world projects. After this, the lecturer returned and asked the students to rate the PhD students on the attributes likeability and intelligence using a six-point Likert scale. The ratings were then immediately calculated and the experimental design was revealed. Students were also asked if they suspected that voice-morphing had been going on as, after all, it was partly the topic of the lecture. This was followed by a discussion of the results and what they revealed about the groups' stereotypical views of males and females.

The first group that was given the lecture strongly suspected that some form of voice morphing was taking place (13/20) and hence these results were discarded. In the second lecture we modified the design so that instead of taking two distinct turns, the 'PhD students' gave the lecture together in a more conversational fashion, sometimes commenting on each other and asking questions. This was made possible by wearing two head-sets simultaneously and alternately muting the microphone on one head-set depending on which avatar was supposedly speaking. In this second group no one suspected that the doctoral students were the same person (the lecturer) and there was a significant difference between how the students evaluated the male and the female PhD avatars. The male was evaluated as slightly more intelligent (approaching significance, $p = 0.07$ using a t-test) while the female was deemed as significantly more likeable ($p = 0.001$ using a t-test).

The most favourable results, however, were the responses to the question of what the students had learnt, posed in the post-event survey:

- 'I learned how easy it was to influence people's thoughts on somebody's identity/personality [. . .]. It creates a whole new look on how we judge people by looks and gender!'
- 'I think it's very interesting how male and female can be so different even though they are the "same" person.'
- 'Yes, I learned that even though I think gender isn't important in the vision you have of a person it plays a big role in your valuation of a person [. . .] in the real world too I guess.'
- 'I think most of us learned that our judgements [. . .] were mostly influenced based on exterior features and voice rather than the information that they gave to us. I think it brought some kind of awareness that you have to look further than only the exterior of a person.'

As an exercise in language awareness-raising this last experiment was actually the most successful and we have used this model to similar effect on several occasions after this initial trial. One of the big advantages is that it is relatively efficient and can be conducted during a double lecture. Secondly, since the students do not have to enter the virtual world themselves, it is less technically challenging to 'administer'. Also, as a result of this, we think that the students can be totally focused on the actual language event, thereby maximising language-awareness and raising impact.

DISCUSSION: LOOKING AHEAD

The main aim of the case studies described above was to create an 'aha' (or revelatory) experience among the students so that they could relate to the theory of language, identity and stereotypical beliefs in a more realistic fashion. As the presentation has shown, this is by no means an easy task. As the project developed, different set-ups were tested and the presentation reflects the chronology of the case studies. Generally speaking, the design of the studies developed from the students being the manipulators ('agents'), to us taking those roles and the students instead ending up at the receiving end of the manipulation ('patients'). Table 8.4 briefly outlines the roles and activities in the four case studies.

The development of the case studies was the result of our analyses of each case study with regard to a number of parameters relevant to the educational frame in which they were set and to prior research. Three aspects turned out to be particularly important:

- time
- ethical issues
- quality of data.

Table 8.4 Roles actions and locations in the four case studies

Case study	Arena for manipulation	'Agent'	Action by 'agent'	'Patient'	Activity for 'patient'	Arena for 'patient'
Match-guise experiments	Second Life	Students	Recording	Anonymous judges	Reacting to recordings	Online
Students' gender-bending	Second Life	Students	Interacting with peers	The students' peers	Group discussions	Second Life
Evaluation of teacher assistants in SL	Second Life	Teacher	Assisting in group discussions	Students	Group discussions	Second Life
The lecture model	Second Life	Teacher	Lecturing	Students	Listening to lecture	In lecture hall, watching screen

From a teaching perspective the time issue cannot be ignored. In our analyses of the case studies, we found that it was far too time-consuming to set up environments for students and give them the necessary guidance to create and manipulate their avatars and voices. The gains were simply too small in relation to the amount of time invested. As previously mentioned, the ethical issues in letting students manipulate their identity should not be taken lightly. The effect of the experience of a different identity on a student is difficult to predict and always beyond the control of the teacher. Nor is it possible to control the effects of peer-to-peer interactions when gender issues are destabilised. For these two reasons alone, students' gender manipulation was decided against.

Another aspect of the case studies that turned out to be problematic was the quality of the data. In the two studies where we relied on students' performances, these were simply too inconsistent to generate reliable data. Either the technology itself (voice-morphing) was not reliable, or, as in the second case, the students' use of the technology was rather awkward. Thus, although it appeared to be a good idea to let students subjectively experience stereotypical expectations in different roles, the harsh reality was that this kind of manipulation is difficult to achieve with good quality.

In moving the agency of the manipulation to the teacher and making the students the recipients of the treatment – 'patients' as it were – we hoped to have solved the problems we experienced and to have created a more effective and efficient set-up. Indeed, there are some interesting patterns in the data shown above. However, when evaluating and analysing the data from the design and the students' answers from the debriefing session, we still found that the environment itself created too much of a distraction in the case study where the teaching assistants acted as facilitators in group discussions in SL. As some students were hardly aware of the impact of the assistants, their evaluation of the assistants did not have the desired effect in terms of how they related to the revelation of the manipulation. In short, the debriefing session did not generate the intensity and impact we had hoped for.

In our final case study, we therefore created a scenario in which the students were outside the SL environment and could devote their full attention to the assistants. Such a design guarantees much more control and provides data with limited or no interference from other aspects. Accordingly, this case study gave us a model with the control and focus required to generate stable data. Further, the model demonstrated the value of, immediately after the presentations, recording students' impressions and then following them up in a debriefing session. The easily retrieved quantitative data generated qualitative data in the ensuing discussions. Moreover, the students experienced this simple exercise as rewarding and enlightening. To sum up our experiences so far, we can say that although the technology invites all sorts of interesting ideas for awareness-raising activities, complex and slightly dirty data may be the result, so there is a good case for keeping it simple – less does indeed seem to be more.

Looking forward, we ask ourselves whether it would not be possible to explore the potential inherent in the Digital Humanities and virtual experiences in such a fashion that we could raise people's awareness of stereotypes in a more fundamental way. In a new project, *Raising Awareness through Virtual Experiencing* (RAVE), funded by the Swedish Research Council, we aim to do exactly that by building on the experiences from the case studies and creating a model that goes beyond the momentary 'aha' experience. Thus we hope to achieve a more pronounced change in our students' awareness of the intricate interaction between social categories, linguistic markers and stereotypical assumptions.

In order to monitor and analyse the long-term effects of awareness-raising activities, a rigorous design is necessary in which independent tests generate data so that we can follow the development of the subjects after the 'treatment'. This is a new step. Previous studies involving match-guise experiments (Giles and Powesland 1975; Young 2003; Cavarallo and Ng 2009; our own reported above) have had a descriptive approach and recorded people's beliefs linked to the specific event with different representations. Because it was not part of the aims of these studies to follow the subjects' development, no calibration was used that was linked to an independent test.

The design of the RAVE project includes three independent testing points (pre-test, post-test and delayed post-test), two 'treatments' and two debriefings, of which the second has an extended format and takes place sometime after the 'treatments' in order to allow for higher-level and more mature reflections (Watson and Williams 2004). In recording the debriefing sessions and interviewing participants, the ambition of the project is to assemble qualitative data which will give insights into students' reasoning around theory and reality with regard to stereotypical beliefs linked to language use, and how such reasoning can be changed. Thus the total data comprises both quantitative and qualitative data which make possible a detailed analysis and comparisons of how awareness-raising activities affect students over time. The ambition is of course that such knowledge, in turn, can help develop procedures for the training of teachers and other professionals working regularly with human contacts so that factual knowledge develops into internalised knowledge – theory could become practice.

NOTE

1. For an example of what this may sound like see <http://www.youtube.com/watch?v=tyXlT3cNHRk> (last accessed 30 August 2015).

REFERENCES

Abel, M. H. and Meltzer, A. L. (2007) 'Student ratings of a male and female professors' lecture on sex discrimination in the workforce', *Sex Roles*, 57: 3–4, 173–80.

Abrams, D. and Rutland, A. (2008) 'The development of subjective group dynamics', in M. Killen and Levy, S. R. (eds), *Intergroup Attitudes and Relations in Childhood Through Adulthood*. New York and Oxford: Oxford University Press, pp. 47–65.

Andrews, D. R. (2003) 'Gender effects in a Russian and American matched-guise study: a sociolinguistic comparison', *Russian Linguistics*, 27 (3): 287–311.

Atherton, J. S. (2013) 'Doceo; Language Codes' [online UK], available at <http://www.doceo.co.uk/background/language_codes.htm> (last accessed 16 April 2015).

Bachen, C. M., McLoughlin, M. M. and S. S. Garcia (1999) 'Assessing the role of gender in college students' evaluations of faculty', *Communication Education*, 48 (3): 193–210.

Basow, S. A. (1995) 'Student evaluations of college professors: when gender matters', *Journal of Educational Psychology*, 87 (4): 656–65.

Bennett, S. K. (1982) 'Student perceptions of and expectations for male and female instructors: evidence relating to the question of gender bias in teaching evaluation', *Journal of Educational Psychology*, 74 (2): 170–9.

Bernstein, B. (1971) *Class, Codes and Control*, Vol.1. London: Routledge & Kegan Paul.

Bojarska, K. (2013) 'Responding to lexical stimuli with gender associations: a cognitive–cultural model', *Journal of Language and Social Psychology*, 32 (1): 46–61.

Boyd, S. (2003) 'Foreign-born teachers in the multilingual classroom in Sweden: the role of attitudes to foreign accent', *International Journal of Bilingual Education and Bilingualism*, 6: 283–95.

Bresnahan, M. J., Ohashi, R., Nebashi, R. et al. (2002) 'Attitudinal and affective response toward accented English', *Language and Communication*, 22 (2): 171–85.

Cavallaro, F. and Ng, B. C. (2009) 'Between status and solidarity in Singapore', *World Englishes*, 28 (2): 143–59.

Centra, J. A. and Gaubatz, N. B. (2000) 'Is there gender bias in student evaluations of teaching?', *Journal of Higher Education*, 71 (1): 17–33.

Chen, E. S. L. and Rao, N. (2011) 'Gender socialization in Chinese kindergartens: teachers' contributions', *Sex Roles*, 64 (1–2): 103–16.

Chester, A. and Gwynne, G. (1998) 'Online teaching: encouraging collaboration through anonymity', *Journal of Computer Mediated Communication*, 4 (2): n.p. [online].

Collins, E. C., Biernat, M. and Eidelman, S. (2009) 'Stereotypes in the communication and translation of person impressions', *Journal of Experimental Social Psychology*, 45 (2): 368–74.

Collins, K. A. and Clement, R. (2012) 'Language and prejudice: direct and moderated effects', *Journal of Language and Social Psychology*, 31 (4): 376–96.

Crawford, M. (1995) *Talking Difference: On Gender and Language*. London: Sage.

Crumpacker, L. and Vander Haegen, E. (1987) 'Pedagogy and prejudice: strategies for confronting homophobia in the classroom', *Women's Studies Quarterly*, 15 (3–4): 65–73.

Deutschmann, M., Steinvall, A. and Lagerström, A. (2011) 'Gender-bending in virtual space: using voice-morphing in second life to raise sociolinguistic gender awareness', in S. Czepielewski (ed.), *Learning a Language in Virtual Worlds: A Review of Innovation and ICT In Language Teaching Methodology*. Warsaw: Warsaw Academy of Computer Science, Management and Administration, International Conference, Warsaw, 17 November, pp. 54–61.

Edlund, A., Erson, E. and Milles, K. (2007) *Språk och kön* [*Language and Gender*]. Falun, Sweden: Norstedts Akademiska Förlag.

Edwards, J. (1999) 'Refining our understanding of language attitudes', *Journal of Language and Social Psychology*, 18 (1): 101–10.

Fuertes, J. N., Gottdiener, W. H., Martin, H., Gilbert, T. C. and H. Giles (2012) 'A meta-analysis of the effects of speaker's accents on interpersonal evaluations', *European Journal of Social Psychology*, 42 (1): 120–33.

Giles, H. and Powesland, P. F. (1975) *Speech Style and Social Evaluation*. London: Academic Press.

Goodwin, L. D. and Stevens, E. A. (1993) 'The influence of gender on university faculty members' perceptions of "good" teaching', *Journal of Higher Education*, 64 (2): 166–85.

Gutierrez y Muhs, G., Niemann, Y. F., Gonzalez, C. G. and Harris, A. P. (eds) (2012) *Presumed Incompetent: The Intersections of Race and Class for Women in Academia*. Boulder: Utah State University Press.

Hawisher, G. E. and Selfe, C. L. (1992) 'Voices in college classrooms: the dynamics of electronic discussion', *Quarterly of the National Writing Project and the Center for the Study of Writing and Literacy*, 14 (3): 24–8.

Kavas, A. and Kavas, A. (2008) 'An exploratory study of undergraduate college students' perceptions and attitudes toward foreign accented faculty', *College Student Journal*, 42 (3): 879–90.

Killen, M. and Levy, S. R. (eds) (2008) *Intergroup Attitudes and Relations in Childhood Through Adulthood*. New York: Oxford University Press.

Labov, W. (1972) 'Academic ignorance and black intelligence', *Atlantic Monthly* (digital edition), available at <http://www.theatlantic.com/past/docs/issues/95sep/ets/labo.htm> (last accessed 17 September 2013).

Lambert, W. E., Hodgson, R. C., Gardner, R. C. and Fillenbaum, S. (1960) 'Evaluational reactions to spoken language', *Journal of Abnormal and Social Psychology*, 60 (1): 44–51.

Lindemann, S. (2003) 'Koreans, Chinese or Indians? Attitudes and ideologies about non-native English speakers in the United States', *Journal of Sociolinguistics*, 7 (3): 348–64.

Lindemann, S. (2005) 'Who speaks "broken English"? US undergraduates' perception of non-native English', *International Journal of Applied Linguistics*, 15 (2): 187–212.

Lippi-Green, R. (1997) *English with Accents: Language, Ideology, and Discrimination in the United States*. New York: Routledge.

Littlejohn, S. (2002) *Theories of Human Communication*. Albuquerque: Wadsworth.

Rakić, T., Steffens, M. C. and Mummendey, A. (2011) 'Blinded by the accent! The minor role of looks in ethnic categorization', *Journal of Personality and Social Psychology*, 100 (1): 16–29.

Sherman, J. W., Stroessner, S. J., Conrey, F. R. and Azam, O. A. (2005) 'Prejudice and stereotype maintenance processes: attention, attribution, and individuation', *Journal of Personality and Social Psychology*, 89 (4): 607–22.

Slaughter-Defoe, D. T. (2012) *Racial Stereotyping and Child Development*. Basel: Karger.

Sprague, J. and Massoni, K. (2005) 'Student evaluations and gendered expectations: what we can't count can hurt us', *Sex Roles*, 53 (11–12): 779–93.

Sunderland, J. (2000) 'New understandings of gender and language classroom research: texts, teacher talk and student talk', *Language Teaching Research*, 4 (2): 149–73.

Sunderland, J. (2004) *Gendered Discourses*. London: Palgrave Macmillan.

Talbot, M. (2003) 'Gender stereotypes: reproduction and challenge', in J. Holmes and M. Meyerhoff (eds), *The Handbook of Language and Gender*. Oxford: Blackwell, pp. 468–86.

Universitets- och högskolerådet (2011) *Higher Education Ordinance – Högskoleförordningen in translation, Annex 2*, at <http://www.uhr.se/sv/Information-in-English/Laws-and-regulations/The-Higher-Education-Ordinance/Annex-2/> (last accessed 25 September 2013).

Warburton, S. (2009) 'Second life in higher education: assessing the potential for and the barriers to deploying virtual worlds in learning and teaching', *British Journal of Educational Technology*, 40 (3): 414–26.

Watson, A. and Williams, M. (2004) 'Post-lesson debriefing: delayed or immediate? An investigation of student teacher talk', *Journal of Education for Teaching: International Research and Pedagogy*, 30 (2): 85–96.

Young, C. E. (2003) 'College students' reactions to accents of L2 learners of Spanish and English', in L. Sayahi (ed.), *Selected Proceedings of the First Workshop on Spanish Sociolinguistics*, pp. 107–111, available at <http://www.lingref.com/cpp/wss/1/paper1013.pdf> (last accessed 17 April 2015).

CHAPTER 9

A World of Possibilities: Digitisation and the Humanities

Marilyn Deegan

Tanner et al.'s chapter at the beginning of this volume established the benefits of creating digital versions of primary and secondary sources for the arts and humanities, and the many choices that need to be made when embarking on such endeavours. This chapter will examine a range of Digital Humanities projects that have digitised sources in different media, or are planning to do so, and have worked with these choices and opportunities to create rich, sustainable scholarly products that greatly enhance arts and humanities scholarship and teaching, and have usefulness and impact way beyond the academy. Most of the projects discussed here do much more than digitise existing resources, however, demonstrating what can be done with digital sources once they have been captured to a high quality, using robust standards and methods, and also what can be done to sustain and make available these materials for the long term.

OLD BAILEY ONLINE

The Old Bailey Online[1] was launched in 2003, and has been used extensively in research and teaching in academic environments, but there is also a huge range of non-academic users who use the site for anything from historical research to family history, personal learning and leisure. Old Bailey Online makes available a fully searchable, digitised collection of all surviving editions of the Old Bailey Proceedings from 1674 to 1913, and of the Ordinary of Newgate's Accounts between 1676 and 1772. It gives access to over 197,000 trials and the biographical details of approximately 2,500 men and women executed at Tyburn, free of charge for non-commercial use.

The project was initiated by Professors Tim Hitchcock, then at the

University of Hertfordshire and now at the University of Sussex, and Robert Shoemaker at the University of Sheffield. Professor Clive Emsley of the Open University joined the project at its second stage. Hitchcock and Shoemaker defined the project as 'history from below': a source of information about everyday people from the period (Hitchcock and Shoemaker 2006). This is in fact the largest body of texts detailing the lives of non-elite people ever published. The project digitised over 400,000 pages of the Old Bailey proceedings from microfilm and then accurately transcribed and tagged 127 million words of text of 197,745 pre-1834 trial records. Old Bailey Online is still the largest body of freely accessible, accurately transcribed and tagged historical text currently available.

The project leaders realised right from the start that raw, uncorrected text searching of the resource would be inadequate for their key research goals and so they devised an XML mark-up schema with defined tags that categorised the crimes and punishments of the period. The result was a series of tags and naming conventions, of which over ninety are unique to the project. A team of historians based at the Humanities Research Institute (HRI) at the University of Sheffield manually tagged most of the 1674 to 1835 text that had been transcribed from microfilm images. Later text was first run through an automated mark-up process by the HRI and then the results were validated, enhanced and checked manually by a team at the University of Hertfordshire.

The resultant resource is both a detailed and accurate text corpus (rekeyed and quality checked, with an accuracy rate of over 99 per cent) and a database that allows fine-grained analysis of the content in order to generate reports and graphs of information in response to detailed search queries. Having made these early decisions to create accurate text meant that the uses of the resource could grow and change over time, and be accessed by audiences that the project team had not initially envisaged. It has been of particular interest in genealogy. Family historians from global transportation locations such as the USA and Australia are able to search the Old Bailey to find ancestors, discover their demographics, acquire details of their trials and, importantly, find their parish of origin. Researchers can then interrogate digitised parish registers and follow the trail of the family's history without having to travel thousands of miles to view the materials in person. The site has received over 15 million visits since its launch in 2003. Site usage has since levelled off at around 12,000 page impressions per day.

The Old Bailey Online project established a robust and sustainable methodology: the project team already had a great deal of experience in digital projects and they used well understood methods of rekeying and encoding, according to international standards, to deliver excellent data that has already stood the test of time. These methods have been applied successfully in a number of related projects, for instance: London Lives 1690–1800: Crime, Poverty and Social

Policy in the Metropolis;[2] Connected Histories: British History Sources, 1500–1900,[3] which brings together a range of digital resources related to early-modern and nineteenth-century Britain within a single federated search; the Old Bailey Corpus,[4] a balanced subset of the Proceedings with socio-linguistic annotation of every utterance based on speaker data found in the context of the trials (407 Proceedings, *c*.318,000 utterances, *c*.14 million spoken words, *c*.750,000 spoken words/decade), produced by the University of Giessen. This is a particularly interesting development, which shows that a corpus produced by and for one academic discipline (history) can be repurposed for use in another discipline (linguistics). This is only possible given the choices made originally in terms of encoding, standards and meticulous accuracy.

The impact of this project outside academia has been profound: Old Bailey Online material formed the basis of BBC1's hugely successful series *Garrow's Law*, which ran for three series between 2009 and 2011 and won the Royal Television Society Award for best drama. It is listed as a key genealogical resource by many archives, for example in the Newcastle Local Studies Genealogy Guide.[5]

Old Bailey Online is a good example of how the choices made at the outset can not only deliver a world-class resource, but can create data that has a life beyond the original project and a methodology that can be used by other projects. The project leaders took time to ascertain not only how to extract the information that they need from the materials but also to make the data as useful as possible for users with a wide variety of research requirements. It is always important in digital projects to ensure that data is created according to well-supported international standards such as those promoted by the TEI. Data that is created only with local and immediate uses in mind has a limited life. Data that is created in a more open way can be reused for purposes never envisaged by the original creators. By keeping the data open and freely available they were able to facilitate a series of additional projects that could use the data in new ways and make the content available to the broadest possible audience.

CHOPIN'S FIRST EDITIONS ONLINE AND JANE AUSTEN'S FICTION MANUSCRIPTS

The Chopin's First Editions Online (CFEO) project[6] had its origins in the *Annotated Catalogue of Chopin's First Editions* by Christophe Grabowski and John Rink, published (in print) by Cambridge University Press in 2010. The *Catalogue* was the result of almost ten years' research by the authors.

More than fifty institutions hold first editions and impressions of Chopin's works: 4,700 copies, which represent around 1,200 distinct impressions.

Given that it was produced in print, only a little more than 200 images are reproduced in the *Catalogue*. The history of Chopin's first editions is highly complex: copyright problems in Europe in the early nineteenth century forced the composer to use different publishers in France, Germany and England, meaning that there are three 'first editions' of most pieces. This is further complicated by the fact that between each 'edition' Chopin made further revisions and changes, meaning that these versions differ. Between 2004 and 2007, funded by the Arts and Humanities Research Board (AHRB, now the AHRC), CFEO created a freely accessible archive of 5,500 pages of the first editions, drawn from the main holding institutions: the Bibliothèque Nationale de France; the Bodleian Library; the British Library; the Narodowy Instytut Fryderyka Chopina; the University of Chicago Library; the Österreichische Nationalbibliothek; and the New York Public Library. These supplied 5,000 of the images, the other 500 came from fifteen other libraries around the world. The project was directed by Professor John Rink, then of Royal Holloway, University of London, now University of Cambridge, and the technical developments were carried out by the Department of Digital Humanities, King's College London. The project used high-quality digital imaging for the image capture; this had to be monitored carefully to maintain consistency across the images obtained from different institutions. Complex metadata schemata and tools were developed using Text Encoding Initiative-defined XML and other international metadata standards to facilitate online display, manipulation and searching. The technical team also devised an image-display system to allow musicians and musicologists to search and browse images of different sizes; to move easily between and compare multiple editions of a piece; and to retrieve analytical materials in appropriate contexts. Information derived from the *Catalogue* was adapted and expanded, and linked to the images. The virtual unification of this complex corpus has, for the first time, assembled an important body of primary sources, facilitating philological and style-historical investigation, and encouraging new understanding of Chopin's compositional and publication histories. This is a boon to musicians, performers, scholars of Chopin and students, and it offers a model for other complex musical corpora.

The Jane Austen's Fiction Manuscripts Digital Edition[7] (edited by Professor Kathryn Sutherland of Oxford University) is another virtual reunification project: it gathers together in one place 1,100 pages of Austen's manuscript writings for the first time since 1845, when at her sister Cassandra's death they were dispersed among family members, with a second major dispersal, to public institutions and private collections, in the 1920s. These manuscripts are among the first substantial collections of a British novelist's creative writings to survive in the author's own hand. They represent every stage of Austen's writing life, from childhood (aged 11 or 12) to the year of her death (aged 41). The physical manuscripts are held by the British Library, the Bodleian

Library, the Morgan Library New York and King's College Cambridge. At the time of digitisation, one part of the manuscript of *The Watsons* was in private hands and on deposit at Queen Mary, University of London, but this was subsequently purchased by the Bodleian Library.

As with CFEO, high-quality digital imaging was used, and again quality was carefully monitored to ensure consistency between the copies obtained from the different sources. In the case of the Austen project, for the first time complete descriptions of, transcriptions of, analysis of and commentary on the manuscripts in the archive were provided, including details of erasures, handwriting, paper quality, watermarks, ink, binding structures and any ancillary materials held with the holographs as aspects of their physical integrity or provenance. Full diplomatic transcriptions of all texts were produced and marked up using an XML schema developed at the Centre for Computing in the Humanities, King's College London. Austen's handwriting and punctuation are agreed to be of great importance in the understanding of her work but have hitherto been little studied. The mark-up scheme has recorded orthographic variants and punctuation symbols in minute detail for subsequent computational analysis.

Complex structural metadata for each work has been added using the METS standard within the TEI header. Austen prepared many of her writing surfaces with special care, regularly assembling small booklets by cutting and folding large sheets of paper in a particular manner. Structural metadata allows for the online reconstruction and deconstruction of these material surfaces which instantiate in miniature, booklet by home-made booklet, Austen's sense as she wrote of the emerging novel.

The transcription and mark-up proved to be highly challenging. Modern manuscript sources had not previously been studied extensively, so the project developed the Document Type Definition (DTD) in the course of working on the transcriptions. A great deal of research had been done previously in TEI on earlier manuscript sources, but manuscripts from the pre-print era are very different from the working manuscripts of modern authors with their erasures, overwritings, scribbles, etc. Modern working manuscripts have a temporal dimension not generally present in those from before the print era, as they contain within them erasures, additions, glosses, etc. In Austen's time, paper was expensive, so early drafts were not discarded, all the work took place over time on the same manuscript. Austen even pinned patches to manuscripts in order to add text (see, for example, the Bodleian Library manuscript of *The Watsons*, MS. Eng. e. 3764).[8] Representing the evidence of the temporal genesis of the manuscripts in mark-up requires new ways of thinking about both the manuscripts and the mark-up. A highly complex model was established by the project team to handle the various interlocking features, including such elements as document features, topography, handwriting, orthography and genetic markers. The developments in the encoding of the Austen materials have informed some of the thinking of the TEI's Special Interest Group on Manuscripts which has established a sub-group on Documents and Genetic Criticism to address such complex issues[9] (Sutherland and Pierazzo 2012).

CFEO began as a development from a print resource. Jane Austen's Fiction Manuscripts was conceived of as a hybrid edition right from the start, with a major print edition being published by Oxford University Press. The online version is, according to Professor Sutherland, a textual laboratory, while the print edition is an authoritative, stable reference source. As she also points out:

> Print and digital editions realise different solutions to the presentation and interpretation of transcribed manuscript text. Unlike print, digital editions are fundamentally dynamic, allowing text to be displayed from multiple perspectives. This is a particular issue in interpreting evidence from revision, where rewriting regularly transgresses the orderly zones of finished copy, spilling into margins, interlinear spaces, and supplementary leaves. In the digital medium, erased sections, words, or letters can be encoded to reappear when the cursor is passed over them. In print, explanatory annotation offers a clearer solution and adds value, as better suited for continuous and reflective reading. A full textual apparatus recording all revisions, erasures, and changes in the text is therefore being prepared for print as a stable record of features of the dynamic digital edition. (Sutherland 2015, personal communication)

The print edition is in production with Oxford University Press in 2015, where reproducing the layout of the digital edition is proving challenging.

The digital edition has benefited academics all over the world, such as Michelle Levy, an English professor at Simon Fraser University in Canada, who uses the manuscripts with her students. 'They provide a window into the very different writing she produced within and for her domestic circle,' wrote Professor Levy to Kathryn Sutherland. 'This greatly expands our understanding of Austen, and of literary culture in the period generally, which was not all print-based. The edition truly revolutionises the teaching of Austen.'[10] Outside of academe, the author Ali Smith credits the Edition as one of her sources in her work of fiction *Artful* (Smith 2012).

NEWSPAPER DIGITISATION

Newspaper publication has been transformed in the last fifteen or so years, with fewer and fewer readers opting for printed papers and choosing instead to access various news forms online and on personal mobile devices. There is no less of a hunger for news, just a greater array of sources, many of them free, though increasingly digital versions of newspapers are charging for access. Print newspapers are in decline, as are their advertising revenues, and publishers are looking to create new revenue streams. Alongside the massive move online of current news publications, various organisations have been digitising runs of historic papers, right back to the first issue, with the publishers themselves engaging in this on a large scale, hoping to recapture some of their declining income by charging for access to their archives.

Historic newspapers engage a broad audience. No other medium records every aspect of human life over the last 300 years on a daily basis, and newspapers are one of the most important historical sources. They are, however, difficult to manage because of their material fragility, size, variety and volume.

Concerned for the preservation of the national record, major libraries – the Library of Congress and the British Library, for example – have been microfilming newspapers for many decades as well as, or instead of, preserving the print objects. However, microfilm is generally recognised to be a better preservation than access tool, especially when most newspapers are minimally indexed. It is possible to recover information from newspapers in collections of clippings on specific topics; agencies provide this service to government, large companies and other organisations. But extracting content from the text of newspapers without presenting all the supporting linguistic and bibliographic or material information around it – adjacent content, details of layout and typographical arrangement – is an impoverishing exercise. Furthermore, there is serious concern about even the preservation status of microfilm: some of the earliest, from the 1950s and 1960s, is already relatively degraded.

There are a number of reasons for the current range of activity in newspaper digitisation. Scanning of microfilms and large-format originals has become ever cheaper; optical character recognition techniques have improved for degraded content; automated techniques for zoning areas of newspapers and recognising types of content have become more common; search engines that can handle imperfect text have improved, driven by projects like Google Books; increasing bandwidth and better screen technology make for a better reading experience. Probably the most significant reason, however, is the huge market for such content. In the past, dedicated historians (professional and amateur) spent hours, days, weeks turning newspaper pages or scrolling microfilm or fiche in libraries, with the only metadata available being a newspaper title and date of publication. As mentioned above, clippings services could supply content too, but this was usually only on the basis of stories of historical importance or widespread public interest. Making available page images, segmented clippings, and full text for searching gives users the opportunity to find things instantly and to search topics across a range of sources of the same time period, or to examine topics diachronically and see how views and perspectives change over time. Other parts of newspapers come into prominence too: advertisements, announcements, pictures can all now be searched and give an interesting picture of cultural change. For example, a search in cigarette advertisements between 1914 and 1918 in Welsh Newspapers Online gives a very different picture of attitudes to smoking: 'Every man in the firing line is a man you would be proud to hand your cigarette case to', proclaims the *North Wales Chronicle* in August 1915, which goes on to offer to 'send a parcel of smokes from you in your name' to men in the trenches.[11]

The Old Bailey Online and the Jane Austen Edition rekeyed the texts to a very high degree of accuracy: this was possible as the corpora are (relatively speaking compared to newspapers) small and finite, and it was necessary for the kind of scholarly critical edition being produced, where each word or punctuation mark could be of significance. However, in the case of the Jane Austen Edition for example, transcribing 1,100 pages took a considerable amount of time. This level of meticulous accuracy is impossible with newspapers, and probably unnecessary for most uses by most users. Technology generally used for producing searchable text for newspapers is uncorrected Optical Character Recognition (OCR), which, even for originals that are relatively compromised, provides good enough search retrieval. Most library newspaper digitisation projects have concentrated on capturing content from before 1922 for legal and copyright reasons. Publishers scanning their own content have of course been able to bring their digital archives up to date, given that they own the rights to the materials.

Simon Tanner and colleagues carried out an analysis of the accuracy of the OCR in the British Library's 19th Century Newspapers Database (Tanner et al. 2009; see also Holley 2009) and found an accuracy level of around 80 per cent. Rekeying is normally expected to give an accuracy of 99.999 per cent: that is a tolerance of one wrong character in ten thousand. The cost of uncorrected OCR is low, the cost of rekeying at the scale needed for newspapers would be unmanageable. And for most purposes, given that search engines have been developed to handle imperfect data and still return acceptable results, 80 per cent is acceptable. As Tanner et al. point out:

> What this means to the end user experience is clear – the lower the
> significant word accuracy, the lower the likely search result accuracy or
> volume of search result returns. Our experience suggests that should
> the word accuracy be greater than 80%, then most fuzzy search engines
> will be able to sufficiently fill in the gaps or find related words such
> that a high search accuracy (>95–98%) would still be possible from
> newspaper content because of repeated significant words. (Tanner et al.
> 2009)

It is always important when using a digitised resource for scholarship to know what choices were made and what the limits of the resource are as a result of those choices. Coming to a digitised resource expecting 99.999 per cent and finding 80 per cent accuracy will result in disappointment; knowing that you have 80 per cent accurate underlying text and knowing how to maximise retrieval despite that limitation will give results that are acceptable. For instance, in a newspaper article of any length, significant words will be repeated more than once. So an article about Churchill may miss four out of ten instances of the name, but will still find the article. As with any digital content, it is vital always to remember that not everything you might want is going to be there – not even the world's greatest libraries can offer that. But if the advanced search features on offer in online newspapers are employed to good effect, excellent results can be obtained. There are now many newspaper digitisation projects all around the world, and millions upon millions of pages of content are available. ICON, the International Coalition on Newspapers,[12] lists almost 200 projects in the US alone, and well over 200 in the rest of the world.

Publishers themselves make available entire archives of their own titles; major libraries offer a whole range of titles ranging from national dailies to local weeklies to specialist titles. Aggregators offer cross-searching of different titles. Newspaperarchive.com, which claims to be the world's largest newspaper archive, has more than two billion searchable articles across more than 400 years of papers from all US states and twenty-two other countries. Their content is aimed firmly at the genealogy market. The British Newspaper Archive,[13] a partnership between the British Library and findmypast, a UK-based online genealogy company,[14] to digitise up to 40 million newspaper pages from the British Library's collection over ten years, has currently more than 11 million pages online from 460 titles. It too is aimed at the genealogy market, as well as research and teaching. Welsh Newspapers Online,[15] an initiative of the National Library of Wales, makes available 1,100,000 pages from nearly 120 newspaper publications up to around 1910. Newspaperarchive and British Newspapers Online charge for services; Welsh Newspapers Online is free.

The National Library of Australia was an early pioneer in the digitisation of periodical content, and currently there are almost 1,000 titles created by the Australian Newspapers Digitisation Program, available on the Trove website.[16] As of 5 August 2015 there are 17,995,679 pages consisting of 177,358,665 articles available to search. This was the first newspaper project to use crowdsourcing to correct the OCR, and to date 168,120,011 lines of print have been corrected. Other newspaper projects have followed suit, and some use crowdsourced effort to transcribe complete articles. For instance, the University of Louisville in the US has digitised the *Louisville Leader*, an African American community newspaper which began publication in Louisville, Kentucky in 1917.[17] Anyone can go to their website and transcribe an article; no registration or passwords are needed. They have captured 14,678 articles to date – small by Australian standards but still a useful amount of data.

Europeana,[18] a multi-lingual online collection of millions of digitised items from European museums, libraries, archives and multimedia collections, and the European Library have been running a project from 2012 to 2015 to aggregate newspapers from across Europe (currently titles from ten European countries are included) in the Europeana Historic Newspapers Collection.[19] Some 18 million pages have been made available, with 10 million pages searchable via uncorrected OCR. Some of the titles (for example, those from the National Library of Wales) are not available on the Europeana site, but they can be cross-searched, with the user then directed to the National Library of Wales to view page images. This kind of access provision gives a new dimension to historical research, given that events, individuals and occasions can be seen from very different perspectives. Language is of course an issue.

The Library of Congress Chronicling America programme in the US is developing a searchable database of US newspapers available online with descriptive information and select digitisation of historic pages. The timeframe is 1836 to 1922, and page images and searchable text are available for 1,841 titles. Also searchable via Chronicling America is the U.S. Newspaper Directory, 1690–Present which has metadata for 153,029 titles.[20]

DIGITAL SUDAN

So far, this chapter has considered the content being digitised and the choices made for individual projects and institutions. I want to move now to a much larger and more varied endeavour, creating digitisation plans and projects for the preservation and access of the cultural heritage of a whole nation: Sudan.

Sudan is a country rich in artefacts that go back millennia: archaeological remains, art, manuscripts that date back to the beginning of Islam, books, archival documents, documentary film, hundreds of thousands of hours of sound recordings, video, television and radio, millions of photographs. The National Archives alone hold 12 million photographic negatives. This rich heritage is at risk, from the heat, dust and humidity, from the obsolescence of the media – the documentary film in the film archive, for instance, can only be accessed on ancient and deteriorating equipment, for which no spare parts for repair can be found – and, of course, at risk from human agency in a country that is plagued with strife. These materials record the history and the culture of the country that are fast disappearing in the modern world. If these artefacts themselves are lost, so too would be the knowledge of a way of life: much of the material records traditional song, music, dance, children's games, knowledge of plant life and traditional foods, dialects, oral literature. For example, the Sudanese Folk Life Documentation Centre, started in 1972, aims to document all aspects of the life of the Sudanese people in video and sound recordings. Some of the recordings are more than forty years old and are in urgent need of attention. The Folklore Archive at the University of Khartoum holds mostly sound and film. There are more than 5,000 sound tapes (cassette and reel-to-reel), and there around 2,000 films on video and DVD. Around 4,000 tapes of different formats have already been digitised and metadata is being added. This is a protracted task as it is necessary to listen to the tapes to find out what they are about. The materials cover music, folklore, religion and history from different parts of Sudan. There is film of dance, materials from Nubia, the Hawasama tribes, the Halfa from northern Sudan, the Sufis. There are also materials captured in natural contexts, for instance songs of coffee where coffee grinding instruments are used to make music.

The aim of Digital Sudan is to transform Sudanese intellectual content into modern digital media which will be safer to preserve and easier to retrieve, and will ensure the survival of the cultural memory of the country. Digital Sudan is also intended to show a different picture of Sudan to the world: not just a country of strife and death, but one that is forward-looking, a knowledge economy. There have been a number of projects digitising Sudanese cultural content in the last few years, in particular at the University of Durham. The Sudan Archive in Durham, established in the 1950s at the end of the British mandate in the country when the country became independent, has substantial holdings of Sudanese materials. The archive was originally set up to preserve the papers of administrators from the Sudan Political Service, missionaries, soldiers, business men, doctors, agriculturalists, teachers and others who had served or lived in the Sudan during the Anglo–Egyptian period (1898–1955). It has continued to collect materials and now has holdings that reach to the present day. In addition to official and personal papers, collections also include a variety of records in other formats such as photographic images (prints, lantern slides and 35mm slides), cinefilms from the 1920s to the 1960s, sound recordings, maps, museum objects and a large amount of related printed material. Durham has digitised a substantial part of its rare printed materials and makes this freely available online: digitised materials include intelligence reports, annual reports of the governors-general, staff lists, government gazettes, some Arabic materials, maps and films. Unfortunately, some of the visual and photographic materials can only be consulted on-site in Durham because of copyright restrictions.[21]

The goal for a country-wide digitisation effort in cultural heritage was first mooted by the Sudanese Association for Archiving Knowledge (SUDAAK), a Khartoum-based NGO. Together with the National Library, SUDAAK established, in 2013, the National Cultural Heritage Digitisation Team (NCHDT). The NCHDT is led by the National Library and has many other stakeholders: the University of Khartoum, the Sudan Radio and TV Corporation, the National Data Centre, the National Archives, the National Museum, Sudan's largest corporation the DAL Group (who have a major commitment to cultural projects), Africa City of Technology and other universities and cultural heritage organisations. I was approached to be an external consultant for Digital Sudan in 2013, and have been heavily involved in the planning phase and in running workshops.

In planning for Digital Sudan, the country has both advantages and challenges. In terms of advantages, there is an excellent telecommunications infrastructure. It is modern, well-designed, robust and capacious. Sudatel, the main telecommunications company, and the National Information Centre can provide some of the storage, connectivity and bandwidth that will be needed for Digital Sudan and, as the resource grows, the capacity can be increased. In the Ministry of Information and other cultural institutions there is already a great deal of technical knowledge and, more importantly, there is huge enthusiasm for the project and a willingness to make things happen. The National Library was initiated in 1999 and established in 2003 as a library for the written heritage, based on Archives set up by the British in 1903. It is modelled on the famous libraries of the world: Alexandria, the British Library, the Library of Congress, and it hopes to play a significant role in cultural emancipation in Sudan. The Government of Sudan has allocated a plot of 11,000 square metres in Khartoum, next to the National Museum, for a new permanent library building.

A Digital Library Project is proposed as a major component of the National Library in order to realise the specific functions of the library in preserving the national heritage and reflecting the nation's cultural and historical heritage. The digital library will facilitate access to information across many public and commercial sectors, and it will undertake digitisation of old and decaying books, old manuscripts and pictures. Digital Sudan is a massive undertaking, but it has support from the stakeholders and increasingly from relevant government ministries and departments: Information, Education, IT. It also has support from the commercial sector: the DAL Group and Sudatel initially. An Action Plan was agreed in February 2015 and a number of key recommendations were made. In particular, plans need to be put in place for a national framework for digital information management and preservation. The national framework will include legislation or policy that provides clear mandates for all stakeholders and clarifies relationships and the division of responsibilities in the area of the management and preservation of digital information and cultural material. The framework will also include standards, developed or adopted by a suitably knowledgeable technical committee who will provide guidance on the creation, management, use and preservation of source material, digital surrogates and born-digital material, to establish a continuum of care, as well as procedures for all aspects of the work of digitisation and preservation, including the care of source materials. It will also consider needs in the areas of infrastructure and facilities, staffing, training and education.

Digital Sudan has the potential to open up a great deal of rare material to the government and citizens of Sudan, unlocking the informational and cultural value of neglected and in some cases as yet unknown material. It also has the potential to help to build national capacity in the area of digital archives. For instance, it might:

- strengthen the national institutions;
- use international technical standards and encourage their adoption and use in Sudan;
- develop scanning and cataloguing procedures that can be usefully replicated elsewhere;
- introduce technologies for ongoing use by the government and people of Sudan;
- support the development of Africa's first Trusted Digital Repository;
- develop technical expertise and become a training ground for new archivists. For example, a Master's in Archives Management/Digital Preservation could be set up with help from international partners.

A number of projects are now under way; for example, in collaboration with the University of Bergen, the Sudan Radio and TV Corporation (SRTC) has begun a major project to digitise important television recordings.[22] This is a huge and expensive undertaking which has been funded by the Norwegian government. At the time of writing, a media asset management system has been installed in Khartoum and local staff have been trained in its use. Tenders are being evaluated for the digitisation and work on this will start in autumn 2015. The SRTC has also built a new facility to house the cinema archive, funded by the DAL Group, Sudan's largest company.

A pilot project to develop an archive of Sudan laws is also underway. This will prioritise safeguarding older versions of laws and their conversion into digital form. Also to be digitised is the *Sudan Government Gazette* from 1975 to the present date, to complete work done in Durham on the earlier volumes. The necessary software has been installed and training for Ministry of Justice staff will begin soon, to be carried out by the University of Khartoum digital content department. The NCHTD is also working on a project to commence digitisation of the 12 million photographs in the National Archives, with support from the DAL Group.

GACACA ARCHIVE PROJECT, RWANDA

I began this chapter with the examination of a project documenting the crimes and punishments of a distant past: Old Bailey Online. I end it with crime and punishment of the much more recent past: the documents that record the trials of the perpetrators of the Rwandan genocide against the Tutsi in 1994. So recent is this that in fact the documents constitute a working archive, being consulted daily for arrest warrants, case files and other legal documents for ongoing trials and appeals. The fact that the documents in the archive concern current legal processes entails some serious issues of privacy and security.

The Gacaca Archive Project (GAP) is a joint endeavour between the National Commission for the Fight Against Genocide (CNLG, a Rwandan government department) and the Aegis Trust (an international organisation working to prevent genocide with a base in Rwanda) together with a group of international partners: King's College London, the NIOD Institute for War, Holocaust and Genocide Studies (an institute of the Royal Netherlands Academy of Arts and Sciences) and the University of Southern California Shoah Foundation. The Project has been set up to digitise the 60 million pages of records of the Gacaca Courts, the legal system that tried the perpetrators of the Rwandan genocide between 2004 and 2014.

In 1994, Rwanda suffered a genocide of almost unimaginable proportions and consequences, and has faced huge challenges in the wake of it. However, the country is now successfully creating a modern integrated society with a burgeoning economy. One crucial factor in the rebuilding of the nation was the process offered to the pursuit of justice and reconciliation by the Gacaca Courts, which operated in local communities throughout the country and which tried around one million individual cases. Nearly every adult Rwandan participated in Gacaca, described by Phil Clark as 'highly ambitious and innovative'. Clark goes on to say that 'other societies confronting the aftermath of mass conflict could learn much from Rwanda's approach to local justice' (Clark 2012). Gacaca is a traditional method of conflict resolution and reconciliation that was revived and legalised in order to deal with an enormous residual problem: hundreds of thousands of accused perpetrators of the genocide were imprisoned awaiting trial, costing the country an enormous amount of money, but with no adequate judicial structure that could deal with their cases, given that much of the infrastructure had been destroyed. Gacaca is 'justice without lawyers', with justice administered at a very local level – more than twelve thousand courts hearing almost two million cases (gacaca.rw).

The records of the courts form an archive of some 60 million pages of documents, one of the largest archives concerning a mass crime anywhere in the world, which now reside in Kigali, at the National Police Headquarters, and are managed by CNLG. This archive is of unparalleled significance, both to

Rwanda and the world, as a record of the process of justice and reconciliation. However, a feasibility study carried out by the Aegis Trust and the NIOD into genocide-related materials in Rwanda's archives has found that there is a significant risk of information getting lost and/or documents becoming unusable in the future. The use of the archive is also hampered by the lack of tools and documentation to facilitate access, such as archival descriptions, indexes and other finding aids that would enable searching and retrieval.

The British government's Department for International Development funded the initial feasibility study in 2013–14 which recommended some conservation work on the physical archive and the digitisation of all the documents. The Netherlands Embassy in Kigali has funded an initial investigative phase into the practical and technical issues of scanning such a large and fragile archive, and CNLG will be funding year one of the digitisation programme, beginning in July 2015, with a commitment to fund the rest of the project, possibly with help from other funders within and outside Rwanda.

This will be one of the largest single archive digitisation projects in the world, and certainly the largest in Africa. The project is currently designing a highly complex workflow whereby the materials will be organised into specific document types. As metadata exists for the courts and locations of the materials in each box, a system of barcodes is being used to apply that information automatically to all the materials scanned. The resulting scanned images will then be indexed for the trial information so that they can be searched and grouped together into virtual case files on the ultimate database repository.

Most of the material is in the form of modern paper no larger than A4 in size. For this reason sheet feed scanners specifically designed to handle fragile materials are being employed to scan the material at speed. Some materials are in the form of registers which will be scanned using a cradle-based book scanner. As a project this is an excellent example of the application of large-volume scanning techniques from industry to archival materials, with best practice in archiving (physical and digital), quality assurance, metadata and delivery being to the fore at all times. The system chosen to archive the materials and deliver them to the users is Islandora, the open-source Fedora-based software framework designed to help institutions and organisations and their audiences collaboratively manage and discover digital assets. Islandora was originally developed by the University of Prince Edward Island's Robertson Library.[23]

CONCLUSION

The work described here is but a small selection of the enormous activity in digitisation in the arts and humanities throughout the world. Are they digital humanities projects? I prefer to think of such activity as humanities done digitally. These projects are all ones that I or the authors of Tanner et al. have been involved in, and they range from closely analysed and encoded scholarly sources to enormous projects that are attempting to scan millions of objects and make these available, in the best way possible, for the widest range of users.

There are many complex issues to consider in embarking upon such projects, but the technical issues are in fact probably easier to resolve than the economic, legal and political ones. Digital projects are costly. While scanning costs have been dropping dramatically with developments in scanner technology and in software, scanning is only one part of these projects. Creating metadata and transcriptions, indexing, developing systems to deliver content and sustaining resources for the long term all cost much more than the initial capture; creating business models for digital projects so that they have a revenue stream for ongoing costs is not always straightforward. As we see from the projects described here, some are made available for free and others for varying levels of subscription.

The legal issues, too, can often take time to disentangle. Materials may be in copyright and so the rights owners need to be contacted and permission sought: this will often require fees to be paid. Often too the rights to use an image or a text are time-delimited, and these rights need to be renegotiated. This is very different from print publication: once an image or text has been used in a book, it is there for as long as the book exists. Many a project has foundered on the costs for securing rights and the difficulty of so doing. Google has, for example, now greatly scaled down its activity in book scanning,[24] probably because the negotiations with publishers were proving so difficult. Even when materials are not in copyright, if they are held by memory institutions permission has to be sought for use.

Digitisation is not a value-free or politically neutral process. In Sudan digitisation of archival collections is seen as a move towards more openness and democracy, though one must always be aware that, like any other collection policy, digitisation policy and strategies can be manipulated to show a particular view of a country or an organisation. In Rwanda, the Gacaca Archive contains material so sensitive that it is kept under armed guard in the police headquarters. Digitisation could allow easier access to the documents, but only, at the moment, under tightly controlled conditions. These documents record criminal actions involving victims and perpetrators who are still alive themselves or whose families are, and so need to be dealt with under strict legal and physical protection. As time goes on, these will become part of the history of the country and of the genocide, but it is currently too soon for that to occur.

The scale of digitisation in the arts and humanities has increased exponentially in the last ten years, much of this driven by large commercial projects like Google Books. In the 1990s, the Yale Open Book Project,[25] one of the earliest book scanning projects, scanned 2,000 volumes; Google Books has now scanned 30 million. These large-scale scanning efforts create an unimaginable cornucopia of content for scholars, but the smaller-scale projects like Jane Austen's Digital Edition are also revolutionising scholarship. For the first time in a century and a half scholars, students and the general public can see all Austen's extant manuscript writings, from her childhood right up to the end of her life, in one place,. This offers new insights into the author and her working practices, and opens up new research questions and opportunities.

ACKNOWLEDGEMENTS

I'd like to thank my colleagues who have contributed to this chapter in different ways: Badreldin Elhag Musa, Jane Hogan, Geoff Laycock, James Lowry, Kathryn Sutherland and Simon Tanner.

NOTES

1. The Proceedings of the Old Bailey, 1674–1913, available at <http://www.oldbaileyonline.org> (last accessed 7 August 2015).
2. London Lives 1690–1800: Crime, Poverty and Social Policy in the Metropolis, available at http://www.londonlives.org (last accessed 7 August 2015).
3. Connected Histories: British History Sources, 1500–1900, available at <http://www.connectedhistories.org> (last accessed 7 August 2015).
4. The Old Bailey Corpus, available at <http://www.uni-giessen.de/old-baileycorpus/> (last accessed 7 August 2015).
5. There is an extensive list of publications that cite Old Bailey Online, available at <http://www.oldbaileyonline.org/static/Publications.jsp> (last accessed 7 August 2015).
6. Chopin's First Editions Online, available at <http://www.cfeo.org.uk> (last accessed 7 August 2015).
7. Jane Austen's Fiction Manuscripts Digital Edition, available at <http://www.janeausten.ac.uk> (last accessed 7 August 2015).
8. Jane Austen's Fiction Manuscripts, *The Watsons* description, available at <http://www.janeausten.ac.uk/edition/ms/WatsonsHeadNote.html> (last accessed 14 August 2015).
9. TEI Special Interest Group on Documents and Genetic Criticism, available at <http://www.tei-c.org/SIG/Manuscripts/genetic.html> (last accessed 7 August 2015).

10. Quoted in an interview with Professor Sutherland by Caroline Roberts. The interview is to appear in print form on the AHRC website during 2015 to celebrate the tenth anniversary of the Council by highlighting key projects.

11. *North Wales Chronicle*, 13 August 1915, p. 5, available at <http://newspapers.library.wales> (last accessed 7 August 2015).

12. ICON, the International Coalition on Newspapers, available at <http://icon.crl.edu> (last accessed 7 August 2015).

13. The British Newspaper Archive, available at <http://www.britishnewspaperarchive.co.uk> (last accessed 7 August 2015).

14. http://www.findmypast.co.uk (last accessed 14 August 2015).

15. Welsh Newspapers Online, available at <http://newspapers.library.wales> (last accessed 7 August 2015).

16. Australian Newspapers Digitisation Program, available at <http://trove.nla.gov.au> (last accessed 7 August 2015).

17. Louisville Leader, available at <http://digital.library.louisville.edu/cdm/landingpage/collection/leader/> (last accessed 7 August 2015).

18. Europeana, available at <http://www.europeana.eu/portal/> (last accessed 19 August 2015).

19. Europeana Newspapers Collection, available at <http://www.theeuropeanlibrary.org/tel4/newspapers?view=discover> (last accessed 9 August 2015).

20. Chronicling America, available at <http://chroniclingamerica.loc.gov/about/> (last accessed 9 August 2015).

21. Sudan Archive Digitisation Project, University of Durham, available at <https://www.dur.ac.uk/library/asc/projects/jiscsudan/> (last accessed 9 August 2015).

22. See Preserving Sudan's Television Archive, available at <http://www.uib.no/en/news/36409/preserving-sudan's-television-archive> (last accessed 9 August 2015).

23. Islandora, available at <http://islandora.ca> (last accessed 9 August 2015). See also Discovery Garden Inc. which supplies Islandora preconfigured for ease of installation and application. Available at <http://www.discoverygarden.ca> (last accessed 9 August 2015).

24. 'Never trust a corporation to do a library's job', *The Message*, 29 January 2015, available at <https://medium.com/message/never-trust-a-corporation-to-do-a-librarys-job-f58db4673351> (last accessed 14 August 2015).

25. Paul Conway (1996) 'Yale University Library's Project Open Book', *Dlib Magazine*, available at <http://www.dlib.org/dlib/february96/yale/02conway.html> (last accessed 14 August 2015).

REFERENCES

Clark, Phil (2012) 'How Rwanda judged its genocide', *Africa Research Institute*, available at <http://www.africaresearchinstitute.org/publications/coun-terpoints/how-rwanda-judged-its-genocide-new/> (last accessed 9 August 2015).

Grabowski, Christophe and Rink, John (2010) *Annotated Catalogue of Chopin's First Editions*. Cambridge: Cambridge University Press.

Hitchcock, Tim and Shoemaker, Robert (2006) 'Digitising history from below: the Old Bailey Proceedings Online, 1674–1834', *History Compass*, 4 (2), available at <http://uhra.herts.ac.uk/bitstream/handle/2299/38/102846.pdf?sequence=1> (last accessed 9 August 2015).

Holley, Rose (2009) 'How good can it get? Analysing and improving OCR accuracy in large-scale historic newspaper digitisation programs', *Dlib Magazine*, 15 (4/5), available at <http://www.dlib.org/dlib/march09/holley/03holley.html> (last accessed 9 August 2015).

Huber, Magnus, Nissel, Magnus, Maiwald, Patrick and Widlitzki, Bianca (2012) 'The Old Bailey Corpus. Spoken English in the 18th and 19th centuries', available at <http://www.uni-giessen.de/oldbaileycorpus> (last accessed 9 August 2015).

Smith, Ali (2012), *Artful*. Harmondsworth: Penguin.

Sutherland, Kathryn and Pierazzo, Elena (2012) 'The author's hand: from page to screen', in Marilyn Deegan and Willard McCarty (eds), *Collaborative Research in the Digital Humanities*. Farnham: Ashgate, pp. 191–212.

Tanner, Simon, Muñoz, Trevor and Ros, Pich Hemy (2009) 'Measuring mass text digitisation quality and usefulness: lessons learned from assessing the OCR accuracy of the British Library's 19th century online newspaper archive', *Dlib Magazine*, 15 (7/8), available at <http://www.dlib.org/dlib/july09/munoz/07munoz.html> (last accessed 9 August 2015).

Notes on Contributors

Nicholas Bauch is Geographer-in-Residence at the Spatial History Project at Stanford University. He is a cultural geographer whose work brings digital practice to bear on the art of landscape interpretation. He is author of *A Geography of Digestion* (forthcoming, University of California Press) and *Enchanting the Desert* (forthcoming, Stanford University Press). He holds a PhD in Geography from the University of California, Los Angeles.

Marilyn Deegan is Professor Emerita of Digital Humanities at King's College London. Formerly she was the Director of the Centre for Humanities Computing, Oxford University, and the Director of Digital Resources, Refugee Studies Centre, Oxford University (1997–2004). Her extensive publications include *Text Editing, Print and the Digital World* (ed., with Kathryn Sutherland, Ashgate, 2008) and *Transferred Illusions: Digital Technology and the Forms of Print* (with Kathryn Sutherland, Ashgate, 2009).

Mats Deutschmann is Associate Professor in English Didactics and Linguistics at the Department of Language Studies, Umeå University, Sweden. He has published extensively in the fields of socio-linguistics and CALL (computer-assisted language learning) with a focus on digital media for innovative design in language learning and language awareness-raising activities.

Ann-Catrine Eriksson is Senior Lecturer at the Department of Culture and Media Studies, Umeå University. Eriksson holds a PhD in the History and Theory of Art (2003) and her research interests concern various aspects of gender and art. Eriksson's current research focuses on medieval representations of the Virgin Mary with a focus on gender theory, emotion theory and material culture, as well as on digital representations of medieval art and cultural heritage.

Mel Evans is Lecturer in English Language at the University of Birmingham. Her research interests combine linguistic and literary areas of study. She is especially interested in the idiolect (the language of an individual), historical socio-linguistics, corpus linguistics and sixteenth-century England (and English). Her past research examines the language and style of Queen Elizabeth I, based on her extant correspondence, speeches and translations. Her publications include *The Language of Queen Elizabeth I: A Sociolinguistic Perspective on Royal Style and Identity* (Transactions of the Philological Society Monograph Series 45, Oxford: Wiley-Blackwell, 2013).

Laura Kate Gibson is a PhD candidate in Digital Humanities at King's College London. She previously managed the Digitisation & Collections Management Project at the Luthuli Museum National Legacy Project, South Africa. Her work builds upon interests and skills developed during her undergraduate degree in History at the University of Durham (UK) and Master's degree in African Studies with Public Culture from the University of Cape Town (South Africa), and courses in Museum Studies at the University of Toronto (Canada). She also has experience working in the area of collections management at Canada's Royal Ontario Museum and South Africa's Iziko South African National Gallery.

Zephyr Frank is Professor of History and Director of the Program on Urban Studies at Stanford University. He is also the founding director of the Center for Spatial and Textual Analysis (CESTA). His research interests focus on Brazilian social and cultural history, the study of wealth and inequality, and the Digital Humanities. His most recent book, entitled *Reading Rio de Janeiro: Literature and Society in the Nineteenth Century*, will be published by Stanford University Press in January 2016.

Gabriele Griffin is Professor of Gender Research at Uppsala University, Sweden. She was previously Professor of Women's Studies at the University of York, UK. She has a long-standing research interest in research methods for the Humanities, and in women's cultural production. Recent publications include *The Emotional Politics of Research Collaboration* (co-ed.; Routledge 2013) and *The Social Politics of Research Collaboration* (co-ed.; Routledge 2013).

Matt Hayler is a Lecturer in Post-1980s Literature at the University of Birmingham specialising in Digital and Cyberculture Studies, specifically (post)phenomenology and cognitive science-influenced approaches to e-reading and to technology more broadly. Recent publications include *Challenging the Phenomena of Technology* (Palgrave, 2015) and chapters on technology and the Digital Humanities in forthcoming volumes on *Futures for English Studies* (Palgrave, 2016, co-written with Marilyn Deegan) and *Theatre, Performance, and Cognition* (Methuen, 2016). He can be found on Twitter: @cryurchin.

Stephen Hilyard is Professor of Digital Arts at the University of Wisconsin-Madison and a practising digital artist. He has had numerous exhibitions across the USA and elsewhere.

Rebecca Kahn is a researcher in Digital Humanities at King's College London. At the time of writing, she is a Fellow at the Alexander von Humboldt Institute for Internet and Society in Berlin.

Anna Lagerström is a freelance translator and linguistics student at Umeå University, Sweden.

Geoff Laycock is the director of the independent digitisation and information management consultancy firm Scan Data Experts. Geoff has been working in the museum and heritage sector for over fifteen years designing and implementing a wide range of digitisation projects. Formerly the senior consultant for HEDS (the Higher Education Digitisation Service) Geoff has worked on many large-scale digitisation projects including the Old Bailey Online, the Hansard Archive and the digitisation of the Design Museum Collection. Geoff is a specialist in digital imaging, project design and the use of metadata with database systems to deliver open access digital content online.

Cecilia Lindhé is Senior Lecturer and Director of HUMlab, Umeå University. She holds a PhD in Comparative Literature from Uppsala University (2008). Lindhé works with issues that involve digital research infrastructure, information technology and pedagogy. Her current research spans ancient/medieval rhetorical and aesthetic theory in relation to digital representations of cultural heritage, screen culture and digital literature and art.

Mattis Lindmark works as a computer technician in HUMlab, Umeå University. Lindmark's interests concern 3D visualisations and game programming in combination with a special interest in how gaming technology can be used as infrastructure in various art and research projects.

Thomas Nygren, PhD, is a Researcher and Associate Senior Lecturer at the Department of Education, Uppsala University. During the academic year 2014–15 he was Visiting Scholar in Digital Humanities at the Center for Spatial and Textual Analysis (CESTA) at Stanford University, funded by the Knut and Alice Wallenberg Foundation. His research interests focus on, for example, the digital impact on history education, historiography, critical thinking and human rights education. His previous research, also conducted at Umeå University, has been published in books and journals of history, education and the Digital Humanities.

Lisa Otty is a Lecturer in English Literature and Digital Humanities at the University of Edinburgh. She was previously an AHRC Early Career Fellow at the Centre for the History of the Book, and a Postdoctoral Research fellow on the AHRC-funded project 'Poetry Beyond Text: Vision, Text and Cognition'.

Jim Robertsson has a degree in Media Engineering and works as a computer technician at HUMlab, Umeå University. His field of interest ranges from sensor technology to physical computing.

Erik Steiner is the Creative Director of the Spatial History Project at the Center for Spatial and Textual Analysis (CESTA) at Stanford University. His research and design interests are at the intersection of technology, creative arts and academic scholarship in the humanities and social and environmental sciences. He is a past president of the North American Cartography Information Society.

Anders Steinvall is Senior Lecturer in English Linguistics at the Department of Language Studies, Umeå University, Sweden. He is an experienced educator, with more than fifteen years of practice teaching online. In his everyday teaching, Steinvall frequently makes use of ICT as a tool for stimulating discussions and debriefings.

Simon Tanner is Director of Digital Consulting at King's College, London. Tanner has an academic background in Library and Information Science. He has a wide ranging interest in cross-disciplinary thinking and collaborative approaches that reflect a fascination with interactions between memory organisation collections (libraries, museum, archives, media and publishing) and the humanities. His research into charging models and rights policy for digital images in art museums has had a transformative effect on open content policy in the international museum sector. His publications include 'The Role of Digital Collections in Shaping National Identity in Africa' (with R. Kahn), in T. Barringer and M. Wallace (eds), *African Studies in the Digital Age* (Brill, 2014) and *Measuring the Impact of Digital Resources: The Balanced*

Value Impact Model, King's College London, October 2012 (available online at <http:// www.kdcs.kcl.ac.uk/innovation/impact.html>).

Tara Thomson is a Research Fellow in the School of Literatures, Languages and Cultures at the University of Edinburgh, and Director of the Scottish Universities' International Summer School.

Index